SUPREME
BAR REVIEW

MPRE Review

for the *Multistate Professional Responsibility Exam*

Supreme Bar Review
30539 Pinetree Road, Suite 224
Cleveland, Ohio 44124

(866) BAR-PREP (toll-free)

www.SupremeBarReview.com

SUMMARY OF CONTENTS

How To Use This MPRE Review Program

As you begin your preparation for the *Multistate Professional Responsibility Exam*, please keep in mind that the MPRE is designed to test your knowledge and understanding of a detailed set of rules and legal principles. You cannot expect to pass this examination without a thorough understanding of these concepts and how to apply them. Therefore, we have designed this comprehensive *MPRE Review* program to give you everything you need to be successful on this exam.

We suggest the following approach to using these materials:

1)   **Read the Outline.** Review the comprehensive **MPRE Subject Outline** (Section 1 of this booklet), which details the essential points of law tested on the MPRE.

2)   **Watch the MPRE Web Video Lecture**, which is available online at:
     http://MPRE.SupremeBarReview.com

     Have your book open in front of you so that you can follow along in the **MPRE Subject Outline** (Section 1) and take notes in the margin.

3)   **Practice Testing.** Once you have completed your substantive review of the legal concepts, test your knowledge and understanding by answering practice questions from your set of **MPRE Sample Questions** (Section 2). These are 150 actual MPRE questions provided by the *National Conference of Bar Examiners* (the people who administer the MPRE). Check your responses against the **Explanatory Answers** at the end of Section 2, referring back to the relevant sections of the outline if you need further review of a particular topic. Also, you can use the **MPRE Web Video Lecture**'s menu-driven system to instantly review particular topics. The list of video topics on the website correspond with the headings in your outline materials to enable you to conveniently review any areas that you missed during your practice testing.

4)   **Simulate the MPRE Exam.** Once you have finished the practice questions, complete the full-length **MPRE Practice Test** (Section 3) under timed conditions (2 hours and 5 minutes). Compare your answers with the **Explanatory Answers** provided at the end of Section 3.

In the past, students who have used these materials, applying the approach described above, have achieved excellent results on the MPRE. You can too.

Good luck.

Please note: While we refer to particular rules and code sections in these materials, it is *not* necessary to memorize these rule numbers or code sections. You simply need to understand the concepts and how to apply them to the fact patterns on the MPRE.

Section 1
MPRE Subject Outline

TABLE OF CONTENTS

I. THE MULTISTATE PROFESSIONAL RESPONSIBILITY EXAMINATION

A. APPLICABLE LAW

1. American Bar Association Model Rules of Professional Conduct ("MRPC")

a) The MRPC were promulgated by the American Bar Association ("ABA") in 1983 and have been amended on several occasions since then. The MRPC replaced the ABA's Model Code of Professional Responsibility of 1969 and have since been adopted by a majority of the states. The MRPC govern the Multistate Professional Responsibility Examination (MPRE).

b) Unlike the superseded Model Code of Professional Responsibility which had three categories of rules (Canons, Ethical Considerations and Disciplinary Rules) the MRPC have only a single category of "Rules." Some of the Rules are equivalent to what had previously been referred to as "Disciplinary Rules" in that violation subjects the offending lawyer to the risk of discipline. Other Rules are equivalent to the superseded "Ethical Considerations" or "Canons" in that they are aspirational in tone, stating what is considered to be proper or improper, appropriate or inappropriate conduct for a lawyer.

c) Although the MRPC have only a single category of Rule, each of the Rules is followed by one or more "Comments." The Comments often use the word "should." Comments do not add formal obligations to the Rules but elaborate upon and often explain the language of the Rules. They provide guidance for practicing in compliance with the Rules.

2. American Bar Association Model Code of Judicial Conduct ("CJC")

The current version of the CJC was adopted by the ABA in 1990 and subsequently amended. It contains four "Canons," broad statements of principle, followed by specific Rules and a "Commentary." The Rules expand upon the principles of the Canons. The Canons and Rules are "authoritative" while the Commentary is not; it provides "guidance by explanation and example."

3. General Principles of Law Practice

Most of the questions on the MPRE deal with disciplinary rules of the MRPC. However, controlling federal constitutional decisions and generally accepted principles of law and practice, established by leading federal and state cases and by the Federal Rules of Civil Procedure ("FRCP") and the Federal Rules of Evidence ("FRE") also play a role. This is because a lawyer's "punishment" for violating a disciplinary rule or other ethical standard might consist of things other than disbarment, suspension or reprimand resulting from a disciplinary proceeding. The lawyer may be subject, for instance, to a civil suit by a client, a criminal prosecution by the government, contempt findings by a court, penalties assessed under FRCP 11, disqualification from representation, suppression of evidence, dismissal of a claim or defense, loss of fee or reversal of conviction.

B. FORMAT OF THE MULTISTATE PROFESSIONAL RESPONSIBILITY EXAMINATION

1. Length of Exam

The MPRE consists of sixty (60) multiple choice questions. Ten of them are "test questions" that do not count in the examinee's score, but those ten are indistinguishable from the fifty questions that do count. The examination is two hours and five minutes long, meaning that there are 125 minutes allocated to the sixty questions to be completed. On average, therefore, an examinee has slightly more than two minutes to answer each question.

2. Approach to Answering Questions

Each of the sixty questions provides a factual situation followed by four possible answer choices. The examinee generally must pick the "best" of the four choices. It is usually more effective to attempt to eliminate incorrect choices than to first choose the best. If three choices can be eliminated, the choice remaining will be the "right" answer even if the examinee would not otherwise be certain that it is correct. There is no penalty for guessing; a blank answer is just as "wrong" as an incorrect choice. Even if only two choices can be eliminated, and the examinee has no idea of which of the two remaining is correct, there is still a fifty percent (rather than twenty-five percent) chance of getting credit for that particular question.

3. Format of Questions

a) **"Subject to discipline"** asks whether the conduct described would subject the lawyer to discipline under the MRPC, or, in the case of a judge, if he or she would be subject to discipline under either the MRPC or the CJC. The words "must" or "must not" have the same significance as "subject to discipline"; a question asking whether a lawyer "must" engage in certain conduct is asking whether that lawyer would be subject to discipline for not doing so.

b) **"May"** or **"Proper"** asks whether the conduct described is professionally appropriate in that it:

i)   would not subject the lawyer or judge to discipline, and

ii) is not inconsistent with anything else contained in the MRPC, CJC or with general principles of law practice.

c) **"Subject to litigation sanction"** asks whether the conduct described would subject the lawyer or law firm to sanction by a tribunal, such as contempt, fine, fee forfeiture or disqualification.

d) **"Subject to disqualification"** asks whether the conduct described would subject the lawyer or law firm to disqualification as counsel in a civil or criminal matter.

e) **"Subject to civil liability"** asks whether the conduct described would subject the lawyer or law firm to civil liability, such as that for malpractice, misrepresentation or breach of fiduciary duty.

f) **"Subject to criminal liability"** asks whether the conduct described would subject the lawyer to criminal liability for participation in, or aiding and abetting criminal acts, such as insurance fraud, tax fraud, destruction of evidence, perjury, suborning perjury, or obstruction of justice.

II. BECOMING A LAWYER AND LOSING THE RIGHT TO BE A LAWYER

A. BECOMING A LAWYER

To be admitted to the Bar of a particular jurisdiction a person must, in addition to other factors relating to competence, be psychologically and morally fit to practice law. Information sought by Bar authorities with regard to an applicant's admission must be rationally connected to that fitness and so must purported misconduct, in order to be relevant. The burden of proof is on the applicant to demonstrate the necessary fitness. Bar authorities seek information as to that fitness from the applicant and from other persons.

1. Information From the Applicant

a) The applicant must not make any false statement of material fact in connection with the application.

b) The applicant must not fail to disclose a fact necessary to correct a misapprehension known by him or her to have arisen in the matter.

c) The applicant must not fail to disclose any material fact requested in connection with the application (unless such fact is protected by the rules governing confidential communications). Questions such as "Have you ever been a party to any legal action or proceeding?" must be answered truthfully and completely, even if the action was dismissed or the judgment eventually expunged.

d) The applicant may invoke the Fifth Amendment privilege against self-incrimination but must do so openly ("I refuse to answer ....") rather than using the right of nondisclosure as justification for failing to comply with the obligations of the rule by leaving out the incriminating information, or by lying about it.

e) Violation of the provisions above may, of course, if discovered prior to admission to the Bar, prevent that admission. If the applicant is admitted to the Bar prior to such discovery, however, he or she is still subject to discipline as a lawyer for having violated the provisions.

f) Violations discovered either before or after admission to the Bar may also be used by other jurisdictions to deny admission or discipline lawyers already admitted.

2. Information From Others

a) The applicant is usually required to provide recommendations from other persons familiar with his or her character and fitness. Some of these persons, generally, are members of the Bar. Those lawyers are subject to rules identical to those impacting on the applicant. It is, therefore, a violation of a disciplinary rule for a lawyer to make a false statement of material fact with regard to another's application to the Bar, to fail to disclose a fact necessary to correct a misapprehension the lawyer knows has arisen in such a matter or to fail to disclose any material fact requested in connection with the application (again, subject to rules governing confidentiality).

b) The rule above, governing lawyers recommending applicants for admission to the Bar, also governs lawyers with regard to disciplinary proceedings, whether brought against others or against themselves.

B. LOSING THE RIGHT TO BE A LAWYER (GROUNDS OF MISCONDUCT; SANCTIONS)

1. Grounds of Misconduct
It is professional misconduct for a lawyer to:

a) Violate or attempt to violate any of the disciplinary rules of the MRPC, to knowingly assist or induce another to do so, or to do so through the acts of another. A lawyer, for instance, who uses a friend, employee or client to solicit, in person, new clients when a significant motive for the lawyer's doing so is pecuniary gain, is guilty of misconduct.

b) Commit a criminal act that reflects adversely on the lawyer's honesty, trustworthiness or fitness as a lawyer in other respects. Some crimes may involve what older codes have called "moral turpitude" yet relate more to personal than professional morality. Crimes such as adultery or gambling have little specific connection to the practice of law and would probably not constitute a violation of this section of the rule. Other crimes, however, such as those involving violence, dishonesty, breach of trust, or serious interference with the administration of justice indicate probable violation, as does a pattern of repeated offenses, even those of minor significance when considered separately.

Watch Out!

The fact that a lawyer has been punished by the criminal justice system does not protect against further action by disciplinary authorities.

c) Engage in conduct involving dishonesty, fraud, deceit or misrepresentation. Said conduct, to constitute a violation of the rule, need not be criminal in nature.

d) Engage in conduct prejudicial to the administration of justice. Said conduct, to constitute a violation of the rule, need not be criminal nor dishonest in nature. Conduct in violation of the rule may include the knowing manifestation, while representing a client, of bias or prejudice based upon race, sex, religion, national origin, disability, age, sexual orientation or socioeconomic status, although legitimate advocacy respecting those factors is not forbidden.

e) State or imply an ability to influence improperly a government agency or official. A lawyer who induces a client to believe that an ex parte conversation with the judge hearing the case will occur is in violation of this rule, even though the conversation never takes place and the lawyer never really intended that it would.

f) Knowingly assist a judge or judicial officer in conduct that is a violation of applicable rules of judicial conduct or other law.

2. **Misconduct Not Connected with the Practice of Law**
With the exception of the biased or prejudiced professional activity referred to in sub-paragraph (d) above, a lawyer does not have to be engaged in the practice of law to run afoul of the provisions defining misconduct. A lawyer convicted of willful failure to pay income taxes has likely committed misconduct even though the failure to pay had nothing to do with representation of any client. Similarly, engaging in a fraudulent sales scheme not criminal in nature and not having anything to do with the practice of law is also misconduct.

3. **Misconduct Outside of the State**
Any of the misconduct mentioned above subjects the offending lawyer to discipline in any jurisdiction where he or she is admitted to practice, even if the misconduct did not take place in that jurisdiction.

4. Misconduct Committed by Others

a) Generally, a lawyer is subject to discipline for acts of misconduct committed by another only if the lawyer:

   i) orders the misconduct,

   ii) with knowledge of the specific conduct, ratifies it, or

   iii) as a partner in a firm in which the other lawyer practices (or as a lawyer with direct supervisory authority over the other lawyer) knows of the conduct at a time when its consequences can be avoided or mitigated but fails to take reasonable remedial action.

b) Partners in a law firm must make reasonable efforts to ensure the firm has measures in place that give reasonable assurance that all lawyers in the firm conform to the MRPC and that the conduct of all non-lawyer personnel is compatible with those rules.

c) A lawyer having direct supervisory authority over another lawyer must make reasonable efforts to ensure that the other lawyer's conduct conforms to the MRPC.

d) A lawyer having direct supervisory authority over a non-lawyer must make reasonable efforts to ensure that the person's conduct is compatible with the MRPC. (Non-lawyers must be instructed, particularly, of the need to maintain confidential communications.) The lawyer is responsible for conduct of such person that would constitute a violation of the MRPC if engaged in by a lawyer if:

   i) the lawyer orders, or, with knowledge of the specific conduct, ratifies it, or

   ii) the lawyer knows of the conduct at a time when its consequences can be avoided or mitigated but fails to take reasonable remedial action.

e) Subordinate lawyers are **not** exempted from the duty to conform to the MRPC even while acting at the direction of a supervising lawyer. The subordinate lawyer is not in violation of the MRPC, however, if that lawyer acts in accordance with a:

   i) **reasonable** resolution of an

   ii) **arguable** question of professional duty.

5. **Sanctions for Misconduct**

   Disciplinary Procedures: The MRPC do not prescribe particular sanctions or the procedures for applying them; these are left for individual states to determine. Generally, punishments range from permanent disbarment (reserved for the most serious offenses, or for a pattern of lesser offenses), through suspension from practice for either indefinite or for fixed periods of time, to public or private censure or reprimand. Procedures provided lawyers must conform to due process and other constitutional strictures. The burden of proving misconduct is generally on the disciplinary authorities.

III. THE LAWYER'S RELATIONSHIP WITH THE CLIENT

A. OBTAINING THE CLIENT THROUGH SOLICITATION AND ADVERTISING

The MRPC draw a distinction between these two terms. The **general** rule is that non-misleading advertising is allowed but that "solicitation" is not. The definition of "solicitation" has been limited to in-person, live telephone, or real-time electronic contact with a prospective client, in whole or in part for pecuniary gain. Other means of obtaining clients generally fall into the category of "advertising."

B. ADVERTISING

1. **Basic Rule**

   The basic and most important rule is that **"A lawyer must not make a false or misleading communication about the lawyer or the lawyer's services."**

   a) This rule applies to all communications relating to the lawyer's services made by the lawyer, directly or indirectly. It applies not only to advertising but also to the few instances of solicitation allowed by the rules.

   b) A communication is "false or misleading" if it:

      i) contains a material misrepresentation of law or fact, or

      ii) omits a fact necessary to make the statement as a whole not materially misleading.

   c) Because false statements are relatively easy to identify, many questions in this area of the MPRE will focus on statements not technically false but rather those that violate the MRPC as being misleading. Examples of statements likely to be in **violation** of the rules include those:

      i) likely to create an unjustified expectation about results the lawyer can achieve; e.g., "I got $1,000,000 for John Jones. Let's see what I can get for you."

    ii) implying the lawyer can achieve results by violating the MRPC or other law; e.g., "I am the friend and confidant of many judges in this state."

    iii) omitting significant information; e.g., "I have won 90% of the matrimonial cases I have filed in the past ten years" when 95% of those cases were uncontested.

    iv) using specific client endorsements of the lawyer's professional skills.

    v) comparing the lawyer's services to those of other lawyers unless the comparison can be factually substantiated. What would be harmless puffery in the context of other occupations is a violation of the MRPC; e.g., "Lawyer Smith is the finest workman's compensation lawyer in the county."

d) While the MPRE is likely to contain questions involving violations of the advertising rules, some instances of permitted statements may be presented. Such statements, provided they are not false or misleading, may be made through public media, including telephone directories, legal directories, newspapers or other periodicals, radio, television, movie and outdoor advertising, and any other communication not involving in-person, live telephone or real-time electronic contact. They include:

    i) **Particular statements relating to specialization:** In communications concerning the lawyer's services, he or she may state (if truthful) that the lawyer:

        A) practices only in certain fields,

        B) will not accept matters except in certain fields, or

        C) is a "specialist," "practices a specialty" or "specializes in" certain fields. Note, however, that a lawyer must **not** claim **recognition** or **certification** by an organization or authority as a specialist except in limited circumstances:

            1) The lawyer may use the designation "Patent Attorney" or a substantially similar designation **if** admitted to engage in patent practice before the U.S. Patent and Trademark Office,

            2) The lawyer may use the designation "Admiralty," "Proctor in Admiralty" or a substantially similar designation if engaged in admiralty practice, and

3) The lawyer may claim recognition or certification as a specialist in fields other than patent and admiralty practice **if** actually **granted certification** by a regulatory authority or approved organization in the jurisdiction, **or** by the ABA, and the name of the certifying organization is clearly identified in the communication.

ii) **Statements regarding admission in other jurisdictions:** A firm with offices in more than one jurisdiction may use the same firm name in each, but if it does so it must indicate which of the partners are **not** licensed to practice in a particular jurisdiction.

2. **Particular Rules**
   Particular rules governing the otherwise acceptable lawyer advertising listed above:

   a) The advertisement must contain the **name and address** of at least one lawyer or law firm responsible for the content of the advertisement.

   b) Although client endorsements of the lawyer's professional skills are inappropriate (as mentioned above), a lawyer or law firm **may** include the name of a client in an advertisement **if**:

      i) the client is or has been represented by the lawyer or firm **and**

      ii) the client consents.

   c) Generally, a lawyer must **not give anything of value** to any person for recommending the lawyer's services. A lawyer may, however, pay the reasonable cost of advertising and may also pay the usual charges for nonprofit lawyer referral services or other legal service organizations.

   d) Written or recorded communications such as mail, e-mail, fax, telephone recordings and television advertisements made to persons known to need legal services in particular matters must be labeled "Advertising Material" on the outside of the envelope or at the beginning and ending of any recording.

   e) A lawyer must not communicate with or contact any prospective client through any written, recorded or electronic communication or by in-person or telephone contact if:

      i) the communication or contact involves any coercion, duress or harassment, or

      ii) the prospective client has made known to the lawyer a desire not to be contacted by the lawyer.

3. Rules Governing Firm Names and Trade Names

a) A lawyer must not use any firm name, letterhead, business card or other professional designation that is false or misleading. Two lawyers not legally affiliated who share office space, a secretary and a receptionist could not have "Johnson and Patterson" painted on their office door, nor could they allow the receptionist to answer the telephone, "Law offices of Johnson and Patterson," since that might imply partnership. Lawyers must never state, expressly or impliedly, that they are partners or otherwise affiliated when they are not.

b) While older codes prohibited lawyers from using trade names (e.g., "Trial Verdicts Store"), the MRPC allow them, provided they are not misleading and do not imply a connection with a government agency or charitable or legal services organization.

c) A law firm must not use the name of a **public official** presently or formerly associated with the firm during any significant period in which he or she holds public office and is not actively and regularly practicing law as a member of the firm.

C. SOLICITATION

1. Definition
As mentioned above, solicitation, defined as **in-person**, **live telephone, or real-time electronic** contact with a prospective client, is **generally not** allowed. Written communications, faxes and most e-mails, therefore, do **not** fall under the definition of solicitation, although they are, of course, subject to the rules on lawyer advertising mentioned above.

2. Solicitation By Others Not Excused If Directed by Lawyer
Prohibited solicitation is not excused by virtue of being carried out by another person, provided the lawyer **directs** that communication. If a lawyer, for instance, asks a hospital emergency room attendant to distribute his business card to any persons who might need legal services in connection with their injuries, the lawyer is guilty of prohibited solicitation. If, on the other hand, a satisfied client asks the lawyer for some business cards so that he might give them to friends needing representation, the lawyer may do so because the satisfied client's communication is not directed by the lawyer.

3. Exceptions To the Rule Prohibiting Solicitation
The lawyer may solicit when:

a) The lawyer has a **family or close personal relationship** with the prospective client;

b) The lawyer has a **prior professional relationship** with the prospective client (including both former clients and other present and former business associates);

c) The lawyer's **pecuniary gain** is **not** a significant motive for seeking the representation; **or**

d) The lawyer participates in a group or prepaid legal service plan that markets its services by in-person or live telephone contact, **if** the persons contacted are not known to need legal services in a particular matter covered by the plan **and** the lawyer does not own or direct the organization.

4. Limits To The Exceptions

Even when the exceptions mentioned above exist, a lawyer must not communicate or contact any prospective client:

a) in a manner involving any coercion, duress or harassment, or

b) in **any** manner if the prospective client has expressed a desire not to be solicited.

D. MAINTAINING THE LAWYER-CLIENT RELATIONSHIP

1. Competence

A lawyer must provide competent representation to the client, utilizing the legal knowledge, skill, thoroughness and preparation reasonably necessary for the representation. A lawyer lacking such necessary knowledge or experience must make one of the following three choices:

a) **Decline representation or withdraw from representation**. If the lawyer has undertaken representation and chooses to withdraw, the client's interests must be protected by, for instance, the lawyer ensuring the retaining of other competent counsel.

b) **Make himself or herself competent** without unreasonable delay or expense to the client.

c) **Associate with competent counsel**.

The choices above do **not** include having the client consent to the less-than-competent representation. Despite client consent (perhaps obtained because the lawyer's services are offered at a low or non-existent fee or because the lawyer and client are friends), the lawyer providing incompetent service is subject to discipline. (Emergency situations may provide a temporary and limited exception; e.g., a lawyer told on short notice to secure a continuance because a partner is too ill to attend court is informed by the court that the continuance is denied and the motion must be argued. Arguing the motion in less than a competent manner will **not** subject the lawyer to discipline.)

2. **Disciplinary Actions and Civil Liability**

   If a lawyer is initially competent, becomes competent within reasonable time and expense limits or associates with competent counsel, he or she will **not** be subject to discipline for subsequently acting incompetently in the case. Civil liability for malpractice may, however, still be imposed, and the lawyer may be subject to discipline for failing to act with reasonable diligence or promptness.

3. **Limiting Malpractice Liability**

   A lawyer seeking to limit malpractice liability is subject to discipline for making an agreement prospectively limiting that liability to a client unless the particular jurisdiction's law makes provision for such agreements and the client is represented by another lawyer in making the agreement. The lawyer is also subject to discipline for settling a malpractice claim with an unrepresented client or former client **unless** the person has first been advised, **in writing**, that independent representation is appropriate.

4. **Fees**

   a) The basis or rate for fees charged must be communicated to the client before or within a reasonable period of time after beginning the representation, unless the lawyer has regularly represented the client. It is **preferable** (but not mandatory unless the fee is contingent) that the fee agreement be reduced to writing. Fees charged must be **reasonable**. The fee is reasonable if an ordinarily prudent lawyer in the geographic area would consider it not clearly excessive. The MRPC state that the factors determining the issue include (but are not limited to):

      i) the time and labor required, the novelty and difficulty involved and the skill necessary to perform the services,

ii) the likelihood, if apparent to the client, that the lawyer's representation will likely preclude other employment,

iii) the fee customarily charged in the locality for similar services,

iv) the amount involved and the result obtained,

v) time limitations imposed by the client or the circumstances,

vi) the nature and length of the professional relationship with the client,

vii) the experience, reputation and ability of the lawyer(s) performing the services, and

viii) whether the fee is fixed or contingent.

b) **Fee-splitting:** Lawyers in the same firm, by agreement, legitimately share or "split" fees earned by any of them, both during their tenure with the firm and upon retirement. Lawyers **not** in the same firm, however, are restricted in sharing fees by the MRPC. They may share fees only if **all three** of the following conditions are satisfied:

i) The total fee charged the client is reasonable, meaning that the client will not be charged more merely because there are more lawyers to compensate.

ii) The client gives informed consent in writing to the participation and fee-share of all lawyers involved, **and**

iii) **Either** the division of fees among the lawyers is:

A) in proportion to the **services** performed by each lawyer, **or**

B) **each** lawyer assumes joint **responsibility** for the representation.

c) Because of the outlined requirements above, a lawyer who refers a case to another lawyer and receives a portion of the fee earned without having done any work on the case or having assumed any responsibility for it is subject to discipline. The other lawyer who provides services to the client, receives a fee and then forwards part of it to the referring lawyer is also subject to discipline. **Pure referral fees violate the rule on fee-splitting.**

d) **Contingent Fees**

i) Subject to the factors relating to reasonableness contingent fees are generally allowed but they are prohibited in two instances:

A) **Criminal cases.** An agreement that the lawyer will be paid $50,000 for an acquittal, $25,000 for conviction of a misdemeanor and only $5,000 for conviction of a felony is a forbidden contingent fee.

B) **Domestic relations matters** in which the fee is contingent upon securing a divorce or upon the amount of alimony, support or property settlement in lieu of such alimony or support.

ii) A contingent fee must be in **writing**. The writing must include the method by which the fee is determined, the percentages accruing to the lawyer upon settlement, trial or appeal, the litigation and other expenses that will be deducted from the recovery and whether such expenses are to be deducted before or after the contingent fee is calculated.

5. **Client Funds**

Particular rules apply to all situations in which a lawyer handles property in which the client has an ownership interest, in whole or in part.

a) Typical MPRE fact patterns raising client fund issues include:

i) The client **pre-pays** legal fees to the lawyer who has not yet performed any services. The funds, possessed by the lawyer, belong to the client. (If money was paid to the lawyer as a **retainer**, however, it belongs to the lawyer. A retainer is non-refundable compensation paid a lawyer in exchange for **agreeing** to be available to provide representation, not for the services that are actually provided.)

ii) The lawyer receives a settlement payment from an opponent. At least a portion of this payment, possessed by the lawyer, belongs to the **client**.

b) A lawyer handling any client funds must establish and use a **trust fund account**. This is generally a single account into which all funds of all clients and third parties are deposited. The lawyer's own funds, whether personal or professional, are kept separate and apart from the lawyer's trust fund account. **A lawyer must not commingle client funds with his or her own funds.**

c) A lawyer may withdraw from the trust fund account **expenses** as needed for the representation and **must withdraw fees as earned** (with notice to the client). Any funds as to which there is a **dispute** as to proper ownership must **remain** in the trust fund account until the dispute is resolved.

d) **Record-keeping obligations for client funds**

i) The lawyer receiving client funds must give prompt notice of that receipt and deposit the funds in the trust fund account.

ii) The lawyer must maintain complete records of client funds and, if requested, render a full accounting to the client.

iii) The lawyer must promptly deliver funds the client is entitled to receive.

e) **Misappropriation of client funds:** This is one of the most serious offenses a lawyer can commit and often leads to disbarment, the most serious of lawyer sanctions, in addition to prosecution under the criminal law.

6. **Conflicts of Interest**

The professional judgment of a lawyer must be exercised, within the bounds of the law, solely for the benefit of the client and free of compromising influences and loyalties. The three most common areas of conflict are between the lawyer and client, between the client and other clients, and between the client and third parties.

a) **Conflicts between lawyer and client**

i) There is no absolute bar on representation when a potential conflict exists between the interests of the lawyer and the client. If, however, the representation may be **materially limited** by the lawyer's own interests, the lawyer must not represent the client unless:

A) the lawyer **reasonably believes** the representation will not be adversely affected (this is both a subjective and objective standard), and

B) the client consents, in writing, after consultation.

ii) Financial dealings with client (apart from legal fees) will presumably create a conflict situation **unless** four tests are met:

A) The transaction must be objectively fair and reasonable,

B) The client must be informed in a writing understandable to a layperson of the terms of the agreement.

C) The client must be given a reasonable opportunity to seek independent counsel, and

D) The client must consent, in writing.

iii) **Gifts from clients** are frowned upon because they raise the possibility of the lawyer's undue influence but they are not generally prohibited. What is **prohibited**, however, is a lawyer preparing an instrument (will, trust agreement, deed, etc.) giving the lawyer or lawyer's parent, child, sibling or spouse any substantial inter vivos or testamentary gift. (The rule does **not** apply if the recipient of the gift is **closely related** to the client.)

iv) **Book and media rights:** Prior to the conclusion of representation a lawyer must not make or negotiate an agreement giving the lawyer literary or media rights to a portrayal or account based in substantial part on information relating to the representation, unless the representation itself involves that literary property. (A lawyer's judgment as to whether to recommend to his accused client acceptance of a plea agreement might be clouded by the knowledge that a book or movie about the case will likely be more marketable if it goes to trial, whether the client is convicted or acquitted.)

v) **Standard commercial transactions** between lawyer and client are permitted. If the client has a car for sale, the lawyer may purchase it as may any other customer.

vi) **Financial assistance to client:** Lawyers are **not** generally allowed to provide financial assistance to clients in connection with pending or planned litigation. **Litigation costs,** however, are an exception to the rule; the **lawyer may advance or guarantee** those costs and, although the **client must remain ultimately liable** for them, repayment may be made **contingent** on the outcome of the case.

Watch Out!

An attorney is permitted to lend money to a client as long as there is no litigation pending or proposed. It is only a violation if an attorney lends money to a client *during pending litigation or in contemplation of potential litigation.*

vii) **Proprietary interest in cause of action:** A lawyer must not obtain a proprietary interest in the cause of action or subject matter of litigation in which the client is represented, with two exceptions:

A) The lawyer may acquire a lien granted by law to secure payment of a fee.

B) The lawyer may enter into a contract for a reasonable contingent fee (but **not** in **criminal** or **matrimonial** cases, as mentioned above).

viii) **The lawyer as witness:** Because the role of advocate is different from, and in some cases in conflict with, the role of witness, a lawyer generally must not act as advocate at a trial in which he or she is likely to be a necessary witness. Three exceptions exist:

   A) The lawyer's testimony relates to an uncontested matter or one of formality as to which there is no reason to believe substantial evidence will be offered in opposition.

   B) The lawyer's testimony relates to the nature and value of legal services rendered in the case.

   C) Disqualification of the lawyer would work substantial hardship on the client because of the lawyer's unique qualifications.

  ix) **Sex with the client:** A lawyer shall not have sexual relations with a client unless a consensual sexual relationship existed between them when the client-lawyer relationship commenced.

b) **Conflicts between the client and other clients**

  i) **Present clients, general rule:** A lawyer must not represent one client if that representation will be either:

   A) directly adverse to another client, or

   B) materially limited by the lawyer's responsibilities to another client.

  ii) **Present clients, exception:** The lawyer may represent more than one present client if both of the following conditions are met:

   A) The affected clients **consent**, after consultation, **and**

   B) The lawyer **reasonably believes** that **none** of the potentially conflicting representations will be **adversely affected**.

Watch Out!

Both subjective and objective standards apply; if a **disinterested** lawyer would conclude that either of the affected clients should not agree to representation under the circumstances, the lawyer involved cannot have the requisite "reasonable" belief.

iii) **Opposing parties** in the **same** lawsuit or same transaction: A lawyer must not represent both parties, under any circumstances.

iv) **Co-parties** in the **same** lawsuit:

    A) **Criminal:** Because the potential for conflict of interest in this situation is so great lawyers **should not** represent more than one defendant in any criminal case. There is, however, no independent rule forbidding the lawyer from doing so in every situation so the lawyer would not necessarily be subject to discipline for the joint representation.

    B) **Civil:** As in criminal cases there is no independent rule forbidding the joint representation and subjecting the lawyer to discipline for it but the MRPC enjoin lawyers to be very careful in undertaking such representation. The lawyer **should not** represent in litigation multiple clients with **differing interests** although there may be some situations in which a lawyer would be acting properly in representing multiple clients with **potentially** differing interests.

v) **Settlements involving co-parties:** Even if a lawyer has acted properly in representing co-parties in a case, proposed settlements raise additional issues. The lawyer may participate in the making of an **aggregate settlement** only if **both** of the following requirements are satisfied:

    A) The lawyer must consult with **each** client, disclosing the nature and extent of all claims and pleas and the participation of each person in the settlement, **and**

    B) **Each client**, after such consultation and disclosure, must **consent**.

vi) **Unrelated lawsuits; present clients:** The general rule is that the duty of loyalty owed a client by a lawyer precludes the lawyer from acting as **advocate** against that client in another matter, **even if** that other matter is wholly unrelated to the first representation. Under some very **rare** circumstances such representation may be proper; almost always it is not.

vii) **Lawyer as third party neutral:** Lawyers may assist two or more persons **not** clients to resolve a dispute or other matter. The lawyer must inform unrepresented parties that the lawyer is not representing them.

viii) **Former clients, general rule:** Once a lawyer has terminated representation of a client, he or she may represent a different client even if that new client's interests are adverse to those of the former client, but **not** if either sub-paragraph (A) or (B) is applicable:

A) The lawyer received confidences in the former representation that could be used in the present representation to the disadvantage of the former client, **unless** the former client consents in writing after consultation **or** the subject information:

    1) has already been revealed, **or**

    2) is generally known.

B) The issues in the two representations are substantially related and the former client does not consent in writing after consultation. "Substantially related" means that the two representations involve, at least in part, the same material subject matter, transactions, occurrences or information.

ix) **Lawyer who has left government for private practice:** In this instance the government or governmental agency is the former client. Generally, the lawyer may represent a private party against an agency of the government, even when the lawyer has previously represented the same agency, but in certain instances, where **all three** of the following sub-paragraphs are applicable, the new representation will not be allowed:

A) The present private representation involves the **same matter** in which the lawyer was involved while working for the government,

B) The lawyer participated **personally and substantially** in that matter while employed by the government, **and**

C) The affected governmental agency does **not consent,** after consultation, to the new representation.

x) **Lawyer Contemplating leaving government for private employment:** Lawyers working for the government are generally allowed to leave to obtain private sector employment but must not **negotiate** for private employment if two conditions exist:

A) The person negotiating with the government lawyer is a party or represents a party in a matter in which the government lawyer is involved, **and**

B) The government lawyer is participating personally and substantially in that matter. (A limited exception exists for law clerks to judges who notify the judge of the negotiations.)

xi) **Judicial officer leaving for private practice:** A lawyer must not represent any client in connection with a matter in which the lawyer participated **personally and substantially** as a judge, magistrate, administrative judge, arbitrator or law clerk. Exceptions are as follows:

A) Where **all parties consent, in writing,** after disclosure, or

B) Where an **arbitrator** was selected as a **partisan in a multi-member panel** and seeks to represent the selecting party.

 Watch Out!

Where a lawyer was formerly a member of a **multi-judge court** before which the matter was pending but did **not participate** in hearing the matter or did so only in some remote administrative fashion, there existed no **personal and substantial** participation.

c) **Conflicts between the client and third parties**

   i) **Lawyer's fee paid by third party:** A lawyer generally may accept payment for representation from someone other than the client being represented, but only if all three of the following conditions exist:

   A) The client must give informed consent;

   B) There is no interference with the lawyer's professional judgment; and

   C) Lawyer-client confidentiality must be preserved.

   ii) **Specific third-party problems frequently tested on the MPRE:**

   A) **Parental payment for representation of a son or daughter:** The son or daughter (if competent), not the parent, is the client whose expressed interests govern.

   B) **Legal aid and legal services offices.**

   C) **Corporate legal departments:** The corporation is the client, not the corporate board members, officers, directors or employees. Many of the officers and board members who make the corporation's decisions will be non-lawyers. The lawyer representing the corporate client must not accept direction of his or her professional judgment from non-lawyers, although the lawyer will be required to work with them in serving the best interests of the client. **Conflicts of interest** must be avoided:

1) **Dual representation:** A lawyer is permitted to represent both the corporation and individual constituents if such representation is not inconsistent with the usual conflict of interests rules. If the rules require corporate consent to the joint representation, such consent must be given by a person other than the individual constituent to be represented.

2) If the corporation's interest becomes **adverse** to the interests of an individual constituent, the lawyer **must** explain to the individual constituent that the organization is the client. The individual constituent **should** be advised that the lawyer cannot represent that person, that he or she may wish to obtain individual counsel, and that future discussions between the individual constituent and the lawyer may no longer be privileged.

3) If a lawyer for an organization knows that an officer, employee or other person associated with the organization is engaged in action or a refusal to act in a matter related to the representation and likely to result in substantial injury to the organization, the lawyer shall proceed as is reasonably necessary in the best interest of the organization.

   a. Unless the lawyer reasonably believes that it is not necessary in the best interest of the organization to do so, the lawyer **shall** refer the matter to higher authority in the organization, including, if warranted by the circumstances, to the highest authority that can act on behalf of the organization. If, despite the lawyer's efforts, the highest authority insists upon or fails to address in a timely and appropriate manner an action or a refusal to act, that is **clearly** a violation of law and likely to result in substantial injury to the organization, the lawyer **may reveal otherwise confidential information** relating to the representation, reasonably believed necessary to prevent that substantial injury. (The last sentence does not apply with respect to information relating to a lawyer's representation of an organization to investigate an alleged violation of law, or to defend the organization or one of its constituents against a claim arising out of the alleged violation.)

D) **Insurance companies:** Many policies provide for legal representation of the insured. A lawyer retained by an insurance company to represent an insured is being paid by the insurance company but primary loyalty is owed the client (the insured). If a settlement offer favorable to the client is made by a plaintiff-claimant, the lawyer must recommend that the client accept it, even if acceptance would work against the interests of the insurance company.

iii) Lawyer's interactions with third parties

A) **Communication with third party represented by counsel:** A lawyer representing a client must not communicate about the subject of the representation with a third person the lawyer knows is represented by counsel, **unless:**

1) the third person's lawyer **consents**, or

2) the communication is **authorized by law**.

B) **When the third party is a corporation or other organization,** the above rule prohibiting communications applies to anyone:

1) with managerial authority, or

2) whose act or omission relating to the representation may be imputed to the organization civilly or criminally.

C) **Communication with third party not represented by counsel:** A lawyer representing a client must **not** state or imply that the lawyer is disinterested. The lawyer should make reasonable efforts to correct any misunderstanding of the lawyer's role by the third party. The **only advice** the lawyer should give that person is to **obtain counsel.**

D) **Truthfulness to third parties:** While a lawyer generally is under no affirmative duty to inform an opposing party of relevant facts, the lawyer, in representing a client, must not knowingly:

1) make false statements of fact or law, expressly or impliedly, to third parties (statements of **opinion** are not included: "My client will not settle for that amount" when the lawyer knows the opposite is considered to be an expression of opinion as to the speaker's valuation of the claim), or

2) fail to disclose a material fact to a third party when disclosure is necessary to avoid assisting a criminal or fraudulent act, unless disclosure is prohibited by the duty of confidentiality.

E) A lawyer representing a client must not disregard the rights of third parties by using means having no substantial purpose other than to embarrass, delay or burden that person or to use methods of obtaining evidence violating that person's legal rights.

F) A lawyer who receives a document relating to the representation of the lawyer's client and knows or reasonably should know that the document was inadvertently sent shall promptly notify the sender.

d) **Vicarious (or imputed) disqualification**

i) Generally, if one member of a law firm is disqualified from accepting representation, all lawyers in the firm are vicariously disqualified.

ii) A "law firm," for purposes of vicarious disqualification, may consist of traditional groupings, such as partners and associates, corporate legal departments and legal aid organizations. Lawyers who work in close physical proximity, sharing office space, clerical help and research materials, although not formally associated, may be held to the strictures of this rule if they conduct themselves in such a way as to lead a client to believe they are formally associated. Lawyers in a single office of a legal aid organization, or of a prosecutorial authority, are considered a "law firm" under this rule; in certain specific cases separate offices may be so closely related (leadership, exchange of information, lawyers shifting from office to office, etc.) that all such offices might be considered a single firm.

iii) **Lawyers moving from one private firm to another:**

A) The moving lawyer (and all members of the firm *to which* the move is made) are disqualified and forbidden from representing a new client (and must seek to withdraw from any such ongoing representation) if:

1) the moving lawyer formerly represented a person whose interests were **materially adverse** to those of the new client,

2) in a matter **identical or substantially related** to the representation sought by the new client.

B) If the former client **consents** in writing after consultation, however, the new representation may go forward.

C) If the moving lawyer had **not actually represented** the former client but had only been a member of a firm in which another lawyer had represented that client, and the moving lawyer had never possessed confidential information about the former client, the moving lawyer (and the firm to which he or she moved) will **not** be disqualified or forbidden from the new representation.

D) Lawyers in the firm **from which** the moving lawyer left will not be prevented from undertaking representation of a client with interests directly adverse to those of the former client of that moving lawyer **unless** the matter is substantially related to that in which the formerly associated lawyer represented the client **and** any lawyer remaining in the firm possesses confidential information material to the matter (and in that instance client **consent**, in writing, after consultation, will cure the conflict).

iv) **Family relations and other personal interests:** A lawyer may be disqualified from representing a client if the lawyer's parent, child, sibling or spouse represents a person with interests directly adverse to the affected lawyer's client. There will be no disqualification, however,

A) of the affected lawyer if the involved client consents in writing after consultation.

B) of the **non-related** lawyers in the same firm, even if there is no consent, since this disqualification is personal to the affected lawyer.

v) **Lawyer as witness:** If a lawyer is disqualified from representation as a potential witness in a case, that lawyer's associates are **not** vicariously disqualified.

vi) **Sexual relation with client:** If a lawyer is disqualified from representation due to a sexual relationship with a client other members of that lawyer's firm will not necessarily be imputedly disqualified, since the primary lawyer's disqualification is considered personal to that lawyer.

vii) **Screening**

A) Some jurisdictions have allowed private law firms to avoid imputed or vicarious disqualification by "screening" or "screening off" the lawyer whose conflict of interest would otherwise be imputed to the entire firm in which the lawyer presently practices.

B) The MRPC did not generally recognize screening as a means for avoiding conflicts of interest caused by lawyers moving **between private firms**, until 2009, when the rules were amended to allow it in appropriate cases, analogous to those in paragraph (C) (1) below.

C) The MRPC have traditionally recognized screening as a means for avoiding conflicts of interest (through imputed or vicarious disqualification) caused by lawyers moving **between public and private employment:**

1) where a lawyer or judge moving from governmental to private employment is disqualified from representation of a private client against the government agency with which the lawyer formerly practiced (under the circumstances mentioned earlier), other members of the lawyer's new firm will **not** be disqualified **if** the disqualified lawyer is **screened** from any participation in the matter (meaning that the lawyer speaks to no one in the firm about the case and no one in the firm speaks to the lawyer about it), is apportioned **no specific portion of the fee therefrom,** and **written notice** is promptly given to the appropriate government agency.

2) where a lawyer is disqualified from representing a private client because of the lawyer's former role as **judicial officer** (under the circumstances mentioned earlier), other members of the lawyer's new firm will **not** be disqualified if the same requirements listed in the sub-paragraph immediately above are met.

e) Given a conflict of interest, a lawyer must not undertake new representation. If the conflict manifests itself **after** the commencement of the representation, the lawyer must attempt to **withdraw** from the representation.

7. Withdrawal From Representation

In certain instances a lawyer **must** seek to withdraw from representation ("mandatory withdrawal"). In other instances the lawyer **may** seek to withdraw ("permissive withdrawal"). Outside of these instances a lawyer is forbidden from attempting to withdraw from representation; a lawyer is seldom required to **undertake** representation but once the lawyer does so it is difficult to terminate. If a lawyer **with** grounds to withdraw has appeared before a court or other tribunal or that tribunal in some other way has taken jurisdiction over the matter, the lawyer must secure the **permission** of the tribunal prior to withdrawal.

a) **Mandatory withdrawal:** A lawyer **must** seek to withdraw if:

i) the lawyer **knows** that continued representation will result in a violation of the MRPC or other law,

ii) the lawyer's physical or mental condition materially impairs the ability to represent the client, or

iii) the client, for **any reason** or no reason, discharges the lawyer. Unlike the lawyer's (presumably) ongoing obligation to the client, the client can fire the lawyer at any time. The lawyer will have legal rights to the recovery of fees corresponding to the time spent in the representation up until discharge but does **not** have the right to stay on the case. (If the case is before a court, however, the **judge** has the power to prevent the lawyer's discharge, if it would cause undue delay in the proceeding.)

b) **Permissive withdrawal:** A lawyer **may** seek to withdraw if:

    i)   the client persists in a course of action the lawyer **reasonably believes** is criminal or fraudulent,

    ii) the client has used the lawyer's services to perpetrate a crime or fraud,

    iii) the client insists upon pursuing an objective the lawyer considers repugnant or imprudent,

    iv) the client fails substantially to fulfill an obligation to the lawyer regarding the lawyer's services and has been given reasonable warning that the lawyer will withdraw unless the obligation is fulfilled,

    v) continued representation will result in an unreasonable financial burden on the lawyer or has been rendered unreasonably difficult by the client,

    vi) other good cause for withdrawal exists, or

    vii) (without any "good cause"): withdrawal may be accomplished **without any material adverse effect** on the interests of the client.

c) Where a lawyer has withdrawn from representation, he or she must take reasonable steps to protect the client's interests, such as giving reasonable notice, allowing time to retain other counsel, returning property or papers to which the client is entitled, and **refunding any unearned advanced fee payments.**

8. **Selling A Law Practice**
   A lawyer or law firm may sell an entire law practice (i.e., "withdraw" from the private practice of law in that location) and another lawyer, firm or firms may purchase that practice but only if all of the following conditions are met:

a) The sale must be to purchasers **of the entire practice** or of the entirety of a particular kind of case within that practice (except where certain representation must be declined because of other rules of the MRPC (e.g., conflicts of interest).

b) The seller must **cease** the private practice of law or of that particular kind of case in that location, except for practicing as an employee of a public agency, legal services entity or business (i.e., in-house counsel) and except if unexpected circumstances arise leading to a legitimate need to re-enter the practice of law.

c) Actual **written notice** is given each of the seller's clients and they **consent** (or a court order excuses lack of consent). The notice must include any proposed changes in fee arrangements; the client's right to obtain other counsel and state that the client's consent will be presumed if the client takes no action or fails to object within 90 days.

IV. REPRESENTING A CLIENT WITH ALL THE ZEAL THAT IS DUE

A. DUTY TO ZEALOUSLY REPRESENT
A lawyer has an ethical duty to zealously represent the client, within the bounds of the law, including the MRPC. A lawyer should assume a client's motivation is proper until it is shown not to be. Mere suspicion is not sufficient for a failure to represent zealously.

B. DECISION-MAKING AUTHORITY (SCOPE OF REPRESENTATION)
Who decides what is to be done in a legal matter, the lawyer or the client?

1. Client's Authority
The **client** has the right to make decisions regarding the objectives and goals of the representation, as well as regarding some of the important means toward those ends. Thus, the client has the right to decide whether and how to settle a civil matter, and in a criminal case whether to accept a plea, waive jury trial, or waive the right to testify. The lawyer **should** advise as to these objectives and means, even if the advice goes beyond pure legality.

2. Lawyer's Authority
The **lawyer** has the authority to make most of the decisions relating to the means and methods by which the client's objectives and goals will be achieved, such as what arguments to make, what motions to file, what witnesses to call (subject to the client's wishes if the decisions relate to **expenses** that might be incurred or the client's **concern for third parties** who might be adversely affected). While the lawyer has the final authority to make most of the significant decisions relating to means and methods, **even if the client objects,** the client must still be consulted regarding those matters. (If the client's objections are consistently overruled the remedy might be to **discharge** the lawyer.) As to technical details of the representation where the client need not be consulted the client must still be kept reasonably **informed** about the status of the matter.

C. DUTY TO AVOID IMPROPER CONDUCT
A lawyer must not counsel or assist the client in conduct the lawyer knows is criminal or fraudulent, nor advance any frivolous claim or defense. If the client insists these be done, the lawyer must seek to withdraw.

1. Definition
"Frivolous" means the lawyer is unable to advance a good-faith argument on the merits in support of it under existing law or on the basis of an extension, modification or reversal of existing law.

2. **Burden of Proof On Opponent**

A lawyer is **not** assisting the client in fraudulent conduct or advancing a fraudulent defense when entering a "not guilty" plea on behalf of an accused who has admitted "I'm guilty" to the lawyer. Nor is the lawyer in violation of the MRPC in cross-examining a witness the lawyer knows is testifying truthfully; the lawyer is entitled to make opponents prove every aspect of their cases.

D. DUTY TO AVOID DISHONESTY

A lawyer must not lie to a tribunal about any aspect of law or fact. A lawyer lies when stating something the lawyer knows to be false but is also lying when stating that something is the truth when he or she does not know if it is true or false.

E. DUTY TO REVEAL ADVERSE LAW

A lawyer **must reveal** to the tribunal **legal authority** in the **controlling jurisdiction** known to the lawyer to be directly adverse to the position of the client yet not disclosed by opposing counsel. This obligation goes beyond the avoidance of concealing truthful information or providing false information; it is an obligation to affirmatively reveal information that **hurts** the cause of the lawyer's client. The MRPC state that the court or other tribunal is entitled to this information, even if it must come from the litigant it harms.

F. DUTY TO REVEAL EVIDENCE

Unlike the duty to reveal adverse **law** there is, generally, no obligation for a lawyer to reveal **evidence** or other factual information harmful to the client. There are several exceptions to this statement:

1. **Prosecutor's Special Duties**

In addition to the prosecutor's duty to avoid bringing criminal charges without probable cause the prosecutor must disclose to the defense all evidence or information known to him or her that tends to:

a) Negate the guilt of the defendant,

b) Mitigate the offense, **or**

c) Mitigate the punishment defendant would receive.

Watch Out!

There is no corresponding duty on the part of the defense to provide any information to the government.

2. Ex Parte Proceedings
Under the MRPC (but not the older codes) a lawyer appearing before a tribunal in the absence of an opponent (e.g., requesting a temporary restraining order) must inform the tribunal of all material facts known to the lawyer which will enable the tribunal to make an informed decision, whether or not the facts are adverse.

3. Duty To Disclose A Material Fact To The Tribunal When Necessary To Avoid Assisting A Criminal or Fraudulent Act By The Client.

Examples:

a) Corporate client has destroyed a document proving its liability and refuses to admit the destruction. The lawyer must disclose the fact to the court, if the lawyer, the client or their witness has previously denied that any such document ever existed.

b) Client has given the lawyer the purported murder weapon, a handgun, to hold until the case is over. The gun is evidence, not a confidential communication, and the lawyer must deliver it to the tribunal, or to the prosecutor.

4. Witness Perjury
If the lawyer knows that a witness, **even the client**, has committed perjury during the representation and the witness will not recant, the lawyer must disclose the perjury to the tribunal.

5. Obligation To Disclose Adverse Information
The lawyer's obligation to disclose adverse information lasts until the conclusion of the proceeding and requires disclosure **even if** the information disclosed would otherwise be protected as confidential.

G. A LAWYER MUST BE FAIR TO OPPOSING PARTY AND COUNSEL

1. Duty Not To Conceal Evidence
A lawyer must not unlawfully alter, destroy or conceal a document or other tangible evidence having potential evidentiary value, unlawfully obstruct a party's access to evidence or counsel or assist any other person in doing so.

2. Duty Not To Interfere With Witness Testimony
A lawyer must not alter a witness's testimony, hide a witness or advise or cause the witness to secrete himself or herself.

3. Duty Not To Obstruct Access To Witness
A lawyer must not prevent another party's access to a witness by requesting the witness to refrain from voluntarily giving information. Three exceptions exist; a lawyer may request the following witnesses to not cooperate with another party:

a) The lawyer's client.

b) A relative of the client.

c) An employee or other agent of the client.

4. **Duty Not To Compensate Witness**
A lawyer ordinarily must not pay a witness to testify. In three instances, however, payment may be made (in addition to any court-mandated fee):

a) A lawyer may **compensate** any witness, lay or expert, for the witness's **expenses** in attending trial; e.g., reasonable compensation for room, board and travel. Payment may **not** be made contingent on the testimony or the outcome of the case.

b) A lawyer may **compensate** any witness, lay or expert, for any **wage or salary** lost due to attendance at trial. Payment may **not** be made contingent on the testimony or the outcome of the case.

c) A lawyer may pay a **reasonable fee** to an **expert** witness. The fee may not be made contingent on the testimony or the outcome of the case.

5. **Duty To Use Only Relevant Admissible Evidence**
A lawyer must not refer to any matter at trial the lawyer does not reasonably believe is relevant or that will not be supported by admissible evidence.

6. **Duty To Refrain From Stating Personal Opinions**
A lawyer must not **state** a **personal opinion** to the fact finder as to the justness of a cause, the credibility of a witness, the culpability of a civil litigant or the guilt or innocence of an accused. A lawyer may argue to the fact finder as to how it should decide the case based on the lawyer's analysis of the evidence.

H. A LAWYER MUST NOT INTERFERE WITH THE IMPARTIALITY AND DECORUM OF THE TRIBUNAL

1. **The Lawyer Must Avoid Disruption.**

   Example: Engaging in a fist fight with your adversary may be cathartic but is a violation of the MRPC.

2. **The Lawyer Must Avoid Delay And Make Reasonable Efforts To Expedite Litigation.**

3. **Interaction With Judges and Jurors**

a) A lawyer must not seek to unlawfully influence, e.g., by bribery or threat, a judge, juror, prospective juror, or other court official in a pending case.

b) A lawyer in a pending case must not communicate ex parte with a judge or other court official about that case except as permitted by law.

c) A lawyer in a pending case must not communicate ex parte with a juror or prospective juror. After trial a lawyer may communicate with jurors but may **not** harass or embarrass them or attempt to negatively influence them in connection with future service.

I. TRIAL PUBLICITY

A lawyer must not make a public statement (i.e., an extra-judicial statement that a reasonable person would expect to be disseminated by means of public communication) that has a substantial likelihood of materially prejudicing the proceeding. Matters in the public record and other neutral and non-prejudicial statements and requests for public assistance are presumptively **not** within the prohibition. A lawyer may respond, but only to the extent necessary, to an opponent's violation of this rule.

V. CONFIDENTIALITY

A. NEED FOR CONFIDENTIALITY

The duty to maintain confidential communications goes to the heart of the lawyer's obligation to serve the client's personal as well as legal interests and also to the heart of the adversary system. A lawyer cannot practice competently without knowing the facts of the case and the facts, as known by the client, will not likely be revealed if the client believes revelation will harm the case. To learn all facts known to the client, both good and bad, the lawyer must convince the client that it is in the client's interest to tell the lawyer the truth; this is done by emphasizing the confidential nature of those communications.

B. EXCEPTIONS

A lawyer **must not** reveal information relating to representation of a client **except** that the lawyer **may** (but does not have to) reveal:

1. Impliedly Authorized Statements

Information the disclosure of which is impliedly authorized to carry on the representation, such as statements made within the law firm concerning the case if the client has not expressly requested that only the lawyer to whom the client spoke be party to those disclosures.

2. Informed Consent

Information the disclosure of which is made with the informed **consent** of the client.

3. **Attorney Claims or Defenses**
Information **necessary** to establish a **claim or defense** on behalf of the lawyer or law firm relating to the representation of the client.

4. **Attorney Compliance With MRPC**
Information reasonably believed necessary to secure legal advice about the lawyer's compliance with the MRPC.

5. **Attorney Compliance With Other Law**
Information reasonably believed necessary to comply with other law or a court order.

6. **To Prevent Death or Bodily Harm**
Information reasonably believed necessary to prevent reasonably certain death or substantial bodily harm.

7. **To Prevent Crime or Injury To Property Interests**
Information reasonably believed necessary to prevent the client from committing a crime or fraud reasonably certain to result in substantial injury to the financial interests or property of another or reasonably believed necessary to mitigate or rectify such an injury if the client has used or is using the lawyer's services in furtherance of such crime or fraud.

C. **DURATION**
Confidentiality requirements are not terminated by the end of the representation. They last longer than the lawyer-client relationship and, in fact, last **even after the death of the client.**

D. **COMPARED WITH EVIDENTIARY PRIVILEGE**
The information covered by the lawyer's duty of confidentiality is **broader than the evidentiary privilege** for lawyer-client communications. It consists of "any information relating to representation of a client." This means that **some** of the information covered by the ethical duty (but not the evidential privilege) is discoverable by the opponent pursuant to the applicable civil and criminal rules and also that the judge, at trial, can force the disclosure of that information. But until and unless such disclosure is mandated the lawyer has an ethical duty not to reveal that information and not to use it against the client.

VI. MAINTAINING THE INTEGRITY OF THE LEGAL PROFESSION

A. **UNAUTHORIZED PRACTICE OF LAW**

1. **Only Lawyers Subject to MRPC**
Only persons authorized to practice law may engage in that practice. An unauthorized person who does so is subject to the civil and criminal law but not

the MRPC because that person is not a lawyer. Lawyers are subject to the MRPC and violate its rules when they assist a person in the unauthorized practice of law.

2. **Only Lawyers May Represent Others**

   A non-lawyer representing himself or herself in a legal matter is **not** engaged in the unauthorized practice of law. Nor is any person who is merely using legal knowledge but is not employed in the representation of a client. Only a lawyer, however, may represent or assist **another** person by the exercise of legal judgment applied to that person's specific legal problem.

3. **Practicing Law Outside Jurisdiction**

   A lawyer must not practice law in any jurisdiction where he or she has **not** been admitted to practice. To attempt to do so will subject the offender to sanctions in the non-admitting jurisdiction and also in the jurisdiction in which the offender **is** admitted. A lawyer asked to represent a client in a non-admitting jurisdiction may request a court in that jurisdiction to admit the attorney pro haec vice (for the purpose of that representation only). Granting the request is discretionary with the court but it will usually be granted, on condition that the applicant associate with a local lawyer.

4. **Fee-splitting with Non-Lawyers**

   A lawyer must not share ("split") legal fees with a non-lawyer; doing so assists the unauthorized practice of law. Three exceptions exist:

   a) Wages, compensation plans and retirement plans for non-lawyer employees of the lawyer or law firm, even if they are funded by legal fees or a profit-sharing arrangement.

   b) Payment to the estate of a deceased lawyer of the portion of the fees earned attributable to the work performed by that deceased lawyer.

   c) Payment of death benefits to the estate of a deceased lawyer or to specified persons for a reasonable time after the lawyer's death, pursuant to an agreement to that effect.

5. **Partnerships with Non-Lawyers**

   A lawyer must not enter into a **partnership with a non-lawyer** if any of the activities of the partnership consist of the practice of law. Doing so would assist the unauthorized practice of law by having legal fees shared by the non-lawyer partners. Nor may a lawyer practice with any association authorized to practice law for profit if any non-lawyer owns an interest therein (except for a fiduciary representative of a lawyer's estate for a reasonable time), or is a corporate director or officer, or can exercise control over the professional judgment of a lawyer.

6. **Agreements Restricting Right To Practice**

A lawyer must not participate in the making of **agreements limiting a lawyer's right to practice** law, except for retirement agreements where the retiring lawyer agrees to restrict his or her practice of law incident to the payment of retirement benefits or where an agreement is made to sell a law practice, as mentioned earlier. Examples of prohibited agreements include:

a) A partnership or employment agreement restricting the right of a lawyer to practice after leaving the firm.

b) An agreement settling a controversy between private parties that includes a restriction on a particular lawyer's right to practice law.

B. REPORTING PROFESSIONAL MISCONDUCT

A lawyer who knows that another lawyer or judge has committed a violation of the MRPC or CJC **must report** that violation to the appropriate authority. If the information was acquired in **confidence**, however, it must **not** be disclosed.

C. COMMENTING ON JUDGES AND JUDICIAL CANDIDATES

While a lawyer is permitted to support or to criticize judicial candidates or judges for election or re-election, a lawyer must not make knowingly false statements regarding the qualifications or integrity of the judge or judicial candidate.

D. PUBLIC SERVICE ACTIVITIES

1. **Pro Bono Public Service**

A lawyer **should** aspire to at least 50 hours per year of public service activity by providing professional services at reduced or no fee to persons of limited means and charitable or public service groups, by engaging in activities for improving the law or the legal profession or by providing financial support for legal services organizations. There is no applicable disciplinary rule.

Watch Out!

Failure to comply with the above recommendation does **not** constitute a violation of a disciplinary rule. Nonetheless, if a question asks whether an attorney is "acting properly" if he does **not** do 50 hours of public service activity, the correct answer is "no" he is **not** "acting properly."

2. **Accepting Appointments**

A lawyer must not seek to avoid appointment by a tribunal to represent a person except for "good cause," meaning:

a) representation is likely to result in violation of the MRPC or other law,

b) representation is likely to result in an unreasonable financial burden on the lawyer, or

c) the client or cause is so repugnant to the lawyer as to be likely to impair the lawyer's ability to represent the client.

3. Membership In Legal Services Organization

A lawyer may serve in a legal services organization even if that organization serves persons with interests adverse to the lawyer's client. In doing so, however, the lawyer must not knowingly participate in a decision of the organization when participation would be incompatible with the lawyer's obligations to the client or when the decision could have a material adverse effect on the representation of a client of the organization whose interests are adverse to those of a client of the lawyer.

VII. JUDGES: APPLICATION OF THE CJC

A. JUDGE AS LAWYER

A judge is also a lawyer in most jurisdictions. A judge may be disciplined, therefore, for violation of disciplinary rules in the MRPC or in the CJC.

B. BECOMING A JUDGE

Fair campaigning rules applicable to all judges and judicial candidates:

1. Political Affiliations

A judge or judicial candidate may identify his or her political party affiliation, be listed on election materials along with the names of other candidates for elective public office and may appear in promotions of the ticket, unless prohibited by state law.

2. Political Activities

a) A judge or judicial candidate must not publicly endorse or oppose a candidate for any public office other than the office that judge or candidate holds or seeks.

b) A judge or judicial candidate must not act as leader or hold an office in a political organization, nor may he or she make speeches on behalf of a political organization, nor engage in fundraising activities for a political organization.

3. **False or Misleading Statements**
   A candidate for election or re-election must not make any false or misleading statement regarding the identity, qualifications, present position, or other fact concerning the candidate or the candidate's opponent.

4. **Statements On Issues Likely To Come Before The Court**
   A candidate for election or re-election may speak of a judicial philosophy and may praise or criticize particular decisions and laws, but must **not** make statements appearing to commit the candidate with respect to the merits of cases, controversies, or issues likely to come before the court.

5. **Political Fundraising**
   A candidate for election or re-election must not personally solicit or accept campaign funds or publicly stated political support but must instead solicit funds through a campaign committee. (Candidates for appointive office must **not** solicit in any manner.) Such committee may solicit and accept reasonable campaign contributions, manage the expenditure of funds for the candidate's campaign and obtain public statements of support for his or her candidacy. **Such committees are not prohibited from soliciting and accepting reasonable campaign contributions and public support from lawyers.**

C. ACTING AS A JUDGE

1. **No Use Of Confidences Gained Prior To Taking Bench**
   A judge must not use, without consent, confidential information obtained prior to taking judicial office regarding any lawyer, party or witness appearing before that judge. If the situation arises, the judge must disqualify himself or herself.

2. **No Conflicts Of Interest Or Appearance Of Conflicts Of Interest Or Improprieties**

   a) A judge must not allow family, social, political, or other relationships to influence the judge's conduct or judgment.

   b) A judge must not convey or permit others to convey the impression that they are in a position to influence the judge.

   c) A judge must not lend the prestige of the office to advance the private interests of the judge or of others.

   d) A judge must not **voluntarily** testify as a character witness. Testifying in response to a subpoena, however, is acceptable.

   e) A judge must not accept a gift, loan, favor, or bequest from anyone. The judge **should** also urge members of his or her family not to accept such things. Three exceptions exist:

i) A judge or member of the family residing in the judge's home may accept gifts from **relatives** and **friends** for a **special** occasion.

ii) A judge may accept a gift incident to a **public testimonial**.

iii) A judge may enter into a commercial loan agreement on the same terms offered to the public at large.

f) **Disqualification**.
A judge must disqualify himself or herself in a proceeding in which the judge's impartiality might reasonably be questioned. Such proceedings include those in which:

i) The judge has a personal bias or prejudice concerning a party or party's lawyer, or personal knowledge of disputed evidentiary facts.

ii) The judge served as a lawyer or material witness in the matter, or a lawyer with whom the judge previously practiced law served during the judge's prior association with that lawyer.

iii) The judge knows that he or she, or the judge's spouse, parent or child, or other family member currently residing in the judge's household has an economic interest or any other interest more than de minimus in the proceeding. (The judge has an additional duty to attempt to be informed about the existence of such interests, and the interests referred to in the sub-paragraph following.)

iv) The judge knows that the judge, or judge's spouse, or person within the **third degree** of relationship to either of them, or the spouse of such person, is a party to or a lawyer in the proceeding, or has more than a de minimus interest in it, or is likely to be a material witness. ("Third degree of relationship" means a parent, grandparent, great-grandparent, child, grandchild or great-grandchild, sibling, aunt, uncle, niece or nephew.)

 Watch Out!

Third degree of relationship does **not** include cousins, not even first cousins.

v) The judge, while a judge or candidate for judicial office, has made a public statement that commits, or appears to commit, the judge with respect to an issue in the proceeding or the controversy in that proceeding.

vi) **Remittal of Disqualification**

A judge otherwise disqualified may disclose on the record the basis of that disqualification and ask the parties and their lawyers to consider, out of the judge's presence, whether to waive disqualification. If the parties and lawyers all agree the judge should not be disqualified, the judge **may**, if he or she wishes, participate further in the proceeding. The agreement must then be incorporated in the record of the proceeding. Such possible remittal of disqualification does **not** apply when the basis for disqualification is personal bias or prejudice concerning a party.

g) A judge must not engage in any extra-judicial activities that cast reasonable doubt on the independence of the judiciary by impairing the judge's capacity to act impartially, that demean the judicial office or that interfere with the proper performance of judicial duties. A judge, therefore, shall not serve as executor, administrator or other personal representative, trustee, guardian, attorney in fact or other fiduciary, except for the estate, trust or person of a member of the judge's family, and then only if such service will not interfere with the proper performance of judicial duties. A judge may, however, speak, write, lecture, teach and participate in other extra-judicial activities concerning the law, the legal system, the administration of justice and non-legal subjects as long as these do not create conflicts of interest or the appearance of impropriety.

h) A judge must avoid even the appearance of impropriety:

i) A judge must avoid unnecessary ex parte communication with parties and their lawyers. Where circumstances require, ex parte communications for scheduling or other administrative purposes, or emergencies, are authorized, provided the judge reasonably believes that no party will gain a procedural or tactical advantage as a result, and that the judge, additionally, promptly notifies all other parties of the ex parte communication and gives them an opportunity to respond.

ii) A judge may obtain the advice of a disinterested expert on the law applicable to a proceeding before the judge, but only if the judge gives notice to the parties of the person consulted and the substance of the advice, and affords the parties a reasonable opportunity to respond. The judge may, of course, consult with other judges and with court staff and officials whose functions are to aid the judge in carrying out adjudicative responsibilities. No notice to the parties is required in such an instance.

iii) A judge shall not hold membership in any organization that practices invidious discrimination on the basis of race, sex, gender, religion, national origin, ethnicity, or sexual orientation.

iv) A judge shall not, in the performance of judicial duties, by words or conduct manifest bias or prejudice, or engage in harassment, including but not limited to race, sex, gender, religion, national origin, ethnicity, disability, age, sexual orientation, marital status, socioeconomic status, or political affiliation, against parties, witnesses, lawyers, or others. The judge must not permit staff, court officials and others subject to the judge's direction and control to manifest such bias or prejudice. The judge must also require lawyers appearing before him or her to avoid such manifestations (but this does not preclude legitimate advocacy when those otherwise prohibited factors are issues in the proceeding).

v) A judge must dispose of all judicial and administrative matters promptly, efficiently, and fairly, and must avoid unnecessary appointments.

vi) A judge must not commend or criticize jurors for their verdict other than in a court order or opinion in a proceeding, but may express appreciation to jurors for their service to the judicial system and the community.

Section 2

MPRE Sample Questions
with Explanatory Answers

Copyright information relative to the *National Conference of Bar Examiners* (NCBE) and *Supreme Bar Review:*

Certain publicly disclosed questions from past MPRE examinations have been included herein with the permission of NCBE, the copyright owner. Permission to use the NCBE's questions does not constitute endorsement by NCBE or otherwise signify that NCBE has reviewed or approved any aspect of these materials or the company or individuals who distribute these materials.

All of the questions included in this set of Sample Questions are questions released by the NCBE and reprinted with permission.

All explanatory answers included in this set of Sample Questions are property of Supreme Bar Review. Copyright © 2012 *Supreme Bar Review*

Supreme Bar Review gratefully acknowledge the assistance of ***the National Conference of Bar Examiners*** in granting permission to reprint the released **MPRE Sample Questions VI,** Copyright © 2002 by the *National Conference of Bar Examiners.* All rights reserved.

MPRE Sample Questions

Questions

This publication consists of 150 questions, some of which have been previously published in MPRE Sample Questions V and others in MPRE Information Booklets. Most of these questions have been administered on actual Multistate Professional Responsibility Examinations, although a few questions are included that were not administered on the MPRE but were written as samples of the kinds of questions that would be included under the test specifications. The questions as a whole cover the eleven major topics in the MPRE subject matter outline, although they do not appear in exactly the same proportions as specified in the outline.

PREFACE

The Multistate Professional Responsibility Examination (MPRE) is assembled and administered by ACT, Inc., on behalf of the National Conference of Bar Examiners. A passing score partially fulfills the requirements for admission to practice law in jurisdictions that require the MPRE. The examination is administered three times per year (March, August, and November) at test centers across the country.

After each test is administered, the MPRE scaled score for each applicant is reported to the jurisdiction designated by the applicant. Because the MPRE requirements, including passing scores, vary from one jurisdiction to another and change over time, applicants should check with the board(s) of bar examiners in each jurisdiction to which they intend to apply to make sure they are in compliance with the requirements. A list of participating jurisdictions and announced passing MPRE scaled scores appears at the NCBE website (www.ncbex.org—in the online MPRE Information Booklet) or in the current printed MPRE Information Booklet.

MPRE application materials are available at law schools or by contacting:

National Conference of Bar Examiners
MPRE Application Department
2255 N. Dubuque Rd.
P.O. Box 4001
Iowa City, Iowa 52243-4001
Phone: 319/341-2500
www.ncbex.org or www.act.org/mpre

DESCRIPTION OF THE MULTISTATE PROFESSIONAL RESPONSIBILITY EXAMINATION

The purpose of the Multistate Professional Responsibility Examination (MPRE) is to measure the examinee's knowledge and understanding of established standards related to a lawyer's professional conduct; thus, the MPRE is not a test to determine an individual's personal ethical values. Lawyers serve in many capacities: for example, as judges, as advocates, as counselors, and in other roles. The law governing the conduct of lawyers in these roles is applied in disciplinary and bar admission procedures, by courts in dealing with issues of appearance, representation, privilege, disqualification, or contempt or other censure, and in lawsuits seeking to establish liability for malpractice or other civil or criminal wrongs committed by a lawyer while acting in a professional capacity.

The law governing the conduct of lawyers is based on the disciplinary rules of professional conduct currently articulated in the American Bar Association (ABA) Model Rules of Professional Conduct (MRPC) and the ABA Model Code of Judicial Conduct (CJC) as well as controlling constitutional decisions and generally accepted principles established in leading federal and state cases and in procedural and evidentiary rules.

The MPRE is developed by a six-member drafting committee comprised of recognized experts in the area of professional responsibility. Before a test item is selected for inclusion in the MPRE, it undergoes a multistage review process that occurs over the course of several years before the test is administered. Besides intensive reviews by the drafting committee and testing specialists, each test item is reviewed by other national and state experts. All test items must successfully pass all reviews before they are included in the MPRE. After an MPRE examination is administered, the statistical performance of each test item is reviewed and evaluated by content and testing experts before the items are included in the computation of examinees' scores. This final statistical review is conducted to ensure that each test item is accurate and psychometrically sound.

The MPRE consists of 50 multiple-choice test items. These test items are followed by 10 test center review items that request the examinee's reactions to the testing conditions. The examination is two hours and five minutes in length.

Test items covering judicial ethics measure applications of the ABA Model Code of Judicial Conduct. Other items will deal with discipline of lawyers by state disciplinary authorities; in these items, the correct answer will be governed by the current ABA Model Rules of Professional Conduct. The remaining items, outside the disciplinary context, are designed to measure an understanding of the generally accepted rules, principles, and common law regulating the legal profession in the United States; in these items, the correct answer will be governed by the view reflected in a majority of cases, statutes, or regulations on the subject. To the extent that questions of professional responsibility arise in the context of procedural or evidentiary issues, such as the availability of litigation sanctions or the scope of the attorney-client evidentiary privilege, the Federal Rules of Civil Procedure and the Federal Rules of Evidence will be assumed to apply, unless otherwise stated.

As a general rule, particular local statutes or rules of court will not be tested in the MPRE. However, a specific test question may include the text of a local statute or rule that must be considered when answering that question. Amendments to the MRPC or the CJC will be reflected in the examination no earlier than one year after the approval of the amendments by the American Bar Association.

Each question contained in the MPRE provides a factual situation along with a specific question and four possible answer choices. Examinees should pick the best answer from the four possible answer choices.

Each question may include, among others, one of the following key words or phrases:

1. <u>Subject to discipline</u> asks whether the conduct described in the question would subject the lawyer to discipline under the provisions of the ABA Model Rules of Professional Conduct. In the case of a judge, the test questions also ask whether the judge would be subject to discipline under the ABA Model Code of Judicial Conduct.

2. <u>May</u> or <u>proper</u> asks whether the conduct referred to or described in the question is professionally appropriate in that it:
    a. would not subject the lawyer or judge to discipline;
    b. is not inconsistent with the Preamble, Comments, or text of the ABA Model Rules of Professional Conduct or the ABA Code of Judicial Conduct; and
    c. is not inconsistent with generally accepted principles of the law of lawyering.

3. <u>Subject to litigation sanction</u> asks whether the conduct described in the question would subject the lawyer or the lawyer's law firm to sanction by a tribunal such as contempt, fine, fee forfeiture, disqualification, or other sanction.

4. <u>Subject to disqualification</u> asks whether the conduct described in the question would subject the lawyer or the lawyer's law firm to disqualification as counsel in a civil or criminal matter.

5. <u>Subject to civil liability</u> asks whether the conduct described in the question would subject the lawyer or the lawyer's law firm to civil liability, such as claims arising from malpractice, misrepresentation, and breach of fiduciary duty.

6. <u>Subject to criminal liability</u> asks whether the conduct described in the question would subject the lawyer to criminal liability for participation in, or aiding and abetting criminal acts, such as prosecution for insurance or tax fraud, destruction of evidence, or obstruction of justice.

When a question refers to discipline by the "bar," "state bar," or "appropriate disciplinary authority," it refers to the agency in the jurisdiction with the authority to administer the standards for admission to practice and for maintenance of professional competence and integrity. Whenever a lawyer is identified as a "certified specialist," that lawyer has been so certified by the appropriate agency in the jurisdiction in which the lawyer practices.

The ABA Model Rules of Professional Conduct, and the ABA Model Code of Judicial Conduct are available from the American Bar Association at 750 N. Lake Shore Dr., Chicago, IL 60611 (312-988-5522 or 800-285-2221) or at www.abanet.org/cpr.

MPRE SUBJECT MATTER OUTLINE

The following subject matter outline indicates the examination's scope of coverage and the approximate percentage of items that are included in each major area. The outline is not intended to list every aspect of a topic mentioned. Although the test items for each MPRE are developed from these categories, each topic is not necessarily tested on each examination.

I.   Regulation of the Legal Profession (8-12%)
     A. Inherent Powers of Courts to Regulate Lawyers
     B. Admission to the Profession
     C. Regulation after Admission
     D. Maintaining Professional Standards—Peer Responsibility
     E. Unauthorized Practice
     F. Fee Division with a Non-Lawyer
     G. The Law Firm
     H. Contractual Restrictions on Practice

II. The Client-Lawyer Relationship (10-14%)
     A. Acceptance or Rejection of Clients
     B. Scope, Objective, and Means of the Representation
     C. Within the Bounds of the Law
     D. Withdrawal
     E. Client-Lawyer Contracts
     F. Fees

III. Privilege and Confidentiality—Clients and Former Clients (6-10%)
     A. Evidentiary Privilege
     B. Professional Obligation of Confidence
     C. Client-Authorized Disclosure
     D. Permissible Disclosure
     E. Special Problems

IV. Independent Professional Judgment—Conflicts of Interest—Client Consent (12-16%)
     A. As Affected by Lawyer's Personal Interest
     B. Lawyer as Witness
     C. Acquiring an Interest in Litigation
     D. Entering into Business Transactions with Client
     E. Conflicting Interests—Current Clients and Former Clients
     F. Influence by Persons Other than Client
     G. Law Firm, Associates, and Related Persons
     H. Lawyer's Service as Arbitrator, Mediator, or Judge

V.   Competence, Legal Malpractice, and Other Civil Liability (8-12%)
     A. Civil Liability, Including Malpractice
     B. Maintaining Competence
     C. Acceptance of Employment

D. Exercise of Diligence and Care
E. Limiting Liability for Malpractice

VI. Litigation and Other Forms of Advocacy (12-16%)
A. Exercise of Professional Judgment
B. Civility, Courtesy, and Decorum
C. Conduct in the Course of Litigation—Claims, Defenses, Testimony, and Evidence
D. Fraud or Perjury
E. Communications in Course of Representation

VII. Different Roles of the Lawyer (4-8%)
A. Lawyer as Advisor
B. Lawyer as Intermediary
C. Lawyer as Evaluator
D. Lawyer as Negotiator
E. Lawyer as Mediator
F. Special Obligations of the Lawyer in Public Service
G. Appearances before Legislative Bodies

VIII. Safekeeping Property and Funds of Clients and Others (4-8%)
A. Lawyer as Trustee of Client Funds
B. Lawyer as Custodian of Client Property
C. Disputed Claims

IX. Communication About Legal Services (6-10%)
A. Public Communications About Services
B. Referrals
C. Group Legal Services
D. Direct Contact With Prospective Clients (Solicitation)
E. Fields of Practice—Limitations of Practice and Specialization

X. Lawyers and the Legal System (2-6%)
A. Lawyer Activity in Improving the Legal System
B. Impropriety Incident to Public Service

XI. Judicial Ethics (6-10%)
A. Upholding the Integrity and Independence of the Judiciary
B. Avoiding Impropriety and the Appearance of Impropriety
C. Duties of Impartiality and Diligence
D. Activities to Improve the Legal System
E. Extra-Judicial Activities
F. Political Activity of Judges
G. Candidate for Judicial Office

GUIDELINES FOR TAKING THE EXAMINATION

The following directions appear on the examination booklet.

Please read the following guidelines carefully. They are designed to help you do your best on the Multistate Professional Responsibility Examination.

1. Listen closely to all directions. Do not hesitate to ask questions if you do not understand what you are to do.

2. Be very precise in marking your answer sheet. Be sure that you blacken the appropriate ovals and that you completely erase any incorrect marks.

3. Your responses must be marked on the answer sheet if you are to receive credit for them.

4. Keep your answer sheet near your test booklet so you can mark answers quickly without moving either the booklet or the answer sheet.

5. Read each question carefully. Pay special attention to such key words or phrases as subject to discipline, may, proper, subject to litigation sanction, subject to disqualification, and subject to civil liability, among others. They are crucial in determining the correct answer.

6. Do not focus solely on the "Yes" or "No" component contained in many answers. Read the entire answer, as the explanations or qualifiers are important in determining the correct answer.

7. Answer each question. There is no penalty for guessing, so use any clues you have in choosing an answer.

8. When you are unsure of the correct answer to a question, first eliminate every wrong answer you can. Each wrong answer eliminated improves your chances of selecting the correct answer.

9. Do not spend too much time on one question. If a question is too hard for you, choose a reasonable answer and go on to the next question. Work quickly, but carefully.

SAMPLE QUESTIONS

The purpose of this publication is to familiarize applicants with the format and nature of MPRE questions. The questions in this publication should not be used for substantive preparation for the MPRE. Because of changes in the law since the time the examination was administered, the questions and their keys may no longer be current.

Each question has four responses from which you are to select the best one. The questions in the MPRE may include qualifications as part of the alternative responses. These qualifications may be essential to the correctness of the response or responses in which they appear and thus to the correct answer to the question. Consequently, you should read each question thoroughly before you select a response. You may check your answers by using the answer key on page 49 of this book.

If you use the questions in this publication as a practice exam, you should not rely on your raw score to identify how well you are doing. MPRE raw scores are converted to scaled scores through an equating procedure that is designed to ensure that the level of difficulty of the examination remains consistent from administration to administration.

Question 1.

State does not require lawyers to participate in continuing legal education courses. Attorneys Alpha, Beta, and Gamma, all lawyers recently admitted to practice, formed a law partnership in State. As they considered what expenses the partnership would pay on behalf of each lawyer, a majority decided that the firm would not pay for continuing legal education courses since they were not required by State. Gamma, who wanted reimbursement for continuing legal education courses, angrily said, "Fine. I won't attend any continuing legal education courses."

Is it proper for Gamma to refuse to attend any continuing legal education courses?

A. Yes, unless the state offers free continuing legal education courses.

B. Yes, if Gamma independently undertakes continuing study and education in the law.

C. No, because Gamma cannot maintain competence without attending continuing legal education courses.

D. No, unless Gamma obtains malpractice insurance.

Question 2.

Client, a new client of Attorney, has asked Attorney to write a letter recommending Client's nephew for admission to the bar. Client has told Attorney that he has no direct contact with the nephew, but that Client's sister (the nephew's mother) has assured Client that the nephew is industrious and honest.

Which of the following would be proper for Attorney?

I.   Write the letter on the basis of Client's assurance.

II. Write the letter on the basis of Client's assurance if Attorney has no unfavorable information about the nephew.

III. Make an independent investigation and write the letter only if Attorney is thereafter satisfied that the nephew is qualified.

A. III only
B. I and II, but not III
C. I and III, but not II
D. I, II, and III

Question 3.

Alpha is a member of the bar in State First and is also licensed as a stockbroker in State Second. In his application for renewal of his stockbroker's license in State Second, Alpha knowingly filed a false financial statement.

Is Alpha subject to discipline in State First for so doing?

A. Yes, because his actions involve dishonesty or misrepresentation.
B. Yes, but only if he is first convicted of a criminal offense in State Second.
C. No, because his action was not in his capacity as an attorney.
D. No, because his action was not in State First.

Question 4.

Attorney is a sole practitioner whose practice is largely in the areas of tax, wills, estates, and trusts. Attorney learned of a new Internal Revenue Service (IRS) regulation that probably affects the trust provisions in a will she prepared for Testatrix two years ago. Attorney has not represented Testatrix since she drew the will.

Is Attorney <u>subject to discipline</u> if she calls Testatrix and advises her of the new IRS ruling and the need to revise the will?

A. Yes, if Attorney has any reason to believe that Testatrix has another lawyer.

B. Yes, because Attorney would be soliciting legal business from a person who is not a current client.

C. No, provided Attorney does not thereafter prepare a new will for Testatrix.

D. No, because Testatrix is a former client of Attorney.

Question 5.

Deft retained Attorney to appeal Deft's criminal conviction and to seek bail pending appeal. The agreed fee for the appearance on the bail hearing was $50 per hour. Attorney received $800 from Deft of which $300 was a deposit to secure Attorney's fee and $500 was for bail costs in the event that bail was obtained. Attorney maintained two office bank accounts: a "Fee Account," in which all fees were deposited and from which all office expenses were paid, and a "Clients' Fund Account." Attorney deposited the $800 in the "Clients' Fund Account" the week before the bail hearing. Attorney expended six hours of time on the bail hearing. The effort to obtain bail was unsuccessful. Dissatisfied, Deft immediately demanded return of the $800.

It is now <u>proper</u> for Attorney to:

A. transfer the $800 to the "Fee Account."

B. transfer $300 to the "Fee Account" and leave $500 in the "Clients' Fund Account" until Attorney's fee for the final appeal is determined.

C. transfer $300 to the "Fee Account" and send Deft a $500 check on the "Clients' Fund Account."

D. send Deft a $500 check and leave $300 in the "Clients' Fund Account" until the matter is resolved with Deft.

Question 6.

Judge Alpha has been assigned to try a criminal prosecution by State against Deft. Ten years previously, Alpha, while serving as a deputy attorney general in State, initiated an investigation of Deft for suspected criminal conduct. The investigation did not establish any basis for prosecution. None of the matters previously investigated is involved in or affects the present prosecution.

Is it <u>proper</u> for Judge Alpha to try the case?

A. Yes, because none of the matters previously investigated is involved in or affects the present case.

B. Yes, unless Alpha might be prejudiced against Deft because of the prior investigation.

C. No, if Alpha had substantial responsibility in initiating the previous investigation of Deft.

D. No, if Alpha had substantial responsibility in determining that the previous investigation did not establish any basis for prosecution.

Question 7.

Attorney represented Landlord in a variety of matters over several years. Plaint, an elderly widow living on public assistance, filed suit against Landlord alleging that Landlord withheld without justification the security deposit on a rental unit that Plaint vacated three years ago. She brought the action for herself, without counsel, in small claims court. Attorney investigated the claim and learned that it was legally barred by the applicable statute of limitations, although Plaint's underlying claim was meritorious. Attorney told Landlord of the legal defense, but emphasized that Plaint's claim was just and that, in all fairness, the security deposit should be returned to Plaint. Attorney told Landlord:

> "I strongly recommend that you pay Plaint the full amount with interest. It is against your long-term business interests to be known in the community as a landlord who routinely withholds security deposits even though the tenant leaves the apartment in good condition. Paying the claim now will prevent future headaches for you."

Was Attorney's conduct <u>proper</u>?

A. Yes, if Landlord did not object to Attorney's advice and paid Plaint's claim.

B. Yes, because Attorney may refer to both legal and nonlegal considerations in advising a client.

C. No, unless Attorney's engagement letter informed Landlord that Attorney's advice on the matter would include both legal and nonlegal considerations.

D. No, because in advising Landlord to pay the full claim, Attorney failed to represent zealously Landlord's legal interests.

Question 8.

Attorney is a member of the bar and a salaried employee of the trust department of Bank. As part of his duties, he prepares a monthly newsletter concerning wills, trusts, estates, and taxes which Bank sends to all of its customers. The newsletter contains a recommendation to the customer to review his or her will in light of the information contained and, if the customer has any questions, to bring the will to Bank's trust department where the trust officer will answer any questions without charge. The trust officer is not a lawyer. If the trust officer is unable to answer the customer's questions, the trust officer refers the customer to Attorney.

Is Attorney subject to discipline for the foregoing?

A. Yes, because Attorney is giving legal advice to persons who are not his clients.

B. Yes, because Attorney is aiding Bank in the unauthorized practice of law.

C. No, because no charge is made for Attorney's advice.

D. No, because Attorney is a member of the bar.

Question 9.

Alpha & Beta is a large firm that employs over 100 lawyers. Attorney Gamma was recently admitted to practice and was hired as a new associate of Alpha & Beta. Gamma was working late one night when he received a telephone call from his cousin Able. Able said that he was calling from the police station where he had just been arrested for possession of cocaine with intent to distribute. He was permitted to make only one phone call, and Gamma was the only lawyer he knew. Gamma responded that he had no criminal law experience and that Alpha & Beta did not handle criminal cases. Nevertheless, Able pleaded with Gamma to come to the police station and see what he could do to get Able out on bail. Gamma replied that he would do what he could.

Gamma went to the police station and using what information he recalled from his criminal law and procedure courses attempted to get Able released on bail. However, as a result of his inexperience, Gamma was unable to secure Able's release that night. The next morning, Gamma found an experienced criminal lawyer for Able, who obtained Able's release within one hour.

Was Gamma's conduct proper?

A. Yes, because neither referral nor consultation was practical under the circumstances.

B. Yes, because Gamma was a close relative of Able.

C. No, because Gamma had no special training or experience in criminal cases.

D. No, because Gamma did not have the requisite level of competence to accept representation in the case.

Question 10.

Attorney wants to make it easier for her clients to pay their bills for her fees.

Which of the following would be proper for Attorney?

I. Accept bank credit cards in payment of Attorney's fees.

II. Arrange for clients to obtain bank loans for the purpose of paying Attorney's fees.

III. If a case is interesting, suggest that the client give Attorney publication rights concerning the case as partial payment of the fee.

A. II only

B. I and II, but not III

C. I, II, and III

D. Neither I, II, nor III

Question 11.

Attorney practices law in a state that has experienced a business recession and where several banks have failed and others are severely pressed to preserve their solvency. Attorney maintains a Clients' Trust Account in Bank and that account is insured by the Federal Deposit Insurance Corporation against losses up to $100,000. Attorney also maintains his regular office account in the same bank and that account is insured to $100,000. During a particularly busy time, Attorney's bookkeeper told Attorney that the balance in the Clients' Trust Account had increased to $150,000. The bookkeeper noted that the office account had a balance of $30,000.

Which of the following courses of action by Attorney would be proper?

I. Leave the Clients' Trust Account as is if the balance is likely to decrease to less than $100,000 within the next ten days.

II. Open another Clients' Trust Account in another bank and transfer some funds to the second Clients' Trust Account to maintain a fully insured balance in both accounts.

III. Temporarily transfer $50,000 from the Clients' Trust Account to the office account so the balance in both accounts is fully within insured limits.

A. I only

B. II only

C. I and II, but not III

D. II and III, but not I

Question 12.

Law Firm, a professional corporation with five lawyer shareholders, employs twenty-five additional lawyers.

Which of the following is(are) <u>proper</u>?

I. Employees who are members of the bar are not made shareholders until they have been with Law Firm ten years.

II. Manager, who is the office manager but not a member of the bar, is executive vice president of Law Firm.

III. Widow, whose husband was a lawyer shareholder in Law Firm until his death two years ago, continues to hold husband's shares in Law Firm, distributed in his estate, until their child completes a law school education.

A. I only
B. I and II, but not III
C. I and III, but not II
D. I, II, and III

Question 13.

Attorney, who was recently admitted to the bar, has been appointed by the court as counsel for Deft, an indigent defendant charged with a felony. After consulting with Deft and attempting for two days to prepare the case for trial, Attorney became convinced that he lacked the knowledge and experience to represent Deft effectively.

Which of the following would be <u>proper</u> for Attorney?

I. Request permission of the court to withdraw from representing Deft because Attorney knows that he is not competent to handle the case.

II. Request the court to appoint experienced co-counsel and grant a continuance to enable co-counsel to prepare the case.

III. Explain the circumstances to Deft and, if Deft consents, proceed to represent Deft alone to the best of Attorney's ability.

A. I only
B. I and II, but not III
C. II and III, but not I
D. I, II, and III

Question 14.

While an assistant district attorney, Attorney Alpha was in charge of the presentation before a grand jury of evidence that led to an indictment charging thirty-two defendants with conspiracy to sell controlled drugs. Shortly after the grand jury returned the indictments, Alpha resigned as assistant district attorney and became an associate in the law office of Attorney Beta, a sole practitioner. At the time of such association, Beta was the attorney for Deft, one of the indicted co-defendants.

Is it <u>proper</u> for Attorney Beta to continue to represent Deft?

A. Yes, if Alpha does not reveal to Beta any confidence or secret learned while an assistant district attorney.
B. Yes, because a public prosecutor must make timely disclosure to the defense attorney of any exculpatory evidence.
C. No, unless Alpha agrees not to participate in the representation of Deft.
D. No, because Alpha had substantial responsibility for the indictment of Deft.

Question 15.

Attorney filed an action on behalf of Client for breach of contract. In fact, Client had no legal basis for the suit, but wanted to harass Defendant. In order to induce Attorney to file the action, Client made certain false statements of material fact to Attorney, which Attorney included in the complaint filed against Defendant.

At the trial of the case, Client took the stand and testified as set forth in the complaint. The trial court ordered judgment for Client. After entry of judgment, Client wrote Attorney a letter marked "Confidential," in which Client admitted that she had lied to Attorney and had testified falsely in the case.

Upon complaint of Defendant, who claimed Attorney had knowingly used false testimony in the case of Client v. Defendant, disciplinary proceedings were instituted against Attorney.

Is it <u>proper</u> for Attorney to use Client's letter to Attorney in Attorney's defense in the disciplinary proceedings?

A. Yes, if it is necessary to do so in order to protect Attorney's rights.
B. Yes, because Client had committed a fraud on the court in which the case was tried.
C. No, because Attorney learned the facts from Client in confidence.
D. No, if disclosure by Attorney could result in Client's prosecution for perjury.

Question 16.

Judge is presently serving on a state intermediate appellate court. This court, in opinions written by her, has decided several controversial cases in which the court has held that the Fourteenth Amendment to the United States Constitution does not guarantee due process protection to state prison inmates who are disciplined by prison authorities for violating the prison's rules of conduct. Judge is now a candidate for election to a vacancy on the state supreme court. She is vigorously opposed by several organizations concerned with the conditions under which prisoners are incarcerated in the state's prison. Judge is scheduled to be interviewed on television and has been informed that questions will be asked of her concerning those decisions and her attitude on the subject of prisoners' rights.

Which of the following is it proper for Judge to say during the interview?

I.   "I believe that the issues raised by the organizations opposing me are appropriate matters for legislative consideration."

II.   "In my opinion, incarceration for the commission of a crime carries with it a loss of civil liberties in prison discipline proceedings."

III. "I am convinced I was right in those cases and will make the same decision in similar cases in the future."

A.   I only
B.   II only
C.   I and II, but not III
D.   I, II, and III

Questions 17-18 are based on the following fact situation.

Attorney was formerly employed by Insurance Company as a lawyer solely to handle fire insurance claims. While so employed she investigated a fire loss claim of Claimant against Insurance Company. Attorney is now in private practice.

Question 17.

Assume the claim has not been settled and Claimant consults Attorney and asks Attorney either to represent him or refer him to another lawyer for suit on the claim.

Which of the following would be proper for Attorney to do?

I.   Refuse to discuss the matter with Claimant.

II.   Represent Claimant.

III. Refer Claimant to an associate in her law firm, provided Attorney does not share in any fee.

IV.   Give Claimant a list of lawyers who Attorney knows are competent and specialize in such claims.

A.   I only
B.   I and II, but not III or IV
C.   I and III, but not II or IV
D.   I and IV, but not II or III

Question 18.

Assume that the original claim was settled. One year after Attorney left the employ of Insurance Company, Claimant slipped and fell in Insurance Company's office. Claimant now asks Attorney to represent him or refer him to another lawyer for suit on the "slip and fall" claim.

Which of the following would be proper for Attorney to do?

I.   Refuse to discuss the matter with Claimant.

II.   Represent Claimant.

III. Give Claimant a list of lawyers who Attorney knows are competent and specialize in such claims.

A.   I only
B.   I and II, but not III
C.   I and III, but not II
D.   I, II, and III

Question 19.

Client has retained Attorney to represent Client in a contract suit. Attorney's retainer agreement provided that Attorney's fees would be based on a fixed hourly rate, payable at the end of each calendar month. Two months before trial, Client fell behind in the payment of Attorney's monthly billing for fees. Attorney included the following statement on Attorney's last billing to Client:

"Your account is more than thirty days past due. If amounts due are not paid promptly in accordance with our agreement, I will terminate the representation. If you cannot pay the amount due, I will accept an assignment of your cause of action as security for your fee to me."

Two weeks after the last billing, Attorney telephoned Client and told Client that Attorney would withdraw from representing Client if the bill was not paid within forty-eight hours or adequate security given for its payment.

If the bill remains unpaid or unsecured after forty-eight hours, it would be <u>proper</u> for Attorney to:

I.   upon notice to Client, move the court for permission to withdraw.

II.   turn Client's file over to another experienced lawyer in town and notify Client that Attorney no longer represents Client.

III. accept an assignment of Client's cause of action as security for Attorney's fee.

A.   I only
B.   II only
C.   I and II, but not III
D.   I, II, and III

Question 20.

Attorney's advertisement in the local newspaper includes the following information, all of which is true:

I.   Attorney, B.A., magna cum laude, Eastern College; J.D., summa cum laude, State Law School; LL.M., Eastern Law School.

II.   My offices are open Monday through Friday from 9:00 a.m. to 5:00 p.m., but you may call my answering service twenty-four hours a day, seven days a week.

III. I speak modern Greek fluently.

For which, if any, of these statements is Attorney <u>subject to discipline</u>?

A.   III only
B.   I and II, but not III
C.   I, II, and III
D.   Neither I, II, nor III

Question 21.

Alpha represents Defendant in bitter and protracted litigation. Alpha, at Defendant's request, has made several offers of settlement to Plaintiff's lawyer Beta, all of which have been rejected.

During a week's recess in the trial, Alpha and Plaintiff were both present at a cocktail party. Plaintiff went over to Alpha and said: "Why can't we settle that case for $50,000? This trial is costing both sides more than it's worth."

Which of the following is a <u>proper</u> response by Alpha?

I.   "I can't discuss the matter with you."

II.   "If that's the way you feel, why don't you and Defendant get together."

III. "I agree. We already have made several offers to settle this matter."

A.   I only
B.   I and II, but not III
C.   II and III, but not I
D.   I, II, and III

Question 22.

The law firm of Alpha and Beta has a radio commercial which states:

> "Do you have a legal problem? Are you being sued? Consult Alpha and Beta, licensed attorneys at law. Initial conference charge is $25 for one hour. Act now and protect your interests. Call at 1234 Main Street; telephone area code (101) 123-4567."

Are Alpha and Beta <u>subject to discipline</u> for the commercial?

A.   Yes, because the qualifications of the lawyers are not stated.

B.   Yes, because the radio broadcast may encourage litigation.

C.   No, if all the statements in the radio broadcast are true.

D.   No, unless the radio broadcast is heard outside the state in which they are licensed.

Question 23.

Attorney Alpha represents Client, the plaintiff in a medical malpractice case. Alpha's contract with Client provides for a contingent fee of 20% of the recovery by settlement and 30% if the case is tried, with a total fee not to exceed $50,000. Alpha associated Attorney Beta, a sole practitioner, in the case, with Client's written consent and after full disclosure of the fee agreement between Alpha and Beta. Beta is both a medical doctor and a lawyer and is well qualified by experience and training to try medical malpractice cases.

The fee agreement between Alpha and Beta reads as follows:

> "The total fee in this case is 20% of recovery by settlement and 30%, if tried, with a maximum fee of $50,000. Alpha will help with discovery and will be the liaison person with Client. Beta will prepare the case and try it if it is not settled. Alpha and Beta will divide the fee, 40% to Alpha and 60% to Beta."

Are Alpha and Beta <u>subject to discipline</u> for their agreement for division of the fee?

A. Yes, unless Client's consent is in writing.
B. Yes, because Alpha will not try the case.
C. No, if the division of the fee between Alpha and Beta is in proportion to actual work done by each.
D. No, because the total fee does not differ from that contracted for by Alpha with Client.

Question 24.

Attorney Alpha was retained by Client to incorporate Client's business, which previously had been operated as a sole proprietorship. Alpha noticed in Client's file copies of some correspondence from Client to Attorney Beta concerning the possibility of Beta's incorporating Client's business. Alpha questioned Client to make certain that any attorney-client relationship between Beta and Client had been terminated. Client told Alpha,

> "It certainly has been terminated. When I discussed the matter with Beta six months ago, he asked for a retainer of $1,000, which I paid him. He did absolutely nothing after he got the money, even though I called him weekly, and finally, last week when I again complained, he returned the retainer. But don't say anything about it because Beta is an old friend of my family."

Is Alpha <u>subject to discipline</u> if she does not report her knowledge of Beta's conduct to the appropriate authority?

A. Yes, if Alpha believes Beta clearly was guilty of professional misconduct.
B. Yes, unless Alpha believes Beta does not usually neglect matters entrusted to him.
C. No, if Client was satisfied by Beta's return of the retainer.
D. No, unless Client agrees that Alpha may report the information.

Question 25.

Alpha & Beta, a general partnership, is a litigation firm practicing in State. It hires new law school graduates as associates. These new lawyers are largely left to their own resources to practice law. Alpha & Beta accepts many small litigation matters and assigns them to the associates for training purposes. No senior partners are assigned to supervise this work. It is assumed that if an associate needs help on a case, he or she will seek the guidance of a more senior attorney.

Client retained Alpha & Beta to pursue a claim for breach of contract against City. Associate, a first year associate, was assigned Client's case. Associate failed to comply with the applicable 30-day notice requirement for filing a complaint against City, and Client lost the chance to recover $5,000 owed to Client by City. When the complaint was dismissed for failure to comply with the notice requirement, Associate instead told Client that the case was dismissed on the merits.

Which of the following statements are correct?

I.   The law firm of Alpha & Beta is subject to discipline for failure to supervise Associate.

II. The individual partners of Alpha & Beta are subject to discipline for failure to make reasonable efforts to establish a system providing reasonable assurance that all lawyers in the firm comply with the rules of professional conduct.

III. Associate, an unsupervised subordinate lawyer, is subject to discipline for making misrepresentations to Client.

IV. Both the law firm of Alpha & Beta and Associate are subject to civil liability for Client's loss.

A.   II and IV, but not I or III
B.   I, III, and IV, but not II
C.   II, III, and IV, but not I
D.   I, II, III, and IV

Question 26.

Attorney, who represented Plaintiff, received a check from Deft payable to Attorney's order in the sum of $10,000 in settlement of Plaintiff's claim against Deft. Plaintiff had previously paid Attorney a fee so no part of the $10,000 was owed to Attorney.

Which of the following would be proper?

I.   Endorse the check and send it to Plaintiff

II. Deposit the check in Attorney's personal bank account and send Attorney's personal check for $10,000 to Plaintiff

III. Deposit the check in a Clients' Trust Account, advise Plaintiff, and forward a check drawn on that account to Plaintiff

A.   I only
B.   III only
C.   I and III, but not II
D.   I, II, and III

Question 27.

Attorney Alpha has tried many contested cases before Judge Gamma. Alpha believes the judge is lacking both in knowledge of the law and in good judgment and that Attorney Beta would make an excellent judge. Alpha wishes to defeat Judge Gamma and assist Beta in getting elected.

Alpha intends to contribute $5,000 to Beta's campaign.

Is it proper for Alpha to do so?

A.   Yes, Alpha may give $5,000 to Beta personally for his campaign.
B.   Yes, if Alpha's contribution to Beta is made anonymously.
C.   No, because Alpha is practicing before the court to which Beta seeks election.
D.   No, unless Alpha gives the $5,000 to a committee formed to further Beta's election.

11

Question 28.

Attorney represented Seller in negotiating the sale of his ice cream parlor. Seller told Attorney in confidence that, although the business was once very profitable, recent profits have been stable but modest. As the negotiations proceeded, Buyer appeared to be losing interest in the deal. Hoping to restore Buyer's interest, Attorney stated, "The ice cream business is every American's dream: happy kids, steady profits, and a clear conscience." Buyer bought the ice cream parlor but was disappointed when his own profits proved to be modest.

Is Attorney <u>subject to discipline</u>?

A. Yes, because Attorney made a false statement of fact to Buyer.

B. Yes, because Attorney exaggerated the profitability of the business.

C. No, because Attorney represented Seller, not Buyer.

D. No, because Attorney's statement constitutes acceptable puffing in negotiations.

Question 29.

Attorney Alpha was retained by Passenger, a passenger on a bus, who had been injured in a collision between the bus and a truck. Passenger paid Alpha a retainer of $1,000 and agreed further that Alpha should have a fee of 25% of any recovery before filing suit, 30% of any recovery after suit was filed but before judgment, and 35% of any recovery after trial and judgment. Alpha promptly called the lawyer for the bus company and told him she was representing Passenger and would like to talk about a settlement. Alpha made an appointment to talk to the lawyer for the bus company but did not keep the appointment. Alpha continued to put off talking to the lawyer for the bus company. Meanwhile, Passenger became concerned because she had heard nothing from Alpha. Passenger called Alpha's office but was told Alpha was not in and would not call back. Passenger was told not to worry because Alpha would look after her interests. After ten months had passed, Passenger went to Attorney Beta for advice. Beta advised Passenger that the statute of limitations would run in one week and, with Passenger's consent, immediately filed suit for Passenger. Alpha, upon Passenger's demand, refunded the $1,000 Passenger had paid.

Is Alpha <u>subject to discipline</u>?

A. Yes, unless Alpha's time was completely occupied with work for other clients.

B. Yes, because Alpha neglected the representation of Passenger.

C. No, because Passenger's suit was filed before the statute of limitations ran.

D. No, because Alpha returned the $1,000 retainer to Passenger.

Question 30.

Attorney Alpha filed a personal injury suit on behalf of Plaintiff against Defendant. Defendant was personally served with process. Alpha knows that Defendant is insured by Insco and that Attorney Beta has been retained by Insco to represent Defendant. No responsive pleading has been filed on behalf of Defendant, and the time for filing expired over ten days ago.

Is Alpha <u>subject to discipline</u> if Alpha proceeds to have a default judgment entered?

A. Yes, because Alpha knew that Beta had been retained by Insco to represent Defendant.

B. Yes, because Alpha failed to extend professional courtesy to another lawyer.

C. No, because Alpha is properly representing her client's interests.

D. No, because any judgment will be satisfied by Insco.

Question 31.

Attorney is a candidate in a contested election for judicial office. Her opponent, Judge, is the incumbent and has occupied the bench for many years. The director of the state commission on judicial conduct, upon inquiry by Attorney, erroneously told Attorney that Judge had been reprimanded by the commission for misconduct in office. Attorney, who had confidence in the director, believed him. In fact, Judge had not been reprimanded by the commission; the commission had conducted hearings on Judge's alleged misconduct in office and, by a three to two vote, declined to reprimand Judge.

Decisions of the commission, including reprimands, are not confidential.

Is Attorney <u>subject to discipline</u> for publicly stating that Judge had been reprimanded for misconduct?

A. Yes, because the official records of the commission would have disclosed the truth.

B. Yes, because Judge had not been reprimanded.

C. No, because Attorney reasonably relied on the director's information.

D. No, because Judge was a candidate in a contested election.

Question 32.

Attorney is a well-known, highly skilled litigator. Attorney's practice is in an area of law in which the trial proceedings are heard by the court without a jury.

In an interview with a prospective client, Attorney said, "I make certain that I give the campaign committee of every candidate for elective judicial office more money than any other lawyer gives, whether it's $500 or $5,000. Judges know who helped them get elected." The prospective client did not retain Attorney.

Is Attorney <u>subject to discipline</u>?

A. Yes, if Attorney's contributions are made without consideration of candidates' merits.
B. Yes, because Attorney implied that Attorney receives favored treatment by judges.
C. No, if Attorney's statements were true.
D. No, because the prospective client did not retain Attorney.

Question 33.

Judge is presiding in a case that has, as its main issue, a complicated point of commercial law. The lawyers have not presented the case to Judge's satisfaction, and Judge believes she needs additional legal advice. Judge's former partner in law practice, Attorney, is an expert in the field of law that is at issue. Attorney has no interest in the case.

Is it <u>proper</u> for Judge to consult Attorney?

A. Yes, because Attorney has no interest in the case.
B. Yes, if Judge believes that Attorney's advice is needed to serve the interests of justice.
C. No, unless all parties in the case first give their written consent to Judge's consultation with Attorney.
D. No, unless Judge informs the parties of Attorney's identity and the substance of Attorney's advice, and asks for their responses.

Question 34.

After both parties had completed the presentation of evidence and arguments, Judge took under advisement a case tried in Judge's court without a jury in which Attorney had represented Plaintiff. The case involved a difficult fact issue of causation and a difficult issue of law.

After the case was under advisement for several weeks, Attorney heard rumors that Judge was having difficulty determining the issue of factual causation and was uncertain about the applicable law. Immediately after hearing these rumors, Attorney telephoned Judge, told Judge of the rumors Attorney had heard, and asked if Judge would like to reopen the case for additional evidence and briefing from both parties. Thereafter Judge reopened the case for further testimony and requested supplementary briefs from both parties.

Was it <u>proper</u> for Attorney to communicate with Judge?

A. Yes, because both parties were given full opportunity to present their views on the issues in the case.
B. Yes, because Attorney did not make any suggestion as to how Judge should decide the matter.
C. No, because Attorney communicated with Judge on a pending matter without advising opposing counsel.
D. No, because Attorney caused Judge to reopen a case that had been taken under advisement.

13

Trustco, a trust company, entered into the following arrangement with Attorney, a lawyer newly admitted to the bar.

Trustco would provide Attorney with free office space in the building in which Trustco had its offices. If a customer of Trustco contacted Trustco about a will, an officer of Trustco, who is not a lawyer, would advise the customer and help the customer work out the details of the will. The customer would be informed that the necessary documents would be prepared by Trustco's staff. The completed documents would be submitted by an officer of Trustco to the customer for execution.

Attorney, in accordance with a memorandum from Trustco's trust officer detailing the plan, would prepare the necessary documents. Attorney would never meet with the customer and would not charge the customer for these services. Attorney would be free to engage in private practice, subject only to the limitation that Attorney could not accept employment adverse to Trustco.

Is Attorney subject to discipline for entering into the arrangement with Trustco?

A. Yes, because Attorney is restricting his right to practice.
B. Yes, because Attorney is aiding Trustco in the practice of law.
C. No, because Attorney is not charging the customer for his services.
D. No, because Attorney is not giving advice to Trustco's customers.

Question 36.
Attorney represented Husband and Wife in the purchase of a business financed by contributions from their respective separate funds. The business was jointly operated by Husband and Wife after acquisition. After several years, a dispute arose over the management of the business. Husband and Wife sought Attorney's advice, and the matter was settled on the basis of an agreement drawn by Attorney and signed by Husband and Wife. Later, Wife asked Attorney to represent her in litigation against Husband based on the claim that Husband was guilty of fraud and misrepresentation in the negotiations for the prior settlement agreement.

Is it proper for Attorney to represent Wife in this matter?

A. Yes, if all information relevant to the litigation was received by Attorney in the presence of both Husband and Wife.
B. Yes, if there is reason to believe Husband misled both Wife and Attorney at the time of the prior agreement.
C. No, because Attorney had previously acted for both parties in reaching the agreement now in dispute.
D. No, unless Husband is now represented by independent counsel.

Question 37.
Alpha and Beta are members of the bar in the same community but have never practiced together. Beta is a candidate in a contested election for judicial office. Beta is opposed by Delta, another lawyer in the community. Alpha believes Beta is better qualified than Delta for the judiciary and is supporting Beta's candidacy.

Which of the following would be proper for Alpha?

I. Solicit public endorsements for Beta's candidacy by other attorneys in the community who know Beta, including those who are likely to appear before Beta if Beta becomes a judge.

II. Solicit contributions to Beta's campaign committee from other attorneys in the community, including those who are likely to appear before Beta if Beta becomes a judge.

III. Publicly oppose the candidacy of Delta.

A. I only
B. I and II, but not III
C. I and III, but not II
D. I, II, and III

Question 38.
Attorney advertises on the local television station. In the advertisements, a professional actor says:

> "Do you need a lawyer? Call Attorney—her telephone number is area code 555-555-5555. Her fees might be lower than you think."

Attorney approved the prerecorded advertisement and is keeping in her office files a copy of the recording of the actual transmission and a record of when each transmission was made.

Is the advertisement <u>proper</u>?

A. Yes.
B. No, unless Attorney's fees are lower than those generally charged in the area where she practices.
C. No, because she used a professional actor for the television advertisement.
D. No, if she makes a charge for the initial consultation.

Questions 39 and 40 are based on the following fact situation.
Deft, who has been indicted for auto theft, is represented by Attorney. Prosecutor reasonably believes that Deft committed the offense, but, because of Deft's youth, it is in the interest of justice to permit Deft to plead guilty to the lesser offense of "joy-riding" in return for an agreement by Prosecutor to recommend probation. Prosecutor has so advised Attorney, but Attorney told Prosecutor she would not plea bargain and would insist on a jury trial. Attorney informed Deft of Prosecutor's offer and advised Deft not to accept it. Deft followed Attorney's advice. Attorney is a candidate for public office, and Prosecutor suspects that Attorney is insisting on a trial of the case to secure publicity for herself.

Question 39.
Which of the following would be <u>proper</u> for Prosecutor?

I. Send a member of his staff who is not a lawyer to consult with Deft.

II. Move the trial court to dismiss the indictment and accept a new complaint charging the offense of "joy-riding."

III. Proceed to trial on the indictment and prosecute the case vigorously.

A. II only
B. III only
C. I and II, but not III
D. II and III, but not I

Question 40.
Assume for the purposes of this question ONLY that Deft was tried, convicted, and sentenced to prison for two years.

<u>Must</u> Prosecutor report to the disciplinary authority his suspicions about Attorney's conduct of the case?

A. Yes, because Deft suffered a detriment from Attorney's refusal to plea bargain.
B. Yes, if Attorney in fact received widespread publicity as a result of the trial.
C. No, unless Prosecutor has knowledge that Attorney's refusal to plea bargain was due to personal motives.
D. No, if Attorney zealously and competently represented Deft at the trial.

Question 41.
Driver consulted Attorney and asked Attorney to represent Driver, who was being prosecuted for driving while intoxicated in a jurisdiction in which there is an increased penalty for a second offense. Driver told Attorney that his driver's license had been obtained under an assumed name because his prior license had been suspended for driving while under the influence of alcohol. Driver asked Attorney not to disclose Driver's true name during the course of the representation and told Attorney that, if called as a witness, he would give his assumed name. Attorney informed Driver that, in order properly to defend the case, Attorney must call Driver as a witness.

Attorney called Driver as a witness and, in response to Attorney's question "what is your name?," Driver gave his assumed name and not his true name.

Is Attorney <u>subject to discipline</u>?

A. Yes, because Attorney knowingly used false testimony.
B. Yes, if Driver committed a felony when he obtained the driver's license under an assumed name.
C. No, because Attorney's knowledge of Driver's true name was obtained during the course of representation.
D. No, unless Driver's true name is an issue in the proceeding.

15

Question 42.

Attorney represents Client, a plaintiff in a personal injury action. Wit was an eyewitness to the accident. Wit lives about 500 miles distant from the city where the case will be tried. Attorney interviewed Wit and determined that Wit's testimony would be favorable for Client. Wit asked Attorney to pay Wit, in addition to the statutory witness fees while attending the trial, the following:

I. Reimbursement for actual travel expenses while attending the trial.

II. Reimbursement for lost wages while present at the trial.

III. An amount equal to 5% of any recovery in the matter.

If Attorney agrees to pay Wit the above, for which, if any, is Attorney <u>subject to discipline</u>?

A. III only
B. II and III, but not I
C. I, II, and III
D. Neither I, II, nor III

Question 43.

Judge is a judge of the trial court in City. Judge has served for many years as a director of a charitable organization that maintains a camp for disadvantaged children. The organization has never been involved in litigation. Judge has not received any compensation for her services. The charity has decided to sponsor a public testimonial dinner in Judge's honor. As part of the occasion, the local bar association intends to commission and present to Judge her portrait at a cost of $4,000.

The money to pay for the portrait will come from a "public testimonial fund" that will be raised by the City Bar Association from contributions of lawyers who are members of the association and who practice in the courts of City.

Is it <u>proper</u> for Judge to accept the gift of the portrait?

A. Yes, because the gift is incident to a public testimonial for Judge.
B. Yes, because Judge did not receive compensation for her services to the charitable organization.
C. No, because the cost of the gift exceeds $1,000.
D. No, because the funds for the gift are contributed by lawyers who practice in the courts of City.

Question 44.

Attorney, who had represented Testator for many years, prepared Testator's will and acted as one of the two subscribing witnesses to its execution. The will gave 10% of Testator's estate to Testator's housekeeper, 10% to Testator's son and sole heir, Son, and the residue to charity. Upon Testator's death one year later, Executor, the executor named in the will, asked Attorney to represent him in probating the will and administering the estate. At that time Executor informed Attorney that Son had notified him that he would contest the probate of the will on the grounds that Testator lacked the required mental capacity at the time the will was executed. Attorney believes that Testator was fully competent at all times and will so testify, if called as a witness. The other subscribing witness to Testator's will predeceased Testator.

Is it <u>proper</u> for Attorney to represent Executor in the probate of the will?

A. Yes, because Attorney is the sole surviving witness to the execution of the will.
B. Yes, because Attorney's testimony will support the validity of the will.
C. No, because Attorney will be called to testify on a contested issue of fact.
D. No, because Attorney will be representing an interest adverse to Testator's heir at law.

Question 45.

Attorney represented Buyer in a real estate transaction. Due to Attorney's negligence in drafting the purchase agreement, Buyer was required to pay for a survey that should have been paid by Seller, the other party to the transaction. Attorney fully disclosed this negligence to Buyer, and Buyer suggested that he would be satisfied if Attorney simply reimbursed Buyer for the entire cost of the survey.

Although Buyer might have recovered additional damages if a malpractice action were filed, Attorney reasonably believed that the proposed settlement was fair to Buyer. Accordingly, in order to forestall a malpractice action, Attorney readily agreed to make the reimbursement. Attorney drafted a settlement agreement, and it was executed by both Attorney and Buyer.

Was Attorney's conduct <u>proper</u>?

A. Yes, if Attorney advised Buyer in writing that Buyer should seek independent representation before deciding to enter into the settlement agreement.
B. Yes, because Attorney reasonably believed that the proposed settlement was fair to Buyer.
C. No, because Attorney settled a case involving liability for malpractice while the matter was still ongoing.
D. No, unless Buyer was separately represented in negotiating and finalizing the settlement agreement.

Question 46.

Plaintiff and Defendant are next-door neighbors and bitter personal enemies. Plaintiff is suing Defendant over an alleged trespass. Each party believes, in good faith, in the correctness of his position. Plaintiff is represented by Attorney Alpha, and Defendant is represented by Attorney Beta. After Plaintiff had retained Alpha, he told Alpha "I do not want you to grant any delays or courtesies to Defendant or his lawyer. I want you to insist on every technicality."

Alpha has served Beta with a demand to answer written interrogatories. Beta, because of the illness of his secretary, has asked Alpha for a five-day extension of time within which to answer them.

Is Alpha <u>subject to discipline</u> if she grants Beta's request for a five-day extension?

A. Yes, because Alpha is acting contrary to her client's instructions.

B. Yes, unless Alpha first informs Plaintiff of the request and obtains Plaintiff's consent to grant it.

C. No, unless granting the extension would prejudice Plaintiff's rights.

D. No, because Beta was not at fault in causing the delay.

Question 47.

Judge and Attorney were formerly law partners and during their partnership acquired several parcels of real property as co-tenants. After Judge was elected to the trial court in County, she remained a co-tenant with Attorney, but left the management of the properties to Attorney.

Judge's term of office will expire soon and she is opposed for reelection by two members of the bar. Attorney, who has not discussed the matter with Judge, intends to make a substantial contribution to Judge's campaign for reelection.

Judge is one of fifteen judges sitting as trial court judges in County.

Is Attorney <u>subject to discipline</u> if Attorney contributes $10,000 to Judge's reelection campaign?

A. Yes, if Attorney frequently represents clients in cases tried in the trial court of County.

B. Yes, because Judge and Attorney have not discussed the matter of a campaign contribution.

C. No, if the contribution is made to a campaign committee organized to support Judge's reelection.

D. No, because Attorney and Judge have a long-standing personal and business relationship.

Question 48.

Witness was subpoenaed to appear and testify at a state legislative committee hearing. Witness retained Attorney to represent her at the hearing. During the hearing, Attorney, reasonably believing that it was in Witness's best interest not to answer, advised Witness not to answer certain questions on the grounds that Witness had a constitutional right not to answer. The committee chairperson directed Witness to answer and cautioned her that refusal to answer was a misdemeanor and that criminal prosecution would be instituted if she did not answer.

Upon Attorney's advice, Witness persisted in her refusal to answer. Witness was subsequently convicted for her refusal to answer.

Is Attorney <u>subject to discipline</u>?

A. Yes, because his advice to Witness was not legally sound.

B. Yes, because Witness, in acting on Attorney's advice, committed a crime.

C. No, if the offense Witness committed did not involve moral turpitude.

D. No, if Attorney reasonably believed Witness had a legal right to refuse to answer the questions.

Question 49.

Pros, an elected prosecutor in City, plans to run for reelection in six months. Last year two teenage girls were kidnapped from a shopping center and sexually assaulted. The community was in an uproar about the crime and put pressure on Pros to indict and convict the assailant. Four months ago, Deft was arrested and charged with the crimes. The trial is scheduled to begin next week.

Pros met with the police chief last week to review the evidence in the case. At that time, Pros first learned that, before they were interviewed by the detective in charge of sexual assault crimes, the two victims had been tape-recorded discussing the case between themselves in an interview room. Reviewing the tape, Pros realized that the girls' descriptions of the assailant differed significantly in terms of height, weight and hair color. When officially interviewed, however, their descriptions matched almost perfectly.

Deft's appointed counsel was busy handling a large caseload of indigent defendants and neglected to seek access to the prosecution's investigative file. Pros was virtually certain that Deft's counsel was unaware of the tape recording. Given the other evidence in the case, Pros reasonably believed that the girls accurately identified Deft as their assailant. Pros did not reveal the existence of the tape to defense counsel.

Is Pros subject to discipline?

A. Yes, because the tape raises a legitimate question about the victims' eyewitness identification of Deft as the assailant.
B. Yes, unless Pros reasonably believed that the girls accurately identified Deft as their assailant.
C. No, because under the adversary system of criminal justice, it is expected that each party will marshal the evidence best supporting its own position.
D. No, unless Deft's counsel submitted a request for all mitigating or exculpatory evidence before the start of trial.

Question 50.

Attorney Alpha currently represents Builder, a building contractor who is the plaintiff in a suit to recover for breach of a contract to build a house. Builder also has pending before the zoning commission a petition to rezone property Builder owns. Builder is represented by Attorney Beta in the zoning matter.

Neighbor, who owns property adjoining that of Builder, has asked Alpha to represent Neighbor in opposing Builder's petition for rezoning. Neighbor knows that Alpha represents Builder in the contract action.

Is it proper for Alpha to represent Neighbor in the zoning matter?

A. Yes, if there is no common issue of law or fact between the two matters.
B. Yes, because one matter is a judicial proceeding and the other is an administrative proceeding.
C. No, because Alpha is currently representing Builder in the contract action.
D. No, if there is a possibility that both matters will be appealed to the same court.

Question 51.

Attorney, a sole practitioner, limits his practice to personal injury cases. Attorney regularly places an advertisement in local newspapers. The advertisement contains the following statement: "Practice limited to personal injury cases, including medical malpractice." After seeing one of Attorney's advertisements, Baker approached Attorney for representation in a medical malpractice case. After a 30-minute interview Attorney told Baker:

> "I'm sorry, but I am very busy and your case appears to be very complicated. I would be happy to refer you to another lawyer who regularly practices in that field and who may have more room in her schedule. You should see another lawyer promptly before the statute of limitations expires and you lose your right to bring the lawsuit."

Although Attorney did not charge Baker for the interview, Baker was upset at the waste of 30 minutes of her time. Baker did not contact another lawyer until eight months later, when she learned that the statute of limitations on her claim had expired six months after her interview with Attorney. In fact, Baker had a meritorious medical malpractice claim.

Is Attorney <u>subject to civil liability</u>?

A. Yes, because Attorney falsely advertised his availability for medical malpractice cases.
B. Yes, because Attorney did not advise Baker as to the date the statute of limitations would expire.
C. No, because Attorney did not violate any duty owed to Baker.
D. No, because Attorney offered to refer Baker to another medical malpractice lawyer.

Question 52.

Alpha and Beta practiced law under the firm name of Alpha and Beta. When Beta died, Alpha did not change the firm name. Thereafter, Alpha entered into an arrangement with another attorney, Gamma. Gamma pays Alpha a certain sum each month for office space and use of Alpha's law library and for secretarial services, but Alpha and Gamma each has his own clients, and neither participates in the representation of the other's clients or shares in fees paid. On the entrance to the suite of offices shared by Alpha and Gamma are the words "Law Firm of Alpha, Beta, and Gamma."

Is Alpha <u>subject to discipline</u>?

A. Yes, because Beta was deceased when Alpha made the arrangement with Gamma.
 B. Yes, because Gamma is not a partner of Alpha.
C. No, because Alpha and Beta were partners at the time of Beta's death.
D. No, because Gamma is paying a share of the rent and office expenses.

Question 53.

Attorney was employed as a lawyer by the state Environmental Control Commission (ECC) for ten years. During the last two years of her employment, Attorney spent most of her time in the preparation, trial, and appeal of a case involving the discharge by Deftco of industrial effluent into a river in the state. The judgment in the case, which is now final, contained a finding of a continuing and knowing discharge of a dangerous substance into a major stream by Deftco and assessed a penalty of $25,000.

The governing statute also provides for private actions for damages by persons injured by the discharge of the effluent.

Attorney recently left the employment of ECC and went into private practice. Three landowners have brought private damage actions against Deftco. They claim their truck farms were contaminated because they irrigated them with water that contained effluent from dangerous chemicals discharged by Deftco. Deftco has asked Attorney to represent it in defense of the three pending actions.

Is Attorney <u>subject to discipline</u> if she represents Deftco in these actions?

A. Yes, unless the judgment in the prior case is determinative of Deftco's liability.
B. Yes, because Attorney had substantial responsibility in the matter while employed by ECC.
C. No, because Attorney has acquired special competence in the matter.
D. No, if all information acquired by Attorney while representing ECC is now a matter of public record.

19

Question 54.

Attorney Alpha is skilled in trying personal injury cases. Alpha accepted the representation of Plaintiff in a personal injury case on a contingent fee basis. While preparing the case for trial, Alpha realized that the direct examination and cross-examination of the medical experts would involve medical issues with which Alpha was not familiar and, as a consequence, Alpha might not be able to represent Plaintiff competently.

Without informing Plaintiff, Alpha consulted Beta, who is both a lawyer and a medical doctor and who is a recognized specialist in the care and treatment of injuries of the type sustained by Plaintiff. Alpha and Beta agreed that Beta would participate in the trial to the limited extent of conducting the direct examination and cross-examination of the medical experts and that Alpha would divide the fee in proportion to the services performed and the responsibility assumed by each.

Was the arrangement between Alpha and Beta proper?

A.   Yes, because the fee to be paid by Plaintiff was not increased by reason of Beta's association.
B.   Yes, because the fee would be divided in proportion to the services performed and the responsibility assumed by each.
C.   No, because Plaintiff was not advised of the association of Beta.
D.   No, unless, upon conclusion of the matter, Alpha provides Plaintiff with a written statement setting forth the method of determining both the fee and the division of the fee with Beta.

Question 55.

Attorney represents Client, a famous politician, in an action against Newspaper for libel. The case has attracted much publicity, and a jury trial has been demanded. After one of the pretrial hearings, as Attorney left the courthouse, news reporters interviewed Attorney. In responding to questions, Attorney truthfully stated:

> "The judge has upheld our right to subpoena the reporter involved, identified in our motion as Repo, and question her on her mental impressions when she prepared the article."

Is Attorney subject to discipline for making this statement?

A.   Yes, because Attorney identified a prospective witness in the case.
B.   Yes, because prospective jurors might learn of Attorney's remarks.
C.   No, because the statement relates to a matter of public record.
D.   No, because the trial has not commenced.

Question 56.

Attorney Alpha has been employed as an assistant prosecutor in the district attorney's office during the time that an investigation of Deft was being conducted by that office. Alpha took no part in the investigation and had no knowledge of the facts other than those disclosed in the press. Two months ago, Alpha left the district attorney's office and formed a partnership with Attorney Beta.

Last week, Deft was indicted for offenses allegedly disclosed by the prior investigation. Deft asked Alpha to represent him. Alpha declined to do so, but suggested Beta.

Is Beta subject to discipline if Beta represents Deft?

A.   Yes, because Alpha was employed in the district attorney's office while the investigation of Deft was being conducted.
B.   Yes, unless the district attorney's office is promptly notified and consents to the representation.
C.   No, unless Alpha participates in the representation or shares in the fee.
D.   No, because Alpha had no responsibility for or knowledge of the facts of the investigation of Deft.

Question 57.

Deft was on trial for the murder of Victim, who was killed during a barroom brawl. In the course of closing arguments to the jury, Prosecutor said,

> "Deft's whole defense is based on the testimony of Wit, who said that Victim attacked Deft with a knife before Deft struck him. No other witness testified to such an attack by Victim. I don't believe Wit was telling the truth, and I don't think you believe him either."

Was Prosecutor's statement proper?

A.   Yes, if Prosecutor accurately stated the testimony in the case.
B.   Yes, if Prosecutor, in fact, believed Wit was lying.
C.   No, because Prosecutor alluded to the beliefs of the jurors.
D.   No, because Prosecutor asserted his personal opinion about Wit's credibility.

20

Question 58.

Attorney represents Client, the plaintiff in a civil action that was filed a year ago and is about to be set for trial. Client informed Attorney that he could be available at any time during the months of October, November, and December. In discussing possible trial dates with opposing counsel and the court clerk, Attorney was advised that a trial date on October 5 was available and that the next available trial date would be December 10. Without first consulting Client, Attorney requested the December 10 trial date because she was representing Deft, the defendant in a felony criminal trial that was set for October 20 and she wanted as much time as possible to prepare for that trial.

Was it _proper_ for Attorney to agree to the December trial date without obtaining Client's consent?

A. Yes, unless Client will be prejudiced by the delay.
B. Yes, because a criminal trial takes precedence over a civil trial.
C. No, because Attorney should manage her calendar so that her cases can be tried promptly.
D. No, unless Attorney was court-appointed counsel in the criminal case.

Question 59.

Able, Baker, and Carter had been indicted for the armed robbery of the cashier of a grocery store. Together, Able and Baker met with Attorney and asked Attorney to represent them. Attorney then interviewed Able and Baker separately. Each told Attorney that the robbery had been committed by Carter while Able and Baker sat in Carter's car outside the store, that Carter had said he needed some cigarettes, and that each knew nothing of Carter's plan to rob the cashier. Attorney agreed to represent both Able and Baker. One week prior to the trial date, Able told Attorney that he wanted to plea bargain and that he was prepared to turn state's evidence and testify that Baker had loaned Carter the gun Carter used in the robbery. Able also said that he and Baker had shared in the proceeds of the robbery with Carter.

It is _proper_ for Attorney to:

A. request court approval to withdraw as lawyer for both Able and Baker.
B. continue to represent Baker and, with Able's consent and court approval, withdraw as Able's lawyer.
C. continue to represent Able and, with Baker's consent and court approval, withdraw as Baker's lawyer.
D. continue to represent Able and Baker, but not call Able as a witness.

Question 60.

While presiding over the trial of a highly publicized antitrust case, ABCO v. DEFO, Judge received in the mail a lengthy letter from Attorney, a local lawyer. The letter discussed the law applicable to ABCO v. DEFO. Judge knew that Attorney did not represent either party. Judge read the letter and, without mentioning its receipt to the lawyers in the pending case, filed the letter in his general file on antitrust litigation.

Later, after reading the trial briefs in ABCO v. DEFO, Judge concluded that Attorney's letter better explained the law applicable to the case pending before him than either of the trial briefs. Judge followed Attorney's reasoning in formulating his decision.

Was it _proper_ for Judge to consider Attorney's letter?

A. Yes, because Judge did not initiate the communication with Attorney.
B. Yes, if Attorney did not represent any client whose interests could be affected by the outcome.
C. No, unless Judge, prior to rendering his decision, communicated its contents to all counsel and gave them an opportunity to respond.
D. No, because Attorney is not of record as counsel in the case.

Question 61.

Attorney's recorded radio advertisement stated:

> "For a fee of $600 Attorney will represent a party to a divorce that does not result in a court trial of a contested issue of fact."

Attorney had the advertisement prerecorded and approved by the appropriate bar agency for broadcast. Attorney retained a recording of the actual transmission in her office. Client, who had previously agreed with her husband to an uncontested dissolution of their marriage, heard the broadcast and called on Attorney in Attorney's office. Client told Attorney that she had heard the broadcast and asked Attorney to represent her. Attorney agreed to represent Client. Because of the nature of the parties' property, Attorney spent more time on the tax aspects of the case than Attorney anticipated. The time expended by Attorney, if charged at a reasonable hourly rate, would have resulted in a fee of $2,000. After the decree was entered, Attorney billed Client for $2,000.

Is Attorney _subject to discipline_?

A. No, because Attorney's fee was a reasonable charge for the time expended.
B. No, because Attorney, when the representation was accepted, did not anticipate the tax problems.
C. Yes, unless Client pays the fee without protest.
D. Yes, because Attorney charged a fee in excess of the advertised fee.

Question 62.

Acton, a certified public accountant, has proposed to Attorney, a recognized specialist in the field of tax law, that Acton and Attorney form a partnership for the purpose of providing clients with tax-related legal and accounting services. Both Acton and Attorney have deserved reputations of being competent, honest, and trustworthy. Acton further proposes that the announcement of the proposed partnership, the firm stationery, and all public directory listings clearly state that Acton is a certified public accountant and that Attorney is a lawyer.

Is Attorney <u>subject to discipline</u> if he enters into the proposed partnership with Acton?

A. Yes, because one of the activities of the partnership would be providing legal services to clients.

B. Yes, because Attorney would be receiving fees paid for other than legal services.

C. No, because the partnership will assure to the public high-quality services in the fields of tax law and accounting.

D. No, if Attorney is the only person in the partnership who gives advice on legal matters.

Question 63.

Client, who is under indictment for homicide, is represented by Attorney. In the course of representation, Client told Attorney that Client had previously killed two other persons in homicides completely unrelated to the murder indictment for which Attorney was providing representation. Attorney, with Client's consent, made a tape recording of Client's confession regarding the unrelated homicides. At Attorney's request, Client also drew a map on which he designated the remote locations of the graves of the victims of the unrelated killings. Those bodies have not been found by the police, and Client is not a suspect in either crime, both of which remain unsolved.

Is Attorney <u>subject to discipline</u> for failing to disclose voluntarily to the authorities his knowledge of the two prior murders and the locations of the bodies of the victims?

A. Yes, because as an officer of the court, Attorney must disclose any knowledge that he has, whether privileged or not, concerning the commission of the prior crimes by Client.

B. Yes, because Attorney is impeding the state's access to significant evidence.

C. No, because Attorney did not represent or advise Client with respect to the prior crimes.

D. No, because the information was obtained by Attorney in the course of the representation.

Question 64.

Attorney Alpha is recognized as an expert in securities regulation law. Corp, a corporation, retained Alpha's law firm to qualify Corp's stock for public sale. After accepting the matter, Alpha decided that he preferred to spend his time on cases with larger fee potential, so he assigned responsibility for the Corp matter to Attorney Beta, an associate in Alpha's office who had recently been admitted to the bar.

Beta protested to Alpha that he, Beta, knew nothing about securities regulation law and that he had too little time to prepare himself to handle the Corp matter competently without substantial help from Alpha. Alpha responded, "I don't have time to help you. Everyone has to start somewhere." Alpha directed Beta to proceed.

Was Alpha's conduct <u>proper</u> in this matter?

A. Yes, because as a member of the bar, Beta is licensed to handle any legal matter.

B. Yes, because Alpha may withdraw from a case if work on it would cause him unreasonable financial hardship.

C. No, because Alpha knew Beta was not competent to handle the matter, and Alpha failed to provide supervision adequate to protect the client's interest.

D. No, because Corp had not given Alpha permission to assign Beta to work on the matter.

Question 65.

Attorney represents Bank in its commercial loan transactions. Corp has applied to Bank for a loan of $900,000 to be secured by a lien on Corp's inventory. The inventory, consisting of small items, constantly turns over. The security documents are complex and if improperly drawn could result in an invalid lien. Bank has approved the loan on the condition that Attorney prepare the necessary security instruments and that Corp pay Attorney's fees. This arrangement is customary in the city in which Attorney's law office and Bank are located. It is obvious to Attorney that he can adequately represent the interests of both Corp and Bank. After Corp and Bank consulted with other lawyers, each consented in writing to the representation.

Is it <u>proper</u> for Attorney to prepare the security documents under these circumstances?

A. Yes, because Bank and Corp have given their informed consent to the arrangement.

B. Yes, because the arrangement is customary in the community.

C. No, because Attorney's fees are being paid by Corp not Bank.

D. No, because Corp and Bank have differing interests.

Question 66.

Attorney, recently admitted to practice, opened an office near a residential neighborhood and published the following advertisement in the local newspaper.

```
COUPON

Get Acquainted With
Your Neighborhood Lawyer

A. Attorney

Suite 2 – 1100 Magnolia Avenue
Sunshine City, State 01000
Telephone: (555) 555-5555

In order to acquaint you with our services, we are
offering a one-hour consultation to review your
estate plans, including your wills, trusts, and similar
documents, all at the nominal cost of $25 to anyone
presenting this coupon. Call now for an appointment.
```

Is Attorney subject to discipline?

A. Yes, because Attorney is soliciting business from persons with whom Attorney had no prior relationship.
B. Yes, because Attorney requires the use of a coupon.
C. No, if Attorney provides the services described for the fee stated.
D. No, unless Attorney is seeking business from persons who are already represented by a lawyer.

Question 67.

Attorney represented Plaintiff in Plaintiff's action for defamation against Defendant. After Defendant's lawyer had filed and served an answer, Attorney, at Plaintiff's direction, hired Inv, a licensed private investigator, and instructed Inv to attempt to interview Defendant without revealing his employment. Inv succeeded in interviewing Defendant privately and obtained an admission from Defendant that the statements Defendant had made were based solely on unsubstantiated gossip.

Is Attorney subject to discipline for obtaining the statement from Defendant in this matter?

A. No, because Attorney was following Plaintiff's instructions.
B. No, because the statement obtained was evidence that Defendant's allegations were unfounded.
C. Yes, because Attorney should have interviewed Defendant personally.
D. Yes, because Attorney instructed Inv to interview Defendant.

Question 68.

Attorney and Broker, a licensed real estate broker, entered into an agreement whereby Broker was to recommend Attorney to any customer of Broker who needed legal services, and Attorney was to recommend Broker to any client of Attorney who wished to buy or sell real estate. Attorney's practice is limited almost entirely to real estate law.

Is Attorney subject to discipline for entering into the agreement with Broker?

A. Yes, because Attorney is compensating Broker for recommending Attorney's legal services.
B. Yes, because the arrangement constitutes the practice of law in association with a nonlawyer.
C. No, if neither Attorney nor Broker shares in the other's fees.
D. No, if the fees of Attorney and Broker do not clearly exceed reasonable fees for the services rendered by each.

Question 69.

Judge, prior to her appointment to the probate court, was a partner in Law Firm. Law Firm had an extensive probate practice. At the time of Judge's appointment, Law Firm had pending before the court to which Judge was appointed numerous matters in which requests were being made for allowances for attorney's fees. When Judge left Law Firm, she was paid a cash settlement. She has no further financial interest in any matter handled by Law Firm. Judge is now being asked to rule on these requests for allowances for attorney's fees.

Is it proper for Judge to rule on these requests?

A. Yes, because Judge has no financial interest in the outcome of these cases.
B. Yes, if these requests are not contested.
C. No, unless Judge notes on the record in each case her prior association with Law Firm.
D. No, because Judge was associated with Law Firm when these matters were pending.

Question 70.

Attorney, representing Client, with Client's approval settled a claim against Defendant for $60,000. The settlement agreement provided that one-half would be paid by Insco, Defendant's primary insurance carrier, and one-half by Sureco, a co-insurer. Attorney's agreed fee was 30% of the amount of the settlement. Attorney received Insco's check for $30,000 and a letter from Sureco advising that its check would be sent in two weeks. Attorney promptly advised Client and deposited the $30,000 in her Clients' Trust Account. Client demanded that Attorney send him the entire $30,000 and take her fee out of the funds to be received from Sureco.

Which of the following would now be proper for Attorney?

I.   Send Client $30,000.

II.   Send Client $21,000 and retain $9,000 in her Clients' Trust Account.

III. Send Client $21,000 and transfer $9,000 to her personal account.

A.   I only
B.   I and II, but not III
C.   I and III, but not II
D.   I, II, and III

Question 71.

Attorney is a well-known tax lawyer and author. During congressional hearings on tax reform, Attorney testified to her personal belief and expert opinion on the pending reform package. She failed to disclose in her testimony that she was being paid well by a private client for her appearance. In her testimony, Attorney took the position favored by her client, but the position was one that Attorney believed was in the public interest.

Was it proper for Attorney to present this testimony without identifying her private client?

A.   Yes, because Attorney conscientiously believed that the position she advocated before Congress was in the public interest.
B.   Yes, because Congress is interested in the content of testimony and not who is paying the witness.
C.   No, because a lawyer may not accept a fee for trying to influence legislative action.
D.   No, because a lawyer who appears in a legislative hearing should identify the capacity in which the lawyer appears.

Question 72.

Attorney represented Baker in a claim involving a breach of Baker's employment contract. The case was settled without suit being filed. The proceeds of the settlement were paid directly to Baker, who subsequently paid Attorney in full for Attorney's fee and expenses. Thereafter, Attorney did no other work for Baker.

Baker is now being audited by the Internal Revenue Service (IRS). The IRS has asked Attorney for details of the settlement, including the amount claimed for each item of damage and the amounts paid for the items. Attorney reported the request to Baker who told Attorney not to provide the information to the IRS.

Is it proper for Attorney to furnish the information to the IRS?

A.   Yes, if the information does not involve Attorney's work product.
B.   Yes, because Attorney no longer represents Baker.
C.   No, because Baker told Attorney not to provide the information.
D.   No, unless Attorney believes the disclosure would be beneficial to Baker.

Question 73.

Attorney represents Driver, the plaintiff in an automobile accident case. Two weeks before the date set for trial, Attorney discovered that Witt was an eyewitness to the accident. Attorney interviewed Witt. Witt's version of the accident was contrary to that of Driver and, if believed by the trier of fact, would establish that Driver was at fault. Witt told Attorney that she had not been interviewed by defense counsel.

Witt also told Attorney that she intended to leave for Europe the following week for a month's vacation unless she had an obligation to remain and attend the trial. Attorney told Witt:

> "No one has subpoenaed you yet. You have no legal duty to make yourself available. Trials can be difficult affairs. Witnesses sometimes get very nervous because of the questions asked by the lawyers. Why don't you take the vacation as planned, and, by the time you return, the trial will be over."

Is Attorney subject to discipline?

A.   Yes, because Attorney advised Witt to leave the jurisdiction.
B.   Yes, because Attorney did not subpoena Witt knowing she was an eyewitness.
C.   No, because Witt had not been subpoenaed by the defense.
D.   No, because Attorney did not offer Witt any inducement not to appear at the trial.

Question 74.
Attorney is employed by Client, a fugitive from justice under indictment for armed robbery. Attorney, after thorough legal research and investigation of the facts furnished by Client, reasonably believes the indictment is fatally defective and should be dismissed as a matter of law. Attorney advised Client of his opinion and urged Client to surrender. Client told Attorney that she would not surrender.

Attorney informed the district attorney that he represented Client and that he counseled Client to surrender, but that Client refused to follow his advice. Attorney has not advised Client on how to avoid arrest and prosecution and does not know where Client is hiding.

Is Attorney subject to discipline if he continues to represent Client?

A. Yes, because Client is engaged in continuing illegal conduct.
B. Yes, because client refused to accept Attorney's advice and surrender.
C. No, because Attorney is not counseling Client to avoid arrest and prosecution.
D. No, because Attorney reasonably believes the indictment is defective.

Question 75.
Attorney in his capacity as part-time assistant county attorney represented County in a criminal non-support proceeding against Husband. This proceeding concluded with an order directing Husband to pay or be jailed. Husband refused to pay.

Attorney, pursuant to applicable rules, is permitted to maintain a private law practice. Wife has discovered some assets of Husband. Attorney now has accepted employment from Wife to maintain a civil action against Husband to recover out of those assets arrearages due to Wife under Wife's support decree. Attorney did not obtain consent from the county attorney or from Husband to represent Wife in the civil action.

Is Attorney subject to discipline for accepting employment in Wife's civil action against Husband?

A. Yes, because Attorney did not obtain Husband's consent to the representation.
B. Yes, because Attorney had personal and substantial responsibility in the first proceeding.
C. No, because Attorney's responsibility in his public employment has terminated.
D. No, because Attorney is representing Wife's interest in both the criminal and the civil proceedings.

Question 76.
Attorney is a lawyer for City and advises City on all tort claims filed against it. Attorney's advice is limited to recommending settlement and the amount thereof. If a claim is not settled and suit is filed, defense of the suit is handled either by lawyers for City's insurance carrier or by outside counsel specially retained for that purpose. In connection with any notice of claim and before suit is filed, Attorney arranges for an investigator to call upon the claimant at the claimant's home and, with no one else present, to interview the claimant and endeavor to obtain a signed statement of the claimant's version of the facts.

Claimant has filed a notice of claim against City. Attorney has sent an investigator to interview Claimant.

Is Attorney subject to discipline for arranging an interview with Claimant?

A. Yes, if Claimant was known by Attorney to be represented by counsel.
B. Yes, if the statement taken is later used to Claimant's disadvantage.
C. No, because claimant had not filed suit at the time of the interview.
D. No, because Attorney would not be representing City in any subsequent litigation on Claimant's claim.

Question 77.
Delta, a lawyer, has just joined the Law Offices of Alpha and Beta, a professional corporation engaged solely in the practice of law. Delta is a salaried associate and is not a member or shareholder of the professional corporation. Alpha's spouse, Veep, who is not a lawyer, is vice-president of the corporation and office manager. All of the other officers are lawyers in the firm. All of the corporate shares are held by lawyers in the corporation, except for ten shares held by the executor under the will of a lawyer-member who died one month previously and whose will is now being probated. Delta knows that Veep is an officer and not a lawyer.

Is Delta subject to discipline?

A. Yes, because Veep is an officer of the corporation.
B. Yes, if a nonlawyer holds the stock as the executor of the will of the deceased member.
C. No, because Delta is a salaried employee and not a member or shareholder of the corporation.
D. No, if Veep does not participate in any decision regarding a client or a client's case.

Attorney is representing Plaintiff in a paternity suit against Defendant. Both Plaintiff and Defendant are well-known public figures, and the suit has attracted much publicity. Attorney has been billing Plaintiff at an agreed hourly fee for his services. Recently, Plaintiff told Attorney,

> "I'm going broke paying you. Why don't you let me assign you all media rights to books, movies, or television programs based on my suit as full payment for all services you will render me between now and the conclusion of the suit?"

Attorney replied,

> "I'll consider it, but first you should seek independent advice about whether such an arrangement is in your own best interests. Why don't you do so and call me next week."

Is Attorney <u>subject to discipline</u> if he agrees to Plaintiff's offer?

A.   Yes, because the amount received by Attorney would be contingent on the receipts from the sale of media rights.
B.   Yes, because Attorney has not concluded the representation of Plaintiff.
C.   No, because the paternity suit is a civil and not a criminal matter.
D.   No, if Plaintiff received independent advice before entering into the agreement.

Four years ago, Attorney represented Husband and Wife, both high school teachers, in the purchase of a new home. Since then, Attorney prepared their tax returns and drafted their wills.

Recently, Husband called Attorney and told her that he and Wife had decided to divorce, but wanted the matter to be resolved amicably. Husband stated that they were planning to file and process their own divorce case, utilizing the state's new streamlined divorce procedure, applicable in "no-fault" cases where there are no minor children. Husband asked if Attorney would agree to work with them to prepare a financial settlement agreement that could be presented to the divorce court, reminding Attorney that the couple's assets were modest and that they wanted to "split it all down the middle."

After considering the risks of a conflict of interest arising in this limited representation, Attorney wrote to the couple separately, and advised each that he or she might be better off with separate lawyers, but that Attorney would assist with the financial settlement agreement, charging an hourly fee of $140 per hour, provided that they were in complete agreement and remained so. Attorney advised that if a conflict developed, or if either party was dissatisfied or uncomfortable about continuing with the joint representation, Attorney would withdraw and would not represent either party from that point forward, forcing them to start all over again with separate lawyers. Finally, Attorney cautioned Husband and Wife that Attorney would be representing both of them equally, would not and could not favor one or the other, and that their separate communications to her could not be kept confidential from the other party. Both Husband and Wife signed their individual copy of the letter, consenting to the joint representation, and returned them to Attorney.

Was it <u>proper</u> for Attorney to accept the representation on these terms?

A.   Yes, because there was little risk that the interests of either Husband or Wife would be materially prejudiced if no settlement was reached.
B.   Yes, because Attorney had previously represented Husband and Wife in their joint affairs.
C.   No, because Attorney conditioned representation upon receiving a waiver of client confidentiality.
D.   No, unless Attorney advised both Husband and Wife, in writing, that they should seek independent counsel before agreeing to enter into the financial settlement on the terms proposed.

Question 80.

Attorney represented Client in negotiating a large real estate transaction. Buyer, who purchased the real estate from Client, has filed suit against both Client and Attorney, alleging fraud and violation of the state unfair trade practices statute. Attorney had advised Client by letter against making the statements relied on by Buyer as the basis for Buyer's claim. Attorney and Client are each represented by separate counsel. In responding to a deposition under subpoena, Attorney wishes to reveal, to the extent Attorney reasonably believes necessary to defend herself, confidential information imparted to Attorney by Client that will be favorable to Attorney but damaging to Client.

Is it <u>proper</u> for Attorney to reveal such information?

A. Yes, unless Client objects to the disclosure.
B. Yes, because Attorney may reveal such information to defend herself against a civil claim.
C. No, unless criminal charges have also been brought against Attorney.
D. No, because the disclosure will be detrimental to Client.

Question 81.

Attorney, who is corporate counsel for Company, is investigating a possible theft ring in the parts department of Company. Attorney knows that Employee has worked in the parts department for a long time and believes that Employee is a suspect in the thefts. Attorney believes that if Employee were questioned, Employee would not answer truthfully if she knew the real purpose of the questions. Attorney plans to question Employee and falsely tell her that she is not a suspect and that her answers to the questions will be held in confidence.

Is Attorney <u>subject to discipline</u> if she so questions Employee?

A. Yes, because Attorney's conduct involves misrepresentation.
B. Yes, unless Attorney first advises Employee to obtain counsel to represent Employee.
C. No, because no legal proceedings are now pending.
D. No, because Attorney did not give legal advice to Employee.

Question 82.

Manufacturer sued Partco for Partco's breach of warranty regarding machine components furnished by Partco. Judge, who presided at the nonjury trial, sent Clerk, her law clerk, to Manufacturer's plant to observe the machine that was malfunctioning due to the allegedly defective parts. Clerk returned and told Judge that the machine was indeed malfunctioning and that Engineer, an employee of Manufacturer, had explained to Clerk how the parts delivered by Partco caused the malfunction. There was testimony at the trial that supported what Clerk learned on his visit. Judge rendered a judgment for Manufacturer.

Was Judge's conduct <u>proper</u>?

A. Yes, because Judge's judgment was supported by evidence at the trial.
B. Yes, because Judge has the right to gather facts concerning the trial.
C. No, because Judge has engaged in ex parte contacts that might influence the outcome of litigation.
D. No, unless Engineer was a witness at the trial and subject to cross-examination by Partco.

Question 83.

Attorney regularly represented Client. When Client planned to leave on a world tour, Client delivered to Attorney sufficient money to pay Client's property taxes when they became due. Attorney placed the money in Attorney's Clients' Trust Account. When the tax payment date arrived, Attorney was in need of a temporary loan to close the purchase of a new personal residence. Because the penalty for late payment of taxes was only 2% while the rate for a personal loan was 6%, Attorney withdrew Client's funds from the Clients' Trust Account to cover Attorney's personal check for the closing. Attorney was confident that Client would not object. Ten days later, after the receipt of a large fee previously earned, Attorney paid Client's property taxes and the 2% penalty, fully satisfying Client's tax obligation. After Client returned, Attorney told Client what Attorney had done, and Client approved Attorney's conduct.

Is Attorney <u>subject to discipline</u>?

A. Yes, because Attorney failed to pay Client the ten days of interest at the fair market rate.
B. Yes, because Attorney used Client's funds for a personal purpose.
C. No, because Client was not harmed and Attorney reasonably believed at the time Attorney withdrew the money that Client would not object.
D. No, because when Attorney told Client what he had done, Client approved Attorney's conduct.

Question 84.

Attorney entered into a written retainer agreement with Deft, who was the defendant in a criminal case. Deft agreed in writing to transfer title to Deft's automobile to Attorney if Attorney successfully prevented Deft from going to prison. Later, the charges against Deft were dismissed.

Is Attorney subject to discipline for entering into this retainer agreement?

A. Yes, because Attorney agreed to a fee contingent on the outcome of a criminal case.

B. Yes, because a lawyer may not acquire a proprietary interest in a client's property.

C. No, because the charges against Deft were dismissed.

D. No, because the retainer agreement is in writing.

Question 85.

Attorney Alpha filed a complaint on behalf of Client against Agri, a corporation, alleging that Agri had breached a valid oral contract entered into on Agri's behalf by Pres, the president and chief executive officer of Agri, to sell Client certain merchandise for a specified price. Attorney Beta, representing Agri, has filed an answer denying the contract and asserting the statute of frauds as a defense.

Attorney Beta has given notice to Alpha that he will take the deposition of Pres on the grounds that Pres will be out of the country on the date the case is set for trial. Pres is not a shareholder of Agri. Alpha would like to interview Pres, prior to the taking of the deposition, in order better to prepare her cross-examination.

Is Alpha subject to discipline if she interviews Pres without Beta's knowledge and consent?

A. No, unless Pres will be personally liable to Agri for damages in the event judgment is rendered against Agri.

B. No, because Pres allegedly entered into the contract on behalf of Agri.

C. Yes, because Pres is being called as an adverse witness.

D. Yes, because Pres is the president of Agri.

Question 86.

Attorney represents ten plaintiffs who were injured when a train operated by Railroad was derailed. Railroad has offered Attorney a $500,000 lump sum settlement for the ten plaintiffs. Attorney has determined a division of the $500,000 among the ten plaintiffs with the amount paid each plaintiff dependent on the nature and extent of that person's injuries. Attorney believes the division is fair to each plaintiff.

Railroad will not settle any of the claims unless all are settled. Attorney has told each plaintiff the total amount Railroad is prepared to pay, the amount that the individual will receive, and the basis on which that amount was calculated. Attorney has not told any plaintiff the amount to be received by any other plaintiff. Attorney believes that if Attorney reveals to each plaintiff the amount of each settlement, there is danger that some plaintiffs will think that they are not getting enough in relation to the amounts others will receive and the entire settlement will be upset. Each of the plaintiffs has agreed to his or her settlement.

Is Attorney subject to discipline if Attorney effects such a settlement?

A. Yes, because Attorney is aiding the lawyer for Railroad in making a lump sum settlement.

B. Yes, because no individual plaintiff knows the amount to be received by any other plaintiff.

C. No, if to disclose all settlements to each plaintiff might jeopardize the entire settlement.

D. No, if the amount received by each plaintiff is fair and each plaintiff is satisfied.

Question 87.

Attorney Alpha serves on a bar association committee established to counsel and rehabilitate lawyers who suffer from substance abuse. The day before Alpha was to leave on a fishing trip, Alpha's close friend, Attorney Beta, disclosed to Alpha that, over the preceding two years, Beta had become heavily addicted to cocaine and was afraid he had committed criminal offenses in his banking activities as a result of his addiction. Beta asked Alpha to represent him. Alpha agreed, but explained that Alpha could do little for two weeks and would consult with Beta immediately upon Alpha's return. While on the fishing trip, Cepa, an accountant who knew that Alpha represented Beta, told Alpha that Cepa had been retained by the trust department of Bank, a commercial bank, to audit several substantial trust accounts in which Bank and Beta are co-trustees. Cepa also told Alpha that the audit furnished incontrovertible proof that Beta had embezzled more than $100,000 from the trust accounts.

Must Alpha report Beta's embezzlement to the appropriate disciplinary authority?

A. Yes, because Alpha learned of Beta's embezzlement from Cepa.
B. Yes, because Alpha's failure to report would assist the concealment of Beta's breach of trust.
C. No, because Alpha gained the information while representing Beta.
D. No, because the information will probably be made public by Bank.

Question 88.

The following advertisement appeared in a daily newspaper in a state in which both parties are members of the bar:

A. ALPHA, M.D., J.D.
and
B. BETA, J.D.

Attorneys at Law
1000 "A" Street, City, State, 00000
Telephone (555) 555-5555.

Are Alpha and Beta subject to discipline?

A. No, because both law and medicine are licensed professions.
B. No, if they possess the degree(s) stated.
C. Yes, because the reference to the M.D. degree is self-laudatory.
D. Yes, unless they limit their practice to areas in which a medical degree is relevant.

Question 89.

While working on a complex matter for Client, Attorney Alpha, a partner in the law firm of Alpha and Beta, identified a particularly difficult issue of law that could prove decisive in the dispute. Alpha had not encountered this issue before and was uncertain of its effect. Alpha called Alpha's partner, Attorney Beta, and asked her for assistance.

Was it proper for Alpha to consult with Beta?

A. No, unless the total fee is not increased by the consultation.
B. No, because Client's consent was not previously obtained.
C. Yes, unless Alpha identified Client to Beta.
D. Yes, because Alpha and Beta are partners in the same firm.

Question 90.

Judge, a state court judge, has presided over the pretrial proceedings in a case involving a novel contract question under the Uniform Commercial Code. During the pretrial proceedings, Judge has acquired considerable background knowledge of the facts and law of the matter and, therefore, is particularly well qualified to preside at the trial. Shortly before the trial date, Judge discovered that his brother owns a substantial block of stock in the defendant corporation. He determined that his brother's financial interests would be substantially affected by the outcome of the case. Although Judge believed he would be impartial, he disclosed to the parties, on the record, his brother's interest.

Is it proper for Judge to hear the case?

A. Yes, because Judge is particularly well qualified to preside at the trial.
B. Yes, because Judge believes his judgment will not be affected by his brother's stockholding.
C. No, because disqualification based on a relative's financial interest cannot be waived.
D. No, unless after proper proceedings in which Judge did not participate all parties and their lawyers consent in writing that Judge may hear the case.

Question 91.

Attorney is representing Deft on a charge of armed robbery. Deft claims that the prosecution witness is mistaken in her identification. Deft has produced Baker, who will testify that Deft was in another city 500 miles away when the robbery occurred. Attorney knows that Baker is lying, but Deft insists that Baker be called on Deft's behalf.

Is Attorney <u>subject to discipline</u> if she calls Baker?

A. Yes, unless, before calling Baker, Attorney informs the court of her belief.

B. Yes, because Attorney knows Baker will be testifying falsely.

C. No, unless Attorney relies on the alibi defense in her argument before the jury.

D. No, because Deft has insisted that Baker be called as a witness on Deft's behalf.

Question 92.

Attorney is a candidate for a judicial office that has been occupied by Incumbent for six years. Attorney has conducted a thorough investigation of Incumbent's personal and professional life.

Assume all factual statements are accurate. Which of the following statements is it <u>proper</u> for Attorney to make during the campaign?

I. "Incumbent has been reversed by the appellate courts more than any other judge in the state during the preceding two years."

II. "Incumbent was publicly censured by the state Judicial Qualification Commission on one occasion for his overbearing conduct in court."

III. "Incumbent was given a poor rating for judicial temperament in a county bar association poll."

IV. "During the previous year, the average sentence in armed robbery cases tried in Incumbent's court was 3.5 years, and in murder cases was 8.2 years. If I am elected, I won't be soft on crime."

A. I only

B. I and II, but not III or IV

C. I, II, and III, but not IV

D. I, II, and IV, but not III

Question 93.

The state bar association has offered Judge and her spouse free transportation and lodging to attend its institute on judicial reform. Judge is expected to deliver a banquet speech.

Is it <u>proper</u> for Judge to accept this offer?

A. Yes, unless the value of the transportation and lodging exceeds $500.

B. Yes, because the activity is devoted to the improvement of law.

C. No, if members of the bar association regularly appear in Judge's court.

D. No, because the bar association is offering free transportation to Judge's spouse.

Question 94.

Attorney represents Client, a well-known contractor, before Agency, a state administrative agency. Agency has ordered Client to show cause why Client's license as a contractor should not be revoked for violation of agency regulations. In a newspaper interview prior to the administrative hearing, Attorney truthfully stated that:

I. "Client denies the charge made by Agency that Client engaged in conduct constituting grounds for revocation of Client's license as a contractor."

II. "The next step in the administrative process is the administrative hearing; if Agency is successful, we will appeal, and Agency still cannot revoke Client's license until a court affirms the finding for Agency."

III. "Client needs witnesses who are aware of the incidents that are the subject of the hearing."

Which of these statements would be <u>proper</u>?

A. I only

B. II only

C. III only

D. I, II, and III

Question 95.
Leaving an airport, Attorney, who primarily practices criminal law, shared a cab with Doctor, a medical doctor. The cab was involved in a collision, and Doctor was seriously injured, while Attorney was only shaken up. Attorney accompanied Doctor to the hospital in the ambulance. Doctor believed that she was dying and asked Attorney to prepare a simple will for her. Attorney told Doctor, "I have never prepared a will, but hope that I can remember the basics from law school." Attorney then complied with Doctor's request. Doctor signed the will, and the two paramedics in the ambulance signed as witnesses.

Was it proper for Attorney to prepare the will?

A. Yes, unless Attorney omitted some required formality that rendered the will invalid.
B. Yes, because Attorney provided legal services that were reasonably necessary under the circumstances.
C. No, unless Doctor waived Attorney's malpractice liability.
D. No, because Attorney did not have the skill required for the representation.

Question 96.
Attorney has recently started her own law firm with four other lawyers as associates. The law firm has moved into offices in a new building which is owned by Bank. Attorney has borrowed heavily from Bank to finance her new law firm. In addition, Bank provides the law firm with accounting services through its computer.

At Bank's suggestion, an employee of Bank, who is not a lawyer, serves as a part-time office manager for the law firm without compensation from the firm. The duties of the office manager are to advise the firm generally on fees and time charges, program matters for the computer services, and consult with Attorney on accounting and billing practices to ensure solvency.

Is the arrangement with Bank proper?

A. Yes, unless secrets or confidences of clients may be disclosed to Bank.
B. Yes, because the office manager is paid by Bank.
C. No, because a nonlawyer will be advising the law firm on fees and time charges.
D. No, because Bank will be involved in the practice of law.

Question 97.
Attorney is representing Client, the plaintiff in a personal injury case, on a contingent fee basis. Client is without resources to pay for the expenses of the investigation and the medical examinations necessary to prepare for trial. Client asked Attorney to pay for these expenses. Attorney declined to advance the funds but offered to guarantee Client's promissory note to a local bank in order to secure the funds needed to cover those expenses. Client has agreed to reimburse Attorney in the event Attorney incurs liability on the guaranty.

Is Attorney subject to discipline if she guarantees Client's promissory note?

A. Yes, because Attorney is lending her credit to Client.
B. Yes, because Attorney is helping to finance litigation.
C. No, because the funds will be used for trial preparation.
D. No, because Attorney took the case on a contingent fee basis.

Question 98.
Attorney Alpha represents Defendant in an action for personal injuries. Alpha, pursuant to Defendant's authorization, made an offer of settlement to Attorney Beta, who represents Plaintiff. Beta has not responded to the offer, and Alpha is convinced that Beta has not communicated the offer to Plaintiff. State law authorizes a defendant to move for a settlement conference and to tender an offer of settlement. If such a motion is made and the offer is rejected by Plaintiff and the eventual judgment does not exceed the amount of the offer, Plaintiff must bear all costs of litigation, including reasonable fees, as determined by the court, for Defendant's counsel.

Alpha, with Defendant's consent, filed a motion requesting a settlement conference, tendered an offer to settle for $25,000, and served copies of the motion and tender on Beta and on Plaintiff personally.

Is Alpha subject to discipline for serving Plaintiff with a copy of the motion and tender?

A. Yes, unless service of copies of the motion and tender on Plaintiff were authorized by statute or rule of court.
B. Yes, unless Alpha first informed Beta of Alpha's intention to serve copies of the motion and tender on Plaintiff.
C. No, because the decision to accept or reject a settlement offer rests with the client.
D. No, because the motion and tender became public documents when they were filed in court.

Question 99.

Attorney Alpha represents Wife in a marriage dissolution proceeding that involves bitterly contested issues of property division and child custody. Husband is represented by Attorney Beta. After one day of trial, Husband, through Beta, made a settlement offer. Because of Husband's intense dislike for Alpha, the proposed settlement requires that Alpha agree not to represent Wife in any subsequent proceeding, brought by either party, to modify or enforce the provisions of the decree. Wife wants to accept the offer, and Alpha believes that the settlement offer made by Husband is better than any award Wife would get if the case went to judgment.

Is it proper for Alpha to agree that Alpha will not represent Wife in any subsequent proceeding?

A. Yes, because the restriction on Alpha is limited to subsequent proceedings in the same matter.
B. Yes, if Alpha believes that it is in Wife's best interests to accept the proposed settlement.
C. No, because the proposed settlement would restrict Alpha's right to represent Wife in the future.
D. No, unless Alpha believes that Wife's interests can be adequately protected by another lawyer in the future.

Question 100.

Attorney represented Plaintiff, who was the plaintiff in litigation that was settled, with Plaintiff's approval, for $25,000. Attorney received a check in that amount from Defendant, payable to Attorney's order. Attorney endorsed and deposited the check in Attorney's Clients' Trust Account. Attorney promptly notified Plaintiff and billed Plaintiff $5,000 for legal fees. Plaintiff disputed the amount of the fee and wrote Attorney, stating, "I will agree to pay $3,000 as a reasonable fee for the work you did, but I will not pay anything more than that."

It is proper for Attorney to:

I. retain the entire $25,000 in Attorney's Clients' Trust Account until the fee dispute is settled.

II. send Plaintiff $20,000, transfer $3,000 to Attorney's office account, and retain $2,000 in Attorney's Clients' Trust Account until the dispute is settled.

III. send Plaintiff $20,000 and transfer $5,000 to Attorney's office account.

A. I only
B. II only
C. I and II, but not III
D. I, II, and III

Question 101.

In Attorney's closing statement to the court in a bench trial, Attorney said,

> "Your honor, I drive on the street in question every day and I know that a driver cannot see cars backing out of driveways as the one did in this case. I believe that my client was not negligent, and I ask you to so find."

Was Attorney's closing argument proper?

A. Yes, if Attorney was speaking truthfully and not trying to deceive the court.
B. Yes, because the rules of evidence are very liberal when the trial is before a judge without a jury.
C. No, because Attorney asserted Attorney's personal knowledge of facts in issue.
D. No, if there is no other evidence in the record about the facts asserted by Attorney.

Question 102.

Plaintiff, who is not a lawyer, is representing himself in small claims court in an action to recover his security deposit from his former landlord. Plaintiff told Attorney, a close friend who lived near him, about this case, but did not ask Attorney for any advice. Attorney said,

> "I'll give you some free advice. It would help your case if the new tenants would testify that the apartment was in good shape when they moved in, and, contrary to the allegation of your former landlord, it was not, in fact, repainted for them."

Plaintiff followed Attorney's advice and won his case.

Is Attorney subject to discipline for assisting Plaintiff in preparing for his court appearance?

A. Yes, because Attorney assisted Plaintiff in the practice of law.
B. Yes, because Attorney offered unsolicited, in-person legal advice.
C. No, because Plaintiff was representing himself in the proceedings.
D. No, because Attorney was not compensated for his advice.

Question 103.

Attorney is defending Client, who has been indicted for burglary. During an interview, Client stated to Attorney that before he had consulted Attorney, Client had committed perjury while testifying before the grand jury that indicted him.

Attorney is <u>subject to discipline</u> if she:

A. continues to represent Client.
B. continues to represent Client unless Client admits his perjury.
C. does not inform the authorities of the perjury.
D. informs the authorities of the perjury.

Question 104.

Attorney is employed in the legal department of Electco, a public utility company, and represents that company in litigation. Electco has been sued by a consumer group that alleges Electco is guilty of various acts in violation of its charter. Through its general counsel, Electco has instructed Attorney not to negotiate a settlement but to go to trial under any circumstances since a precedent needs to be established. Attorney believes the case should be settled if possible.

<u>Must</u> Attorney withdraw as counsel in the case?

A. Yes, if Electco is controlling Attorney's judgment in settling the case.
B. Yes, because a lawyer should endeavor to avoid litigation.
C. No, if Electco's defense can be supported by a good faith argument.
D. No, because as an employee, Attorney is bound by the instructions of the general counsel.

Question 105.

Four years ago, Alpha was a judge in a state court of general jurisdiction and heard the civil case of Plaintiff against Defendant in which Plaintiff prevailed and secured a judgment for $50,000 which was sustained on appeal. Since then Alpha has resigned from the bench and returned to private practice. Defendant has filed suit to enjoin enforcement of the judgment on the grounds of extrinsic fraud in its procurement. Plaintiff has now asked Alpha to represent Plaintiff in defending the suit to enjoin enforcement.

Is it <u>proper</u> for Alpha to accept the representation of Plaintiff in this matter?

A. Yes, because Alpha would be upholding the decision of the court.
B. Yes, if Alpha's conduct of the first trial will not be in issue.
C. No, unless Alpha believes the present suit is brought in bad faith.
D. No, because Alpha had acted in a judicial capacity on the merits of the original case.

Question 106.

Attorney Alpha represents Plaintiff in a personal injury action against Defendant, the defendant, who is represented by Attorney Beta. Alpha had heard that Defendant was anxious to settle the case and believed that Beta had not informed Defendant of a reasonable settlement offer made by Alpha. Alpha instructed Alpha's nonlawyer investigator, Inv, to tell Defendant about the settlement offer so Alpha could be sure that Beta does not force the case to trial merely to increase Beta's fee. Inv talked to Defendant as instructed.

Is Alpha <u>subject to discipline</u>?

A. Yes, because Defendant was represented by counsel.
B. Yes, because Alpha was assisting Inv in the unauthorized practice of law.
C. No, because Inv is not a lawyer.
D. No, if Alpha reasonably believed Beta was not keeping Defendant informed.

Question 107.

Attorney served two four-year terms as the governor of State immediately prior to reopening his law office in State. Attorney printed and mailed an announcement of his return to private practice to members of the bar, persons who had previously been his clients, and personal friends whom he had never represented. The printed announcement stated that Attorney had reopened his law office, gave his address and telephone number, and added that he had been governor of State for the past eight years.

Is Attorney <u>subject to discipline</u> for the announcement?

A. Yes, because it was mailed to persons who had not been his clients.
B. Yes, because his service as governor is unrelated to his ability as a lawyer.
C. No, because the information in the announcement is true.
D. No, because all of the information was already in the public domain.

Question 108.

Attorney placed Associate, recently admitted to the bar, in complete charge of the work of the paralegals in Attorney's office. That work consisted of searching titles to real property, an area in which Associate had no familiarity. Attorney instructed Associate to review the searches prepared by the paralegals, and thereafter to sign Attorney's name to the required certifications of title if Associate was satisfied that the search accurately reflected the condition of the title. This arrangement enabled Attorney to lower office operating expenses. Attorney told Associate that Associate should resolve any legal questions that might arise and not to bother Attorney because Attorney was too busy handling major litigation.

Is it proper for Attorney to assign Associate this responsibility?

A. Yes, if the paralegals are experienced in searching titles.
B. Yes, because Attorney is ultimately liable for the accuracy of the title searches.
C. No, unless it enables Attorney to charge lower fees for title certification.
D. No, because Attorney is not adequately supervising the work of Associate.

Question 109.

The law firm of Able & Baker agreed to represent Client in various business matters. The written retainer agreement called for Client to pay Able & Baker's hourly rates of $180 per hour for a partner's time and $110 per hour for an associate's time. The representation proceeded. Able & Baker submitted monthly bills, which Client paid promptly. After two years, Able & Baker decided to increase their hourly rates by $10. Able & Baker thereafter billed Client at their new rates, but did not specifically inform Client of the increase. Client continued to pay monthly bills promptly.

Are Able & Baker subject to discipline?

A. Yes, because the entire original fee agreement was required to be in writing.
B. Yes, because Client did not consent to the increase.
C. No, if the $10 hourly increase is reasonable.
D. No, because Client agreed in writing to pay Able & Baker's hourly rate.

Question 110.

During the closing argument to the jury in a civil tax fraud case, Attorney, representing the government, quoted a portion of Defendant's testimony and then said:

I.   "That testimony of Defendant directly contradicts the testimony of two witnesses for the government."

II. "I ask you, who has the reason to lie, the two witnesses for the government or Defendant?"

III. "I can truthfully say I have never seen a witness less worthy of belief."

Which of the above statements by Attorney would be proper?

A. I only
B. I and II, but not III
C. II and III, but not I
D. I, II, and III

Question 111.

Attorney's standard retainer contract in divorce cases provides for the payment of a fee of one-third of the amount of alimony or property settlement secured by Attorney. Attorney declines to represent clients who do not agree to this arrangement.

Is Attorney's standard retainer contract proper?

A. Yes, because clients often prefer to pay a lawyer a fee based on the outcome of the case.
B. Yes, if a fee of one-third is not excessive.
C. No, because a lawyer may not acquire a proprietary interest in a cause of action.
D. No, because the fee is contingent.

Question 112.

Attorney Alpha was retained by Client to represent Client in defense of an action brought against Client by Plaintiff. In order to obtain ample time for settlement negotiations, Alpha immediately requested and obtained from opposing counsel, Attorney Beta, a stipulation extending Client's time to answer the complaint until ten days after receipt of written demand from Beta. Four months later, no settlement had been reached, and on May 1, Beta wrote Alpha demanding that an answer be filed within ten days. When no answer was filed by May 15, Beta had a default judgment entered in favor of Plaintiff.

Alpha was away on a two-month vacation when Beta's letter was received in her office. When Alpha returned on June 15, she promptly moved to have the default set aside and her motion was granted.

Is Alpha subject to discipline?

A. Yes, unless she makes restitution to Client for any loss sustained by Client.
B. Yes, if she did not make provision for the handling of her pending cases while she was away.
C. No, because the default judgment was set aside.
D. No, unless she knew that Beta had demanded that an answer be filed within ten days.

Question 113.

Attorney represents Defendant, a prominent business-man, in a civil paternity suit brought by Plaintiff, who was formerly Defendant's employee. Blood tests did not exclude Defendant's paternity, and the case is being tried before a jury. The result turns on questions of fact. Defendant has steadfastly denied that he had sexual relations with Plaintiff, while Plaintiff has testified that they had sexual relations while on business trips and in her home. The trial has generated great public interest and is closely followed by the news media.

When Plaintiff completed her testimony, Attorney was interviewed by a newspaper reporter.

Which of the following statements, if believed by Attorney to be true, would be proper for Attorney to make?

I. "As stated in our pleadings, we expect to prove that other men could be the father of Plaintiff's child."

II. "We have scientific medical tests proving that Defendant is sterile."

III. "We have been unable to locate several people whose testimony will be helpful to us, and I implore them to contact me immediately."

A. II only
B. III only
C. I and III, but not II
D. I, II, and III

Question 114.

Attorney Alpha is a lawyer running for election as a state judge. Attorney Beta, who practices law in the same community as Alpha, has frequently observed Alpha's courtroom demeanor in litigated cases. Based on those experiences, Beta believes that Alpha does not have a proper judicial temperament. A local news reporter asked Beta how Beta would rate the candidates, and Beta responded in good faith, "I think Alpha is unsuited for the bench. Alpha lacks the proper judicial temperament and would make a very poor judge." A local newspaper with a wide circulation quoted Beta's remarks.

Were Beta's remarks proper?

A. Yes, because Beta was not seeking judicial office.
B. Yes, because Beta believed Alpha was unsuited for the bench.
C. No, because the remarks serve to bring the judiciary into disrepute.
D. No, because a lawyer should not publicly comment on candidates for judicial office.

Question 115.

Attorney has been representing Client in a matter in litigation. During protracted pretrial proceedings, Client complained bitterly about the time and expense involved and insisted that Attorney take steps to terminate the pretrial proceedings. Attorney believes that to do so would jeopardize Client's interests and has so informed Client. Attorney believes that the case cannot be adequately prepared for trial without further pretrial proceedings that will require an additional six months' delay and involve further expense. Client insists that Attorney forego any further pretrial proceedings and set the case for trial at the earliest available date. There are several other competent lawyers who are willing to undertake the representation.

Is it proper for Attorney to ask leave of the court to withdraw?

A. Yes, because a lawyer may discontinue representation in a civil case at any time before trial.
B. Yes, because Client's conduct makes it unreasonably difficult for Attorney to represent Client effectively and competently.
C. No, because Attorney must follow Client's instructions.
D. No, unless Client consents to Attorney's withdrawal.

Question 116.

The judicial district in which Judge sits has a rule that allows litigants two postponements as a matter of right. After that, a litigant who moves for a postponement must convince the presiding judge that a postponement is appropriate. Judge routinely grants additional postponements because, in her view,

> "What harm is done if one of the litigants wants a postponement? The worst that can happen is that the parties have more time to negotiate and thus are more likely to settle."

Are Judge's actions proper?

A. Yes, because Judge is exercising her judicial discretion.
B. Yes, because a party objecting to a postponement can seek appellate review.
C. No, because judges have no official obligation to encourage private settlements.
D. No, because Judge should expedite the determination of matters before her.

Question 117.

Two years ago, Attorney was employed by State's Department of Transportation (DOT) to search title to several tracts of land. Attorney has not been employed by DOT during the last year. Recently, DOT instituted proceedings to condemn a tract, owned by Owner, for a new highway route. Owner asked Attorney to represent her in obtaining the highest amount of compensation for the condemnation. Owner's tract is one of the tracts on which Attorney searched title two years ago. Attorney remembers that Engineer, a DOT engineer, once drafted a confidential memorandum advising against running a new highway across Owner's land because of potential adverse environmental impact. Because of this information, Attorney believes it is possible to prevent the condemnation of Owner's land or to increase the settlement amount.

It is proper for Attorney to:

A. represent Owner on the issue of damages only and not disclose the information that might prevent the condemnation.
B. represent Owner and attempt to prevent the condemnation by using the information about the adverse environmental impact.
C. refuse to represent Owner but disclose to Owner the information about the adverse environmental impact.
D. refuse to represent Owner and not disclose the information about the adverse environmental impact.

Question 118.

Attorney, who had represented Testator for many years, prepared Testator's will and acted as one of the two subscribing witnesses to its execution. Testator's sister and brother were his sole heirs. The will left Testator's entire estate to his sister and nothing to his brother. Upon Testator's death two years later, Executor, the executor named in the will, asked Attorney to act as his lawyer in the probate of the will and the administration of the estate. At that time, Executor informed Attorney that Testator's brother would concede that the will was properly executed but intended to contest the will on the ground that he had been excluded because of fraud previously practiced on Testator by Testator's sister. The other subscribing witness to the will predeceased Testator, and Attorney will be called as a witness solely for the purpose of establishing the due execution of the will.

Is it proper for Attorney to accept the representation?

A. Yes, if there is no contested issue of fact with respect to the formal execution of the will.
B. Yes, because Executor has no beneficial interest under the will.
C. No, unless Attorney's services are necessary to avoid substantial hardship to Executor.
D. No, because Attorney will be called as a witness in the case.

Question 119.

Attorney has been retained to defend an adult charged with a sex offense involving a minor. Attorney believes that, in order to win the case, she must keep parents of minor children off the jury. Attorney instructed her investigator as follows:

> "Visit the neighborhood of those prospective jurors on the panel with minor children. Ask the neighbors if they know of any kind of unusual sex activity of the prospective juror or any member of the family. This talk will get back to the prospective jurors, and they will think of excuses not to serve. But don't under any circumstances talk directly with any prospective juror or member of the family."

Is Attorney subject to discipline for so instructing her investigator?

A. Yes, unless the prospective jurors investigated are, in fact, selected to serve on the jury in the case.
B. Yes, because the investigation is intended to harass prospective jurors and members of their families.
C. No, if the matters inquired into might be relevant to a prospective juror's qualifications to serve in the case.
D. No, because no prospective juror was directly contacted.

Question 120.

Attorney prepared a will for Client and acted as one of the subscribing witnesses to Client's execution of the will. The will left all of Client's estate to Son, Client's son. Later, at Client's request, Attorney prepared a second will for Client and acted as one of the subscribing witnesses to Client's execution of the second will. The second will left one-half of Client's estate to Son and the other one-half to Housekeeper, Client's housekeeper. Client died and Housekeeper has offered the second will for probate.

If Son requests Attorney to represent him in opposing probate of the second will on the grounds of fraud and undue influence, is it proper for Attorney to do so?

A. Yes, because after Client's death Attorney may represent Son.
B. Yes, because Son is a beneficiary under both wills.
C. No, because an attorney guarantees the validity of a will that he or she prepares.
D. No, because Attorney would be taking a position adverse to a will she prepared and witnessed.

Question 121.

Attorney represented Plaintiff in an action against several defendants. The retainer agreement provided that Plaintiff would pay all costs and expenses of litigation and would, on demand, reimburse Attorney for any costs or expenses advanced by Attorney. After serving process on two defendants, Attorney had difficulty locating and serving the remaining defendants. Plaintiff approved the hiring of an investigator to locate and serve the defendants, and Attorney advanced the costs for the investigator. When Attorney asked Plaintiff for reimbursement, Plaintiff refused to pay. Attorney then told Plaintiff that Attorney would do no more work on the case until Attorney was reimbursed for the amount advanced.

Thereafter, one of the defendants filed a counterclaim that required a responsive pleading within thirty days. Because Attorney had not been paid, Attorney permitted the time to respond to the counterclaim to expire without filing a responsive pleading, and a default was entered on the counterclaim. Later, Plaintiff reimbursed Attorney for the costs Attorney had advanced, and Attorney was successful in having the default on the counterclaim set aside. The case was tried, and Plaintiff prevailed on Plaintiff's complaint, and the counterclaimant recovered nothing.

Is Attorney subject to discipline for not initially filing a responsive pleading to the counterclaim?

A. Yes, because Attorney neglected Plaintiff's cause.
B. Yes, unless Attorney had asked leave of court to withdraw.
C. No, because Plaintiff breached the agreement to reimburse Attorney.
D. No, because Plaintiff did not sustain any prejudice as a result of Attorney's action.

Question 122.

Judge, prior to her recent appointment to the federal court, had been an outspoken and effective opponent of the racial segregation policies of Gov, a foreign country. As part of its worldwide tour, Gov's national soccer team scheduled a soccer match with a team in this country. Several civil rights groups have applied to Judge for an order enjoining the playing of the proposed match. The matter is now pending. Only legal issues are presented. Judge, after painstaking consideration, has privately concluded that she cannot decide the legal questions without bias against the representatives of Gov's government. However, no one has made a motion to disqualify Judge.

Must Judge recuse herself in the pending matter?

A. Yes, unless Judge believes she has greater expertise than other judges on the court in legal issues involving racial segregation.
B. Yes, because Judge believes that she cannot be impartial.
C. No, because the only issues presented for decision are legal questions.
D. No, because none of the interested parties has moved to disqualify Judge.

Question 123.

Client telephoned Attorney, who had previously represented Client. Client described a problem on which he needed advice and made an appointment for the following week to discuss the matter with Attorney. Prior to the appointment, Attorney performed 5 hours of preliminary research on Client's problem. At the end of the appointment, Client agreed that Attorney should pursue the matter, agreed to a fee of $100 per hour, and gave Attorney a check for $5,000 to cover the 5 hours already worked and as an advance on further fees and expenses.

Attorney gave the check to the office bookkeeper with the directions to "Deposit the check in the Clients' Trust Account and immediately transfer $3,000 to our General Office Account to cover the 5 hours of research already conducted plus the 25 additional hours I'll spend on it next week." At that time, Attorney reasonably believed that Attorney would spend 25 additional hours on the case.

The bookkeeper followed these directions. The next week, Attorney worked diligently on the matter for 23 hours. Reasonably believing that no significant work remained to be done on the matter, Attorney directed the bookkeeper to transfer $200 from the General Office Account to the Clients' Trust Account. Attorney then called Client and made an appointment to discuss the status of the matter.

Is Attorney subject to discipline?

A. Yes, because Attorney accepted legal fees in advance of performing the work.
B. Yes, because Attorney transferred funds for unearned fees to the General Office Account.
C. No, because Attorney transferred the $200 owed to Client from the General Office Account to the Clients' Trust Account.
D. No, because Attorney reasonably believed that Attorney would spend 25 additional hours on the case.

Question 124.

Candidate, a member of the bar, is a candidate for judicial office in an election. Candidate personally asked several of his friends to contribute $1,000 each to kick off his campaign. After Candidate's friends made the contributions, Candidate, who was elated by the support, formed a committee to collect more contributions. Candidate then turned over the contributions to the committee and began campaigning in earnest.

Is Candidate subject to discipline?

A. No, because Candidate turned over the funds to his committee.
B. No, unless the committee includes lawyers likely to practice before Candidate.
C. Yes, unless none of the original contributors was a lawyer.
D. Yes, because Candidate personally solicited funds.

Question 125.

Judge Alpha has recently resigned from the state trial court bench. While she was a judge and supervising activity in cases pending before Judge Beta, who was on vacation, Alpha entered an administrative order changing the courtroom in which the case of Able v. Baker was to be tried. After trial and appeal, the case was remanded for a new trial. The plaintiff in Able v. Baker has now decided to change lawyers and has asked Alpha to try the case.

Will Alpha be subject to discipline if she tries this case on behalf of the plaintiff?

A. Yes, because Alpha acted officially as a judge with respect to an aspect of the case.
B. Yes, because Alpha would try the case before a judge of the court on which Alpha previously sat.
C. No, because Alpha did not act as a judge with respect to a substantial matter or on the merits of the case.
D. No, because any information that Alpha learned about the case while acting as a judge was a matter of public record.

Question 126.

Although licensed to practice law in State, Attorney Alpha does not practice law but works as an investment broker. Alpha could have elected inactive status as a member of the bar, but chose not to do so. Recently, in connection with a sale of worthless securities, Alpha made materially false representations to Victim, an investment customer. Victim sued Alpha for civil fraud, and a jury returned a verdict in Victim's favor. Alpha did not appeal.

Is Alpha subject to discipline?

A. Yes, because Alpha was pursuing a non-legal occupation while an active member of the bar.
B. Yes, because Alpha's conduct was fraudulent.
C. No, because Alpha was not convicted of a crime.
D. No, unless the standard of proof in State is the same in lawyer disciplinary cases and civil cases.

Question 127.

Client was an experienced oil and gas developer. Client asked Attorney for representation in a suit to establish Client's ownership of certain oil and gas royalties. Client did not have available the necessary funds to pay Attorney's reasonable hourly rate for undertaking the case. Client proposed instead to pay Attorney an amount in cash equal to 20% of the value of the proceeds received from the first year royalties Client might recover as a result of the suit. Attorney accepted the proposal and took the case.

Is Attorney subject to discipline?

A. Yes, because the agreement gave Attorney a proprietary interest in Client's cause of action.
B. Yes, unless the fee Attorney receives does not exceed that which Attorney would have received by charging a reasonable hourly rate.
C. No, because Client rather than Attorney proposed the fee arrangement.
D. No, because Attorney may contract with Client for a reasonable contingent fee.

Question 128.

Attorney has been hired by Client to represent Client in a civil commitment proceeding initiated by the state. Client is now undergoing psychiatric evaluation to determine whether civil commitment should be ordered. Client told Attorney that Client intends to commit suicide as soon as the tests are completed, and Attorney believes that Client will carry out this threat. Suicide and attempted suicide are crimes in the state.

Is it proper for Attorney to disclose Client's intentions to the authorities?

A. Yes, because the information concerns a future crime and is not protected by the attorney-client evidentiary privilege.
B. Yes, because the information concerns a future crime that is likely to result in Client's imminent death.
C. No, unless Attorney knows that client has attempted suicide in the past.
D. No, because disclosure would aid the state in its civil commitment case against Client.

Question 129.

Attorney is a long-time member of the state legislature and serves on the legislative budget committee that funds the local trial courts in the state. Attorney also maintains a part-time law practice as is permitted in the state. Able, an influential businessperson, who regularly makes significant contributions to Attorney's political campaigns, asked Attorney to help Able's uncle, Baker, who was involved in a bitter divorce. Attorney called the trial judge sitting on Baker's case, a personal friend of Attorney. In discussing some upcoming votes of the budget committee with the judge, Attorney mentioned that Baker was the type of solid citizen and influential person who could help garner support for the budget and thus ensure the economic health of the judicial system.

Is Attorney subject to discipline?

A. Yes, if the trial judge ruled in Baker's favor.
B. Yes, because Attorney used her public position to attempt to influence a tribunal in a pending matter.
C. No, if Attorney called the trial judge in her capacity as a legislator and not as Baker's lawyer.
D. No, because members of the state legislature are permitted by law to engage in part-time legal practice.

Question 130.

Attorney agreed to represent Able, a client, in bringing a lawsuit. Attorney and Able executed Attorney's preprinted retainer form that provides, in part:

> "The client agrees to pay promptly Attorney's fees for services. In addition, the client and Attorney agree to release each other from any and all liability arising from the representation. The client agrees that Attorney need not return the client's file prior to receiving the client's executed release. Attorney agrees to return the client's file promptly upon receipt of all fees owed and of the client's executed release."

During their initial meeting, Attorney recommended that Able consult independent counsel before signing the retainer agreement, but Able chose not to do so. Attorney reasonably believes that his fee is fair and that the quality of his work will be competent.

Is Attorney's retainer agreement with Able proper?

A. Yes, because Attorney furnished consideration by agreeing to release Able from liability and to return Able's files.
B. Yes, because Attorney reasonably believes that his fee is fair and that the quality of his work will be competent.
C. No, because Attorney is attempting to limit prospectively his liability for malpractice.
D. No, because Attorney uses a preprinted form for all retainers.

Question 131.

Attorney represents Corp, a defendant in a product liability case. Engineer, a Corp employee nearing retirement, was likely to be a key witness in the case, as she had been in charge of all of Corp's product safety testing during the relevant period. Engineer had been very critical of Corp's safety testing procedures during that period and had repeatedly complained that the product at issue had not been adequately tested. Engineer's views were reduced to writing and were well known to many employees of Corp. Because of the early stage of the case, however, plaintiff's counsel was not yet aware of Engineer's existence or her views.

Aware of Engineer's views, Attorney approached Corp's officials and recommended that it offer Engineer a special package of severance benefits if she would retire immediately and move to the Bahamas. Attorney believed that if Engineer accepted this offer, she would be beyond the subpoena power of the court in which the suit against Corp was pending. Corp adopted Attorney's recommendation and made the offer. Engineer accepted it. Attorney did not disclose Engineer's identity to plaintiff's counsel.

Is Attorney subject to discipline?

A. Yes, because Attorney caused Engineer to leave the jurisdiction of the court for the purpose of making her unavailable as a witness.
B. Yes, because opposing counsel had not yet had a reasonable opportunity to learn of Engineer's views.
C. No, because Engineer's views were reduced to writing and are well known to many other employees of Corp.
D. No, unless there was a pending request for Engineer's testimony at the time the retirement offer was made to Engineer.

Question 132.

Attorney represented Client in a personal injury action against the driver of the car in which Client was injured while a passenger. The personal injury action was settled, and Attorney received a check in the amount of $10,000 payable to Attorney. Attorney deposited the check in her Clients' Trust Account.

One day later, Attorney received a letter from Bank, which had heard of the settlement of the personal injury lawsuit. Bank informed Attorney that Client had failed to make his monthly mortgage payments for the last three months and demanded that Attorney immediately release $900 of the proceeds of the settlement to Bank or Bank would institute mortgage foreclosure proceedings against Client. Attorney informed Client of Bank's letter. Client responded:

> "I don't care what Bank does. The property is essentially worthless, so let Bank foreclose. If Bank wants to sue me, I'll be easy enough to find. I don't think they'll even bother. You just take your legal fees and turn the rest of the proceeds over to me."

Is Attorney subject to discipline if she follows Client's instructions?

A. Yes, if Client does not dispute the $900 debt to Bank.
B. Yes, because Attorney knew that client was planning to force Bank to sue him.
C. No, unless Attorney had reason to believe that Client would not have sufficient funds to pay any subsequent judgment obtained by Bank.
D. No, because Bank has no established right to the specific proceeds of Client's personal injury judgment.

Question 133.

Three lawyers, Alpha, Beta, and Delta, formed a partnership to practice law with offices in both State First and State Second. Alpha is admitted to practice only in State First. Beta is admitted to practice only in State Second, and Delta is admitted to practice in both States First and Second. The following letterhead is on stationery used by their offices in both states:

Alpha, Beta, and Delta
Attorneys at Law

100 State Street   200 Bank Building
City, State First   City, State Second
(200) 555-5555   (202) 555-5555

Attorney Alpha Admitted
to practice only in State First

Attorney Beta Admitted
to practice only in State Second

Attorney Delta Admitted
to practice in States First and Second

Are the members of the partnership subject to discipline?

A. No, because the letterhead states the jurisdictions in which each partner is admitted.
B. Yes, because there is no jurisdiction in which both Alpha and Beta are admitted to practice.
C. Yes, because the firm name used by each office contains the name of a lawyer not admitted to practice in that jurisdiction.
D. Yes, unless Delta actively practices law in both States First and Second.

Question 134.

Attorney was engaged under a general retainer agreement to represent Corp, a corporation involved in the uranium industry. Under the agreement, Attorney handled all of Corp's legal work, which typically involved regulatory issues and litigation.

Corp told Attorney that a congressional committee was holding hearings concerning the extent of regulation in the copper industry. Because Corp was considering buying a copper mine during the next fiscal year, Corp wanted Attorney to testify that the industry was over-regulated. Attorney subsequently testified before the relevant congressional committee. Attorney registered his appearance under his own name and did not disclose that he was appearing on behalf of a client. Afterward, Attorney billed Corp for fees and expenses related to his testimony.

Was Attorney's conduct <u>proper</u>?

A. Yes, because the duty of confidentiality prevented Attorney from disclosing the identity of his client.

B. Yes, because the attorney-client evidentiary privilege prevented disclosure of the identity of his client in this context.

C. No, because Attorney failed to disclose that he was appearing and testifying in a representative capacity.

D. No, because Attorney accepted compensation in return for his testimony.

Question 135.

Judge is one of three trustees of a trust for the educational benefit of her grandchildren. The trust owns 5,000 shares of stock in Big Oil Company. The stock has been selling for the past year at $10 per share. Big Oil is suing Oil Refining Company for breach of an oil refining agreement, and the case is assigned to Judge for trial. Judge believes that she can be fair and impartial.

<u>Must</u> Judge disqualify herself from the case?

A. Yes, because the trust has more than a de minimus financial interest in Big Oil Company.

B. Yes, unless the outcome of the lawsuit is unlikely to affect the value of the stock.

C. No, unless Judge personally owns stock in either party to the litigation.

D. No, because Judge believes she can remain impartial.

Question 136.

For many years, Attorney has served as outside counsel to Corp, a corporation. Shortly after a change in management, Attorney discovered what she reasonably believed to be a material misstatement in a document she had drafted that Attorney was about to file on Corp's behalf with a government agency. Attorney advised Corp's Board of Directors that filing the document was probably criminal. However, the Board disagreed that there was any material misstatement and directed Attorney to proceed with the filing. When Attorney indicated her intention to resign, Corp argued that a resignation at this time would send a signal that there was a problem with the filing. Corp urged Attorney to continue the representation, but offered to use in-house counsel to complete the work on the filing. Although she does not know for certain that filing the document is illegal, Attorney reasonably believes that it is. In any event, Attorney is personally uncomfortable with the representation and wants to withdraw.

<u>May</u> Attorney withdraw from her representation of Corp?

A. Yes, because withdrawal is permitted but not required when a client insists on conduct which the lawyer reasonably believes, but does not know, will be criminal.

B. Yes, because withdrawal is required when a client insists on conduct which the lawyer reasonably believes, but does not know, will be criminal.

C. No, if Corp is correct that withdrawal would breach confidentiality by sending a signal that the filing is problematic.

D. No, if Attorney's withdrawal as outside counsel might affect Corp's ability to complete the filing in a timely fashion.

Question 137.

Attorney represented Client on a minor personal injury claim against Driver, an uninsured motorist. Attorney represented Client on a 30% contingent fee basis. Pursuant to a negotiated settlement in the amount of $2,000, Driver agreed to send Attorney a $100 check, made payable to Attorney, in each of the ensuing twenty months.

Which of the following dispositions of each monthly check would be <u>proper</u> for Attorney?

I. Deposit the check into her office account and immediately write Client a check for $70 from that account.

II. Deposit the check into a separate account established for Client and immediately request Client to pay Attorney $30.

III. Deposit the check into a trust account in which funds belonging to all Attorney's clients are deposited and immediately write Client a check for $70 and herself a check for $30 from that account.

A. II only
B. III only
C. I and II, but not III
D. II and III, but not I

Question 138.

Attorney Alpha, a partner in the law firm of Alpha & Beta, was retained by Plaint, the plaintiff in a personal injury action against Deft. The jury rendered a verdict in favor of Deft, and Alpha filed an appeal on Plaint's behalf. Alpha reviewed the trial transcript and wrote the brief. The brief stated, "It is uncontroverted that Deft failed to signal before turning left into the intersection." In fact, Wit, a witness called by Deft, testified that Deft did signal before turning. Alpha was aware of this testimony, having read it while reviewing the trial transcript.

Three days before the appeal was scheduled to be argued in the state's intermediate appellate court, Alpha suffered a heart attack. Attorney Beta, one of Alpha's partners, agreed to argue the appeal. Beta knew nothing about the case and had no opportunity to confer with Alpha. In preparing for the argument, Beta read Alpha's brief thoroughly and read as much of the trial transcript as was possible in the limited time available, but did not read Wit's testimony. In oral argument, Beta stated to the court, "Your honors, as stated in our brief, it is uncontroverted that Deft failed to signal before turning left into the intersection." Beta assumed that Alpha's statement in the brief to that effect was correct.

Is Beta <u>subject to discipline</u> for making this statement during oral argument?

A. Yes, because the statement was false.
B. Yes, because Beta did not know whether or not the statement was true.
C. No, because Beta did not know that the statement was false.
D. No, because all Beta did was to truthfully recount the statement made by Alpha in the brief.

Question 139.

Judge needed to obtain a loan to be secured by a second mortgage on his house. Bank offered him a loan at a very favorable interest rate. The vice-president at Bank told Judge:

> "Frankly, we normally don't give such a large loan when the security is a second mortgage, and your interest rate will be 2% less than we charge our other customers. But we know that your salary is inadequate, and we are giving you special consideration."

Is it <u>proper</u> for Judge to accept the loan?

A. Yes, if Judge does not act in any case involving Bank.
B. Yes, if Bank is not likely to be involved in litigation in the court on which Judge sits.
C. No, unless the same terms are available to all judges in the state.
D. No, because the amount of the loan and interest rate were not available to persons who were not judges.

Question 140.

Law Firm has 300 lawyers in 10 states. It has placed the supervision of all routine administrative and financial matters in the hands of Admin, a nonlawyer. Admin is paid a regular monthly salary and a year-end bonus of 1% of Law Firm's net income from fees. Organizationally, Admin reports to Attorney, who is the managing partner of Law Firm. Attorney deals with all issues related to Law Firm's supervision of the practice of law.

Is it proper for Attorney to participate in Law Firm's use of Admin's services in this fashion?

A. Yes, unless Admin has access to client files.
B. Yes, if Admin does not control the professional judgment of the lawyers in the firm.
C. No, because Law Firm is sharing legal fees with a nonlawyer.
D. No, because Law Firm is assisting a nonlawyer in the unauthorized practice of law.

Question 141.

Attorney experienced several instances when clients failed to pay their fees in a timely manner, but it was too late in the representation to withdraw without prejudicing the clients. To avoid a recurrence of this situation, Attorney has drafted a stipulation of consent to withdraw if fees are not paid according to the fee agreement. She proposes to have all clients sign the stipulation at the outset of the representation.

Is it proper for Attorney to use the stipulation to withdraw from representation whenever a client fails to pay fees?

A. Yes, because a lawyer may withdraw when the financial burden of continuing the representation would be substantially greater than the parties anticipated at the time of the fee agreement.
B. Yes, because the clients consented to the withdrawal in the stipulation.
C. No, because a client's failure to pay fees when due may be insufficient in itself to justify withdrawal.
D. No, unless clients are provided an opportunity to seek independent legal advice before signing the stipulation.

Question 142.

Attorney was retained by Defendant to represent him in a paternity suit. Aunt, Defendant's aunt, believed the suit was unfounded and motivated by malice. Aunt sent Attorney a check for $1,000 and asked Attorney to apply it to the payment of Defendant's fee. Aunt told Attorney not to tell Defendant of the payment because "Defendant is too proud to accept gifts, but I know he really needs the money."

Is it proper for Attorney to accept Aunt's check?

A. Yes, if Aunt does not attempt to influence Attorney's conduct of the case.
B. Yes, if Attorney's charges to Defendant are reduced accordingly.
C. No, because Aunt is attempting to finance litigation to which she is not a party.
D. No, unless Attorney first informs Defendant and obtains Defendant's consent to retain the payment.

Question 143.

Attorney has a highly efficient staff of paraprofessional legal assistants, all of whom are graduates of recognized legal assistant educational programs. Recently, the statute of limitations ran against a claim of a client of Attorney's when a legal assistant negligently misplaced Client's file and suit was not filed within the time permitted by law.

Which of the following correctly states Attorney's professional responsibility?

A. Attorney is subject to civil liability and is also subject to discipline on the theory of respondent superior.
B. Attorney is subject to civil liability or is subject to discipline at Client's election.
C. Attorney is subject to civil liability but is NOT subject to discipline unless Attorney failed to supervise the legal assistant adequately.
D. Attorney is NOT subject to civil liability and is NOT subject to discipline if Attorney personally was not negligent.

Question 144.

Attorney represented Plaint, who sued Deft for injuries Plaint sustained in a car accident. Prior to trial, Attorney interviewed Wit, who stated that she had observed Deft drinking heavily hours before the accident. Unfortunately, on the eve of trial, Wit informed Attorney that Wit was ill and could not testify at trial. Attorney tried but could not obtain a continuance. As a result, Plaint's direct case rested solely on Plaint's testimony that Deft was speeding and that Deft's car crossed the center line and hit Plaint's car. Deft testified that he was driving safely in compliance with all rules and that the accident was entirely Plaint's fault. On cross examination, Attorney asked Deft, "Isn't it a fact that you were drinking prior to the accident?" Deft answered that he had not consumed alcoholic beverages on the day of the accident. In summation to the jury, Attorney stated:

> "Ladies and gentlemen of the jury, you and I know that Deft lied when he stated that he had not consumed alcoholic beverages on the day of the accident. We know that he was impaired."

On which of the following grounds, if any, is Attorney subject to discipline?

I. Attorney's question to Deft implying that Deft had consumed alcoholic beverages when Attorney knew that he could not offer evidence of Deft's drinking.

II. Attorney's statement to the jury asserting that Attorney knew that Deft was drunk when no evidence in the record supported this allegation.

III. Attorney's statement asserting a personal belief that Deft was drunk and lying.

A. I and II, but not III
B. II and III, but not I
C. I, II, and III
D. Neither I, II, nor III

Question 145.

Pros, a prosecutor, was assigned to try a criminal case against Deft, who was charged with robbery of a convenience store. Deft denied any involvement, contending he was home watching television with his mother on the night in question. At the trial, Wit, a customer at the convenience store, testified that he had identified Deft in a police line-up and provided other testimony connecting Deft to the crime. In addition, Pros entered into evidence a poor-quality videotape of the robbery as recorded by the store surveillance camera. The jury convicted Deft of the crime charged. Unknown to Deft's court-appointed lawyer, Wit had first identified another person in the police line-up and selected Deft only after encouragement by the detective. Pros was aware of these facts but did not notify Deft's counsel who made no pretrial discovery request to obtain this information.

Is Pros subject to discipline?

A. Yes, unless the jury could make its own identification of Deft from the videotape.
B. Yes, because this information tended to negate Deft's guilt.
C. No, because Deft's counsel made no pretrial discovery request to obtain this information.
D. No, unless it is likely that the jury would have acquitted Deft had it known that Wit first identified someone else.

Question 146.

Attorney and Client entered into a written retainer and hourly fee agreement that required Client to pay $5,000 in advance of any services rendered by Attorney and which required Attorney to return any portion of the $5,000 that was not earned. The agreement further provided that Attorney would render monthly statements and withdraw her fees as billed. The agreement was silent as to whether the $5,000 advance was to be deposited in Attorney's Clients' Trust Account or in a general account. Attorney deposited the entire fund in her Clients' Trust Account, which also contained the funds of other persons which had been entrusted to Attorney. Thereafter, Attorney rendered monthly progress reports and statements for services to Client after services were rendered, showing the balance of Client's fee advance. However, Attorney did not withdraw any of the $5,000 advance until one year later when the matter was concluded to Client's complete satisfaction. At that time, Attorney had billed Client reasonable legal fees of $4,500. Attorney wrote two checks on her Clients' Trust Account: one to herself for $4,500, which she deposited in her general office account, and one for $500 to Client.

Was Attorney's conduct proper?

A. Yes, because Attorney deposited the funds in her Clients' Trust Account.
B. Yes, because Attorney rendered periodic and accurate billings.
C. No, because Attorney's failure to withdraw her fees as billed resulted in an impermissible commingling of her funds and Client's funds.
D. No, because Attorney required an advanced payment against her fee.

Question 147.

Attorney Alpha, a member of the bar, placed a printed flyer in the booth of each artist exhibiting works at a county fair. The face of the flyer contained the following information:

> "I, Alpha, am an attorney, with offices in 800 Bank Building, telephone (555) 555-5555. I have a J.D. degree from State Law School and an M.A. degree in fine arts from State University. My practice includes representing artists in negotiating contracts between artists and dealers and protecting artists' interests. You can find me in the van parked at the fair entrance."

All factual information on the face of the flyer was correct. There was a retainer agreement on the back of the flyer. At the entrance to the fair, Alpha parked a van with a sign that read "Alpha—Attorney at Law."

For which, if any, of the following is Alpha subject to discipline?

I.   Placing copies of the flyer in the booth of each artist.

II. Including a retainer agreement on the back of the flyer.

III. Parking the van with the sign on it at the fair entrance.

A. III only
B. I and II, but not III
C. I, II, and III
D. Neither I, II, nor III

Question 148.

Attorneys Alpha and Beta had been political opponents. Alpha was elected to the state legislature after a bitter race in which Beta had managed the campaign of Alpha's opponent. Alpha had publicly blamed Beta at that time for what Alpha reasonably believed were illegal and unethical campaign practices and later had publicly objected to Beta's appointment as a judge.

Alpha represented Client in a widely publicized case tried in Judge Beta's court. At the conclusion of the trial, Beta ruled against Alpha's client. Alpha then held a press conference and said, "All that you reporters have to do is check your files and you will know what I think about Judge Beta's character and fitness."

Is Alpha subject to discipline for making this statement?

A.   Yes, if Alpha's statement might lessen confidence in the legal system.
B.   Yes, because Alpha's past accusations were unrelated to Beta's legal knowledge.
C.   No, because Alpha reasonably believed that the statements about Beta were true.
D.   No, if Beta had equal access to the press.

Question 149.

Judge, a judge in a criminal trial court of State, wishes to serve as guardian of her father, who has been declared incompetent. Accepting the responsibilities of the position would not interfere with the performance of Judge's official duties. Although the position in all likelihood would not involve contested litigation, it would be necessary for Judge to prepare and sign various pleadings, motions, and other papers and to appear in civil court on her father's behalf.

Would it be proper for Judge to undertake this guardianship?

A.   Yes, unless Judge receives compensation for her services as guardian.
B.   Yes, because the position involves a close family member and will not interfere with Judge's performance of her judicial duties.
C.   No, because the position will require Judge to appear in court.
D.   No, because the position will require Judge to prepare and sign pleadings, motions, and other papers.

Question 150.

Client hired Attorney Alpha to file a lawsuit against Client's former employer, Corp, for wrongful discharge. Alpha filed the suit in federal district court based upon three grounds. It turned out that a unanimous U.S. Supreme Court decision had recently eliminated the third ground as a theory available to plaintiffs in wrongful discharge cases. Attorney Beta, who represents Corp, filed a motion alleging that the complaint was based upon a theory (the third ground) that is no longer supported by existing law and cited the new decision. Within ten days after the filing of the complaint, Alpha withdrew the third ground and continued with the litigation.

Is Alpha subject to litigation sanction?

A.   Yes, unless Alpha discussed the adverse legal authority with Client before filing the complaint.
B.   Yes, because Alpha should have cited the U.S. Supreme Court decision in the complaint.
C.   No, because Alpha withdrew the third ground within ten days after filing the complaint.
D.   No, unless Alpha knew or should have known of the recent decision when the complaint was filed.

MPRE Sample Questions
Explanatory Answers

Explanatory Answer Key to *MPRE Sample Questions VI*

Questions 1 – 150

The MPRE consists of sixty (60) multiple-choice questions. Ten of them are "test questions" that do not count in the examinee's score, but those ten are indistinguishable from the fifty questions that do count. The examination is two hours and five minutes long, meaning that there are 125 minutes allocated to the sixty questions to be completed. On average, therefore, an examinee has slightly more than two minutes to answer each question.

Each of the sixty questions provides a factual situation and then asks that you choose among four possible answers. You must pick the "best" of the four choices. You will be graded on the basis of the number of correct answers, not penalized for an answer that is incorrect. This means that if you are not certain you should **guess** rather than leaving the question unanswered.

The most effective means to follow in choosing the "best" answer is to proceed sequentially through the four options, (A), (B), (C) then (D), attempting to **eliminate incorrect choices**, rather than first attempting to make the correct choice. Sometimes the "best" answer of the four is not the intellectually satisfying choice you want to find, but rather a relatively unsatisfying solution to a murky issue. You are more likely to find it if you have first eliminated choices clearly incorrect. If you can eliminate three choices as incorrect and only one ambiguous choice remains that choice must be the "best." Even if you can eliminate only two choices your guess as between those remaining now has a better chance of being correct.

The explanatory answers to Questions 1 through 150 of the "MPRE Sample Questions VI" that follow will first indicate the correct choice of the four provided and then explain, sequentially, why each possible choice is right or wrong.

Question 1

The correct answer is B.

(A) is incorrect because of its use of the word "unless." Lawyers should maintain their competence by engaging in continued study and education. Continuing legal education courses are not the only means of maintaining that competence. The word "unless" implies that if the state was to offer free continuing legal education courses it would be improper for Gamma to refuse to attend, even if Gamma engaged in continued study and education independently; that is wrong. (Note that if the state did require participation in continuing legal education courses, as many states do, failure to attend would be improper and would subject the attorney to discipline.)

(B) looks to be correct for the reasons stated above regarding choice (A).

(C) is incorrect for the reasons stated above regarding choice (A).

(D) is incorrect because the purchasing of malpractice insurance does not excuse an attorney's lack of competence. Incompetence subjects a lawyer to discipline even if the client is fully compensated for any malpractice.

Because choices (A), (C) and (D) are incorrect only choice (B) can be the correct answer.

Question 2

The correct answer is A.

In a question of this particular format we are called upon to pick the best of the four lettered choices by first determining which of the **numbered** choices are "proper." In the context of the MPRE "proper" means that the proposed course of conduct is not only one that will not subject the lawyer to discipline but also is consistent with other (non-disciplinary) rules of the MRPC, with the Code of Judicial Conduct ("CJC") and with general principles of law practice.

Which of the numbered choices are proper?

I is not proper because a lawyer must make an independent determination as to the qualifications of any person recommended to the Bar in order to be making a truthful statement about that person.

II is not proper for the same reason as in I. Attorney must make an independent determination.

III is proper because it requires an independent investigation that satisfies Attorney that a positive recommendation is appropriate.

Because choices I and II are improper only (A), which offers Choice III alone, is correct.

Question 3

The correct answer is A.

(A) looks to be correct because Alpha's actions do involve dishonesty or misrepresentation.

(B) is incorrect because it rests on the thought that a lawyer is subject to discipline only for offenses that have led to criminal conviction. Dishonest statements, even if not illegal, subject a lawyer to discipline under the MRPC.

(C) is incorrect because it rests on the thought that a lawyer is subject to discipline only for acts done in his or her professional capacity. This is not true.

(D) is incorrect because it rests on the thought that lawyers in a particular jurisdiction can be punished only for acts done in that jurisdiction. This is not true.

Question 4

The correct answer is D.

(A) is incorrect because a lawyer ordinarily is not allowed to contact a person represented by another lawyer "while representing a client" but Attorney is not currently representing a client.

(B) is incorrect because lawyers **are** allowed to solicit former clients.

(C) is incorrect because once Attorney contacts Testatrix and she decides to have Attorney represent her in this matter Attorney is obligated to provide competent service, which may well entail the preparation of a new will.

(D) **must** be the correct answer because the first three choices are incorrect. Even if Attorney's acts constituted "solicitation" under the MRPC it is allowed as to former clients.

Question 5

The correct answer is D.

(A) is incorrect because $500 was for bail, if obtained, not for the lawyer's fee. The "Fee Account" must be limited to compensation for services performed, and not disputed.

(B) is incorrect for two reasons: first, the $300 Attorney put in the "Fee Account" is disputed and must therefore remain in the "Clients' Fund Account" pending the dispute's resolution and second, the $500 must be returned to Deft as it was placed in the "Clients' Fund Account" only to be used for bail and not for an appeal.

(C) is incorrect because the $300 Attorney put in the "Fee Account" is disputed and must therefore remain in the "Clients' Fund Account" pending the dispute's resolution.

(D) **must** be the correct answer because the first three choices are incorrect. Deft is entitled to $500 now and the other $300 is in dispute and so stays in the "Clients' Fund Account."

Question 6

The correct answer is B.

(A) is incorrect because even if no basis for prosecution was established in the investigation ten years ago and even if that investigation is not substantially related to the current case, Judge Alpha might still, in the mind of a reasonable observer, have a bias or prejudice against Deft. If so disqualification is required. **If** the judge is **not** reasonably perceived as biased there is no need for disqualification but choice (A)'s "because" does not state that fact.

(B) looks to be correct because, as mentioned above, it states the correct test.

(C) is not as good an answer as (B). "Substantial responsibility" **might** be the basis for **suspecting** bias or prejudice but (B) goes directly to the point: might or might not a reasonable person believe the judge is prejudiced.

(D) is not as good an answer as (B) because it focuses, as does (C), on the presence or absence of "substantial responsibility" as opposed to going directly to the question of whether there might be a reasonable perception of prejudice.

Since (A) is incorrect and neither (C) nor (D) is as good as (B) only (B) can be correct.

Question 7

The correct answer is B.

(A) is incorrect because of its use of the word "if." Attorney's actions in advising Landlord are either proper or improper independent of Landlord's acceptance or rejection of that advice.

(B) looks to be correct because a lawyer may refer to non-legal as well as legal considerations in advising a client. It is up to Landlord to decide whether to waive the statute of limitations defense and if Landlord decides not to do so Attorney must accept that decision, as part of the zealous representation of a client. Having advised Landlord of the legal situation it is entirely proper for Attorney to provide the non-legal advice as to the consequences of fully pursuing the client's legal rights.

(C) is incorrect because both legal and related non-legal advice is part of the service a lawyer appropriately and ordinarily provides. No formal notification to the client about the provision on non-legal advice is necessary.

(D) is incorrect because Attorney did zealously represent the client's legal interests by advising as to the statute of limitations barring Plaint's claim and by being ready to accept Landlord's refusal to waive that defense if Attorney's non-legal advice was rejected by the client. Landlord, in accepting the advice, chose not to insist zealously on the maintenance of legal interests but rather to maintain business reputational interests.

Because (A), (C) and (D) are incorrect only (B) is correct.

Question 8

The correct answer is B.

(A) is incorrect because it states Attorney is subject to discipline for giving legal advice to non-clients. There is no disciplinary sanction for a lawyer doing that, absent in-person, live telephone or real-time electronic contact and absent any false pretense of disinterestedness toward non-represented persons while engaged in the representation of an existing client.

(B) looks to be correct because Attorney is advising customers to seek assistance by having non-lawyer trust officers review their wills. That assistance is unauthorized practice of law and Attorney's advice is assisting that unauthorized practice, a disciplinary offense.

(C) is incorrect because Attorney is assisting the unauthorized practice of law whether Attorney collects a fee or not.

(D) is incorrect because being a lawyer does not excuse assisting the authorized practice of law; **only a lawyer** is subject to discipline under the MRPC.

Since (A), (C) and (D) are incorrect only (B) can be correct.

Question 9

The correct answer is A.

(A) looks to be correct because of the emergency nature of the situation. Since it was late at night, no opportunity was presented for referral to competent counsel nor for consultation by said counsel. Ordinarily, client consent, even after full disclosure, cannot excuse incompetent representation but this is not the case in an emergency such as that presented here.

(B) is incorrect because the familial relationship between lawyer and client has nothing to do with whether competent service was or was not provided. (Note that if the question was whether or not Gamma acted appropriately in soliciting Able as a client (contrary to the facts presented in this question) the family relationship would then be significant.)

(C) is incorrect because of the emergency nature of the situation, as explained with regard to choice (A) above.

(D) is incorrect because of the emergency nature of the situation, as explained with regard to choice (A) above.

Because (B), (C) and (D) are incorrect only (A) is correct.

Question 10

The correct answer is B.

As in Question 2 we must decide which of the **numbered** choices are "proper."

I is proper because, while a lawyer's fee must be "reasonable," there is no requirement that it be made in any particular form. Bank credit cards are acceptable.

II is proper because, while a lawyer must not provide financial assistance (i.e., advance funds) to a client in connection with litigation except for advances of court costs and litigation expenses, helping the client secure a bank loan is not "provision of financial assistance" by the lawyer.

III is not proper because a lawyer is subject to discipline for receiving publication rights prior to the conclusion of the representation and therefore may not make that suggestion to the client.

Because III is improper and both I and II are proper only (B) is correct.

Question 11

The correct answer is B.

Which of the numbered choices are proper?

I is incorrect because there is a danger, even though slight, of bank failure that would imperil the Clients' Trust Account, and lawyers have a fiduciary obligation to their clients to protect their property. (Bank failure could occur within ten days and even were it to occur at a later time choice (I) indicates that it is only "likely" that within that time the account would diminish sufficiently to be fully insured.)

II looks to be correct because fund transfer that would ensure complete protection through coverage by the FDIC would protect the clients' property in accordance with Attorney's obligation.

III is incorrect because a lawyer must keep client property separate from his or her own personal or professional property. Even though both accounts would be fully insured under this choice the rule on commingling would be violated.

Because choices I and III are improper only (B), limited to the proper choice II, is correct.

Question 12

The correct answer is A.

Which of the numbered choices are proper?

I is proper because Law Firm has discretion as to the necessary qualifications for shareholder status.

II is not proper because no lawyer may practice in a private firm in which a non-lawyer is an officer or director.

III is not proper because there is no indication that Widow is a lawyer. No lawyer may practice in a private firm in which a non-lawyer is a shareholder except for a "reasonable time during administration of an estate" and Widow is holding for an indefinite period of time, "until [her] child completes a law school education."

Because choices II and III are improper only (A), limited to the proper choice I, is correct.

Question 13

The correct answer is B.

Which of the numbered choices are proper?

I is proper because Attorney cannot provide competent representation and continuing on the case could therefore violate the MRPC.

II is proper, and probably preferable, given the imminence of trial. A lawyer not competent to represent a client may continue representation in association with competent counsel.

III is not proper. A lawyer must not render less than competent representation, even with a client's consent, because the client is unable to give an informed consent.

Because choice III is improper while choices I and II are proper, only (B), consisting of I and II but not III, is correct.

Question 14

The correct answer is D.

(A) is incorrect because **Alpha** could not represent Deft, having had substantial authority in representing an adverse interest in the same case prior to associating with Beta, and if Alpha could not represent Deft no current associate of his, i.e., **Beta**, can continue representing Deft. (This is an imputed or vicarious disqualification.) In some instances (since Alpha has left **government** employment to join a private firm) a sufficient "screening" may allow **Beta** to continue the representation of Deft, but that would require assurance to the court that Alpha and Beta would not communicate about the case, that Alpha would receive no funds from Deft's representation and that the district attorney's office was timely notified of the screening. There is no indication in this question of those assurances being made. It is **not** sufficient that Alpha does not reveal any confidential information to Beta.

(B) is incorrect because, although it accurately states one of the obligations imposed on prosecutors by the MRPC, compliance or non-compliance with that obligation has nothing to do with the question posed: Beta's ability to continue representation of Deft.

(C) is incorrect because Alpha's mere agreement not to participate in the case does not eliminate Beta's imputed disqualification; it does not satisfy the requirements for "screening."

(D) must be the correct answer because the first three choices are incorrect. Alpha was substantially involved in a case adverse to Deft; Alpha is now disqualified from representing Deft in that same case and, absent any indicating of sufficient "screening," so is Beta.

Question 15

The correct answer is A.

(A) looks to be correct because a lawyer has the discretion to reveal confidential information when necessary to defend against a charge of improper conduct.

(B) is incorrect because Attorney's obligation to reveal Client's perjury to the court lasts only to the conclusion of the proceeding. The case is now concluded.

(C) is incorrect because even confidential communications may be disclosed by a lawyer when necessary to defend against a charge of improper conduct.

(D) is incorrect because, again, Attorney is defending against a charge of improper conduct. If the possibility of a client being charged with perjury could nullify the lawyer's right to disclose no lawyer would ever be able to report a client's perjury even though the MRPC assumes such report will be made (if discovered prior to the conclusion of the case).

Since (B), (C) and (D) are incorrect (A) must be the correct answer.

Question 16

The correct answer is A.

Which of the numbered choices are proper?

I is proper because it **does** not commit her to a particular position on the merits of a case that might come before her in the future.

II is not proper because it **does** commit the judge to a particular position on the merits of a case that might come before her in the future.

III is not proper for the same reason as II is not proper.

Because only choice I is proper, (A) which offers that choice alone, is correct.

Question 17

The correct answer is D.

Which of the numbered choices are proper?

I is proper because Attorney cannot represent Claimant, having represented an interest adverse to claimant in the same matter. If she cannot represent him she has no obligation to discuss the matter with him.

II is not proper because Attorney is forbidden, as above, from representing Claimant.

III is not proper because any other lawyer in Attorney's present firm is forbidden to represent claimant, by imputed or vicarious disqualification. No "screening" is allowed because Attorney has not transferred from a **governmental** office to this private firm.

IV is proper. Attorney may refer to any competent counsel **outside** her firm.

Because only choices I and IV are proper (D) is the correct answer.

Question 18

The correct answer is D.

Which of the numbered choices are proper?

I is proper because, unless appointed by a tribunal, a lawyer has no obligation to undertake representation of a new client.

II is proper because the first claim was settled and this claim is unrelated to the first.

III is proper because prospective clients may always be referred to competent counsel.

Because choices I, II and III are all proper (D) is the correct answer.

Question 19

The correct answer is A.

Which of the numbered choices are proper?

I looks to be correct because Attorney has given adequate notice to Client that the bill must be paid, it has not been paid, and Attorney has requested permission from the court before which the case is pending to withdraw. (Note that while in some states a lawyer may not withdraw when a client fails to pay fees unless the failure is "deliberate;" i.e., not when failure is due to an inability to pay because of loss of employment, savings, etc., under the MRPC (applicable on this examination) the lawyer may move to withdraw for non-payment no matter what resources are available to the client.)

II is incorrect for two reasons: first, another lawyer may not be retained without the client's prior approval, and second, Attorney may not withdraw from representation without approval by the court before which the case is pending.

III is incorrect because a lawyer is prohibited from acquiring a proprietary interest in the cause of action or subject matter of litigation the lawyer is conducting for a client, with two exceptions neither of which is applicable here: first, a lien on papers and property granted by law to secure a lawyer's fees or expenses and second, a reasonable contingent fee in a civil case.

Because choices II and III are improper only (A), limited to the proper choice I, is correct.

Question 20

The correct answer is D.

Which of the numbered choices represent statements subjecting Attorney to discipline?

I does not subject Attorney to discipline. The statements are informational as to Attorney's background and qualifications, and they are true.

II does not subject Attorney to discipline. The statements are informational as to Attorney's times of availability, and they are true.

III does not subject Attorney to discipline. The statement is informational as to Attorney's language capabilities, and is true.

Because neither I, nor II nor III subject Attorney to discipline only (D) is correct.

Question 21

The correct answer is A.

Which of the numbered choices are proper?

I is proper because a lawyer representing a client must not discuss the matter with the client's opponent without the permission of opponent's counsel (unless specifically authorized by law to do so).

II is not proper because Alpha is now discussing the matter with the opposing party. The impropriety is not cured by the fact that the opposing party initiated the discussion.

III is not proper for the same reason above.

Because choices II and III are improper only (A), limited to choice I, is correct.

Question 22

The correct answer is C.

(A) is incorrect because the lawyers do not have to state their qualifications.

(B) is incorrect because, while any consultation with a lawyer may eventually lead to litigation, no disciplinary rule forbids this kind of advertising, if not misleading, to obtain clients.

(C) looks to be correct, as mentioned above.

(D) is incorrect because the possibility of someone out of state hearing the advertisement is not a violation of any disciplinary rule. It will be assumed until shown otherwise that the lawyers intend to engage in practice only in those jurisdictions to which they are admitted.

Since (A), (B) and (D) are incorrect (C) must be the correct answer.

Question 23

The correct answer is A.

Note: The answer key to "MPRE Sample Questions VI" provided by the National Conference of Bar Examiners (BCBE) in 2002 gave the answer to this question as "C." That answer was correct at the time, prior to the amendments to the MRPC made by the ABA later that year. Under the MRPC as presently constituted (the rules for which we are responsible on all MPRE given in 2004 and in subsequent years) the answer is "A," for the following reasons:

(A) looks to be correct because the present MRPC require that a division of fees between lawyers not in the same firm may be made only if (1) the division is in proportion to the services performed by each **or** each assumes joint responsibility for the representation, (2) the client agrees, in writing, to the arrangement, including the share each lawyer receives **and** (3) the total fee is reasonable. If the client's consent is not in writing, therefore, all three criteria have not been met and the lawyers are subject to discipline.

(B) is incorrect because there is no ethical requirement that the first lawyer hired be the one to try the case.

(C) is incorrect because even though the division of the fee is in proportion to the work done by each, satisfying the first of the three criteria mentioned in (A) above, the other two criteria must also be satisfied and there is no indication that the client has agreed in writing to the arrangement (the second criterion).

(D) is incorrect because although the total fee does not differ from that originally contracted for by Alpha with Client (satisfying the third criterion of reasonableness), the other two criteria must also be satisfied and, again, there is no indication that the client has agreed in writing to the arrangement.

Since (B), (C) and (D) are incorrect (A) must be the correct answer.

Question 24

The correct answer is D.

(A) is incorrect because Beta's neglect of the case might well constitute misconduct, but since the information relates to the representation of Client it is confidential and Alpha cannot report it without Client's consent. It is unlikely that Client will consent to reporting a family friend.

(B) is incorrect because Beta's usual conduct is irrelevant. The particular conduct in this matter is relevant and would have to be reported, provided Client consented, as above.

(C) is incorrect because Client's satisfaction, or lack of same, is irrelevant, as above.

(D) **must** be the correct answer because the first three choices are incorrect. Only if Client consents to disclosure **must** Alpha then report the information.

Question 25

The correct answer is C.

Which of the numbered choices are correct?

I is incorrect because it assumes that a law firm, rather than the individual lawyers within a firm, is subject to discipline. The MRPC are rules designed to ensure the proper behavior of individuals who have been admitted to practice or are seeking that admission. Only individual lawyers, then, may be disciplined for violating those rules. (Note that certain violations of the MRPC may subject an individual lawyer, and all that lawyer's partners and associates, to informal "punishment;" e.g., disqualification from representation in a particular case. In that sense the entire law firm has been "disciplined," but that is not the kind of **professional** discipline (the kind possibly leading to disbarment, suspension, censure or reprimand) referred to in this question.

II looks to be correct because partners in a law firm do have the obligation to make efforts to establish a system within the firm to ensure compliance with the MRPC and they clearly failed to make those efforts in this case.

III looks to be correct because Associate lied to Client, violating the duty of loyalty to a client and violating the rule prohibiting lying to any person. While a subordinate lawyer acting in accordance with a supervising lawyer's reasonable resolution of an arguable question of professional duty is not thereby subjected to discipline, that rule does not help Associate here: it is not arguable that lying to a client is a violation of the MRPC (and no supervisor told Associate to do so).

IV looks to be correct because both Associate and the law firm are subject to civil liability for Associate's malpractice. Associate is liable because he or she acted negligently and the firm is liable vicariously because Associate's actions were within the scope of the firm's business. (Note that while the firm, as an entity, is not subject to discipline (as explained above with regard to choice I) it may, nonetheless, be subject to informal "punishment" such as civil liability.)

Because choice I is incorrect and choices II, II and IV are correct, (C), which incorporates choices II, III and IV, is correct.

Question 26

The correct answer is C.

Which of the numbered choices are proper?

I is proper because the money presumably belongs to Plaintiff (there being no indication in the question that the lawyer has any interest in the money, such as unpaid fees or advanced costs of litigation) and the lawyer is promptly delivering the money to Plaintiff.

II is not proper because it constitutes commingling Plaintiff's money with the lawyer's, even though Plaintiff then has the appropriate amount promptly delivered.

III is proper (and, as a practical matter, **better** than choice I because it creates a record of funds received and disbursed). It constitutes prompt delivery of Plaintiff's money and avoids any commingling of Plaintiff's money with the lawyer's.

Because both choices I and III are **proper** (even though choice III is better as a practical matter) and choice II is not proper, (C) is correct. **Note** that if the question were worded differently, and we were asked "Which of the numbered choices is the **best**?" we would find that choice III is "best" and the answer to this question would then be (B).

Question 27

The correct answer is D.

(A) is incorrect because campaign contributions for a judge may be made only to a duly formed campaign committee, not to the candidate personally.

(B) is incorrect because, anonymous or not, the contribution cannot be made to the candidate personally, as indicated above.

(C) is incorrect because campaign contributions can be made to the campaign committee of any judicial candidate, even if the lawyer practices before a candidate who is already a judge.

(D) must be the correct answer because the first three choices are incorrect. The contribution is improper if given to the candidate personally, but proper if given to the campaign committee.

Question 28

The correct answer is D.

(A) is incorrect because no false statement of fact was made. Attorney made statements of opinion ("... every American's dream: happy kids ... and a clear conscience") and those opinions are considered legitimate in negotiations. "Steady profits" might well be a statement of fact but there is no indication that that statement was not true; profits may be "steady" even if they are also "modest."

(B) is incorrect because Attorney did not exaggerate profitability; he said "steady profits," not "high profits."

(C) is incorrect because if Attorney had engaged in conduct involving dishonesty, fraud, deceit or misrepresentation toward Buyer (which was not the case, as indicated above regarding choices (A) and (B)) the fact that Attorney was representing Seller would not excuse that behavior.

(D) must be correct because all other choices are incorrect. Attorney's statements did not contain false representations, even though they were designed to convince Buyer to complete the sale. They were within the accepted scope of representation in negotiations.

Question 29

The correct answer is B.

(A) is incorrect because if Alpha was too busy with other clients this case should not have been undertaken.

(B) looks to be correct; Alpha appears to have neglected Passenger's case.

(C) is incorrect because Alpha's neglect has harmed Passenger (delay, frustration, a possibility of a more beneficial settlement diminished) regardless of the fact that the harm did not go so far as to entirely void any possible chance of recovery.

(D) is incorrect because return of the retainer, though beneficial to Passenger, does not remove the harm caused by Alpha's neglect, as indicated above.

Since (A), (C) and (D) are incorrect (B) must be the correct answer.

Question 30

The correct answer is C.

(A) is incorrect because a lawyer's duty to be fair to opposing parties and their counsel does not extend to warning them that a deadline is approaching, or has passed.

(B) is incorrect because "professional courtesy" does not require the waiving of a client's rights nor the warning of an opponent as to a deadline, as mentioned above.

(C) looks to be correct as the lawyer's foremost loyalty is to the client and the lawyer's zeal has not led to any violation of a disciplinary rule, as mentioned above.

(D) is incorrect because the existence or non-existence of insurance is not relevant to the lawyer's professional obligations.

Since (A), (B) and (D) are incorrect (C) must be the correct answer.

Question 31

The correct answer is C.

(A) is incorrect because Attorney was reasonable in her reliance on the information she received from the director of the state commission. Candidates for judicial office must not **knowingly** misrepresent a fact concerning an opponent and knowledge may be inferred from the circumstances. In this instance Attorney did not **know** her information was incorrect and it was not unreasonable to rely on the director's statement rather than going further into the commission's records.

(B) is incorrect because Attorney's **knowledge** of the falsity of the information is required in order for discipline to be imposed, as mentioned above.

(C) looks to be correct because Attorney's reliance on the director's statement appears reasonable.

(D) is incorrect because whether the election is contested or uncontested is irrelevant.

Since (A), (B) and (D) are incorrect (C) must be the correct answer.

Question 32

The correct answer is B.

(A) is incorrect because a lawyer's otherwise appropriate contributions to a judicial candidate's campaign committee will not be examined further as to the lawyer's motivation.

(B) looks to be correct because Attorney is impugning the integrity of the entire judiciary. If Attorney's statement is true there has been an attempt to influence a judge by means prohibited by law. If Attorney's statement is false the lie is a violation of the MRPC.

(C) is incorrect because if the statement is true it is a rule violation, as mentioned above.

(D) is incorrect because whether Attorney was retained or not is irrelevant. What is important is that the statement was made.

Since (A), (C) and (D) are incorrect B must be the correct answer.

Question 33

The correct answer is D.

(A) is incorrect because Attorney's disinterest is not sufficient. The judge must notify the parties of the person consulted and the substance of the advice as well as affording the parties reasonable opportunity to respond.

(B) is incorrect because the judge's need for the advice is not sufficient, as mentioned above.

(C) is incorrect because prior consent of the parties is not required by the rule.

(D) must be the correct answer because the first three choices are incorrect. This choice correctly states the rule.

Question 34

The correct answer is C.

(A) is incorrect because lawyers are forbidden from communicating with a judge ex parte; i.e., without advising Attorney's adversary of the impending communication.

(B) is incorrect for the same reason as above.

(C) looks to be correct because it correctly states the relevant rule.

(D) is incorrect because the ex parte communication constitutes the violation of the MRPC, not the fact that a case taken under advisement is reopened.

Since (A), (B) and (D) are incorrect (C) must be the correct answer.

Question 35

The correct answer is B.

(A) is incorrect because Attorney is not restricting his right to practice in violation of the MRPC by agreeing not to accept employment adverse to Trustco. Trustco is in the position of being Attorney's client.

(B) looks to be correct in that Trustco is engaged in the unauthorized practice of law and Attorney, by his agreement, is aiding that unauthorized practice.

(C) is incorrect because if Attorney is assisting the unauthorized practice of law doing so without charging customers for service will not excuse the ethical violation.

(D) is incorrect because if Attorney is assisting the unauthorized practice of law doing so without giving advice himself will not excuse the ethical violation.

Since (A), (C) and (D) are incorrect (B) must be the correct answer.

Question 36

The correct answer is C.

(A) is incorrect because Attorney, having represented **both** parties in the past, is precluded from representing either against the other now; each "other" is a former client, adverse to the proposed client in a case substantially related to the earlier case.

(B) is incorrect because the rule against representing a client against a former client in a substantially related case applies regardless of the bad acts of the former client.

(C) looks to be correct, as mentioned above.

(D) is incorrect because the rule against representing a client against a former client in a substantially related case applies regardless of the former client's new representation.

Since (A), (B) and (D) are incorrect (C) is the correct answer.

Question 37

The correct answer is D.

Which of the numbered choices are proper?

I is proper because it is protected speech under the First Amendment.

II is proper because Alpha can solicit for a judge's campaign committee. (A contribution to the judge personally would be improper.)

III is proper because it is protected speech under the First Amendment.

Because I, II and III are all proper only (D), combining all three, is correct.

Question 38

The correct answer is A.

(A) looks to be correct. Lawyers may advertise through the media as long as the statements made are not misleading and "…might be lower…" is not a misleading promise of fees lower then average, as indicated in (B) below.

(B) is incorrect because the advertisement does not say Attorney's fees are lower than average, only that the recipient might think lawyers are more expensive than she actually is.

(C) is incorrect because no rule states a lawyer cannot use a professional actor in an ad, as long as there is no misrepresentation; e.g., the actor claiming to be Attorney.

(D) is incorrect because nothing in the ad implies there will not be a charge for the initial consultation and such charges are within the rules.

Since (B), (C) and (D) are incorrect (A) must be the correct answer.

Question 39

The correct answer is D.

Which of the numbered choices are proper?

I is improper because a lawyer on a case cannot speak with the opposing party without the consent of the lawyer for that party (unless specifically authorized by law to do so), nor can the lawyer attempt to accomplish that end through the actions of another person.

II is proper because Prosecutor has discretion to re-charge and doing so conforms to his view of appropriate justice in the matter.

III is proper because Prosecutor is an advocate whose **discretion** to seek less than he might reasonably attain does not constitute a mandatory obligation to do so.

Because I is improper and II and III are proper only (D) is correct.

Question 40

The correct answer is C.

(A) is incorrect because the test for a lawyer's obligation to report another lawyer's misconduct is not the degree of harm the misconduct caused the other lawyer's client.

(B) is incorrect because the test for the lawyer's obligation mentioned above is not the degree of publicity gained by the other lawyer.

(C) looks to be correct because Prosecutor should not report Attorney except for a clear violation of the MRPC. **Knowledge** of a refusal to bargain for personal motives (as opposed to the mere suspicion mentioned in the choices above) would constitute a clear violation of Attorney's obligation to Deft and justify Prosecutor reporting him to the disciplinary authority.

(D) is incorrect because **if** Attorney refused to bargain for her client in order to attain publicity for herself she would be in violation of the MRPC even if she also represented Deft at trial with competence and zeal.

Since (A), (B) and (D) are incorrect (C) must be the correct answer.

Question 41

The correct answer is A.

(A) looks to be the correct answer because lawyers are not allowed to knowingly present perjured testimony, even if they are doing so in order to zealously represent a client.

(B) is incorrect because Attorney is subject to discipline, as mentioned above, whether Driver had committed a felony or not in securing the license. It is not Driver's felony that is relevant; it is Attorney's knowing presentation of perjury.

(C) is incorrect because even if the only reason Attorney knows of the planned perjury is a communication made in confidence Attorney cannot present that testimony.

(D) is incorrect because it assumes that Driver's true name might not be an issue at trial when, in fact, it is a central issue regarding the degree of punishment to be inflicted. If it were not an issue at trial it is possible that a court would not consider Driver's testimony "perjury" because it might not be "material." But Attorney would **still** have presented **false evidence**, even if not perjury.

Since (B), (C) and (D) are incorrect (A) must be the correct answer.

Question 42

The correct answer is A.

Which of the numbered choices would subject Attorney to discipline?

I would not subject Attorney to discipline because any witness, lay or expert, may be reimbursed for actual travel expenses, if reasonable.

II would not subject Attorney to discipline because any witness, lay or expert, may be reimbursed for lost wages while attending trial.

III **would** subject Attorney to discipline because no witness, lay or expert, may be paid any fee that is **contingent** on the testimony or on the outcome of the case.

Because choices I and II would not subject Attorney to discipline but choice III **would**, (A) is the correct answer.

Question 43

The correct answer is A.

(A) looks to be correct. The portrait is a gift incident to a public testimonial which may ordinarily be accepted under the CJC. The presenting organization is not one whose members usually represent the same side in litigation nor an organization likely to come before the judge.

(B) is incorrect because although no compensation was given the judge other criteria must be satisfied, such as the charity not engaging in litigation in the judge's courtroom.

(C) is incorrect because the CJC does not set a limit on the value of a testimonial gift.

(D) is incorrect because the mere fact that lawyers appear before a judge does not mean that they cannot contribute to a testimonial gift. If the lawyers have come or will come before the judge and a gift valued at over $150 is given the judge must report the gift.

Since (B), (C) and (D) are incorrect (A) must be the correct answer.

Question 44

The correct answer is C.

(A) is incorrect because the fact that Attorney is a necessary witness means that it is not proper for Attorney to act as an advocate in the case.

(B) is incorrect because of the reason above.

(C) looks to be correct because of the reason above.

(D) is incorrect because **whatever** side Attorney supports as a witness, **being** a witness prevents Attorney from being an advocate.

Since (A), (B) and (D) are incorrect (C) must be the correct answer.

Question 45

The correct answer is A.

(A) looks to be correct because the MRPC require that Attorney advise Buyer, in writing, that independent representation is appropriate in this case. Once that advice is given in such a way as to make the client understand it the lawyer has fulfilled the required duty. When the client thereafter declines independent representation and executes the settlement agreement no MRPC violation has occurred.

(B) is incorrect because it implies that Attorney's conduct would be proper as long as it was based on a reasonable belief that the settlement was fair to Buyer. What makes Attorney's conduct proper, however, is the written notice to the client that independent representation is appropriate. If Attorney believed the settlement fair but did not provide the written notice Attorney would be subject to discipline.

(C) is incorrect because the matter in which the potential malpractice was committed (the real estate transaction) has terminated. There is no longer an ongoing case in which the lawyer's representation may be affected by a conflict with the lawyer's own interest in not being subjected to a malpractice suit. The "claim" involving possible malpractice is ongoing but ongoing claims are the only kind that can be settled; settlement is proper if the lawyer provides the written notice referred to in choices (A) and (B) above.

(D) is incorrect because Buyer need not be separately represented as long as Buyer was given written notice that such representation was appropriate. (Note that an agreement **prospectively** limiting a lawyer's malpractice liability; i.e., limiting it prior to its occurrence, unlike the situation here, does require the actual separate representation of the client, not merely written notice of its appropriateness.)

Because (B), (C) and (D) are all incorrect only (A) is the correct answer.

Question 46

The correct answer is C.

(A) is incorrect because Alpha need not follow client instructions as to tactical decisions within her professional discretion. She should **inform** her client of her actions but need not consult or gain consent. If the client disagrees strongly Alpha can be discharged at will.

(B) is incorrect because of the reasons mentioned above.

(C) looks to be correct. If a tactical decision could actually harm the client it would have to be foregone, but this is not that kind of decision.

(D) is incorrect because Alpha can extend professional courtesy in this matter regardless of Beta's deservedness.

Since (A), (B) and (D) are incorrect (C) must be the correct answer.

Question 47

The correct answer is C.

(A) is incorrect because Attorney is allowed to contribute to Judge's campaign as long as the contribution is made to a campaign committee, not to the judge personally. Attorney frequently represents clients in the trial court of which Judge is a part but Judge is only one of fifteen in the County. There is little appearance of impropriety.

(B) is incorrect because there is no need to discuss the matter of a campaign contribution; in fact, the less discussion the less chance there is for an appearance of impropriety.

(C) looks to be correct since contributions must go through a campaign committee.

(D) is incorrect because a long-standing personal and business relationship does not prevent Attorney from making a contribution; in fact, given the long-standing relationship the monetary contribution takes on less significance, not more.

Since (A), (B) and (D) are incorrect (C) must be the correct answer.

Question 48

The correct answer is D.

(A) is incorrect because Attorney apparently was attempting to act in Witness's best interests in providing his advice. Even assuming Attorney was wrong there is no indication that he was not competent when he undertook the representation.

(B) is incorrect because Attorney was attempting to protect Witness's constitutional rights. This is technically within the definition of "counseling a client to commit a crime" but because reasonable interpretation of constitutional rights were involved a disciplinary charge for doing so is highly unlikely.

(C) is incorrect because it draws a distinction between crimes involving moral turpitude and crimes that do not. The MRPC do not draw this distinction. Attorney cannot, ordinarily, counsel a client to commit any crime, but, as mentioned above, when it is necessary to preserve or assert a constitutional right disciplinary action is highly unlikely.

(D) must be the correct answer because the first three choices are incorrect. As mentioned above, if Attorney believed Witness had a legal right to refuse to answer and that belief was reasonable Attorney should not be liable to discipline.

Question 49

The correct answer is A.

(A) looks to be correct because a prosecutor has a duty to make timely disclosure to the defense of all known evidence or information tending to negate guilt (as well as that tending to mitigate the offense or the sentence) and this information does raise a legitimate question as to proper identification and, therefore, guilt.

(B) is incorrect because of the word "unless." Even though the prosecutor reasonably believed the victims' identification of the defendant was accurate the obligation to disclose the contrary information to the defense still exists.

(C) is incorrect because, even though the adversary system generally requires each party to marshal its own evidence, a prosecutor has the special duty to disclose to the defense the information referred to in choices (A) and (B) above.

(D) is incorrect because the prosecutor's duty to disclose under the MRPC exists independently of any defense request for the information.

Because (B), (C) and (D) are incorrect only (A) is the correct answer.

Question 50

The correct answer is C.

(A) is incorrect because Alpha cannot represent Neighbor against Builder simultaneously with representation of Builder against the defendant in the breach of contract action, regardless of whether the two cases have common issues of law or fact. Alpha's duty of loyalty to Builder, a present client, precludes presently opposing Builder in another case.

(B) is incorrect because loyalty is the issue, and loyalty is violated by simultaneous representation and opposition, whether in two court matters, two administrative matters, or some combination of both.

(C) looks to be correct because it states the points made above.

(D) is incorrect because simultaneous representation and opposition would not be allowed even if there was no chance of the two cases being appealed to the same court.

Since (A), (B) and (D) are incorrect (C) must be the correct answer.

Question 51

The correct answer is C.

(A) is incorrect because Attorney did not advertise falsely; his advertisement did not state, expressly or impliedly, that he would take on every case presented to him.

(B) is incorrect because Attorney's warning of the possibility of losing the claim due to violating the statute of limitations did not require notice as to the exact date of expiration in order to be effective. (The answer might be different if the statute would expire in a matter of days, as opposed to the six months applicable here.)

(C) looks to be correct because Attorney had no duty to Baker once he told her he was not going to take the case and that she should see another lawyer promptly before the statute of limitations expired.

(D) is incorrect because it implies that the reason Attorney is not civilly liable to Baker is that he offered to refer her to another lawyer. Because Attorney violated no duty to Baker (as in (C) above) he would not be liable civilly to her even if he had not offered to refer her to another lawyer.

Because (A), (B) and (D) are incorrect (C) must be the correct answer.

Question 52

The correct answer is B.

(A) is incorrect because the fact that Beta is deceased does not mean that Alpha can no longer use Beta in the firm name; the name of a deceased partner is useful to the public in identifying the firm.

(B) looks to be correct because Alpha has allowed Gamma's name to be used as if Gamma were a partner of Alpha, which he is not. If lawyers are not associated they may not claim, expressly or impliedly, that they are.

(C) is incorrect because the fact that Alpha and Beta were partners at Beta's death does not excuse Alpha's use of **Gamma's** name, as indicated in (B) above.

(D) is incorrect because Gamma's sharing of the rent and office expenses does not excuse Alpha's holding out of Gamma as a partner when he is not.

Because (A), (C) and (D) are incorrect (B) must be the correct answer.

Question 53

The correct answer is B.

(A) is incorrect because Attorney is subject to discipline if she represents Deftco in a matter for which she had personal and substantial responsibility while working for the governmental organization ("ECC"), unless the ECC gives its informed consent, in writing, to the representation. There is no indication in the fact pattern that ECC has consented or will consent. Whether or not the judgment in the prior case is determinative of Deftco's liability is immaterial to Attorney's obligation **not** to represent Deftco in the absence of the ECC's consent.

(B) looks to be correct for the reasons stated in (A) above.

(C) is incorrect. The fact that Attorney has acquired special competence in the matter for which she had personal and substantial responsibility is the very reason that the conflict of interest exists between Deftco and the ECC. Attorney's special competence, therefore, cannot justify her representation of Deftco.

(D) is incorrect because even if all information Attorney acquired while representing ECC is now a matter of public record and therefore not privileged Attorney is still bound by the text of the disciplinary rule set forth in (A) above.

Because (A), (C) and (D) are incorrect (B) must be the correct answer.

Question 54

The correct answer is C.

(A) is incorrect because even if the fee paid by Plaintiff was not increased by reason of Beta's association, Plaintiff, the client, was never informed of Beta's association in the case and so was deprived of the ability to decide whether to consent to that representation. That fact makes Beta's association in the case improper. In addition, if two or more lawyers associate as in this case the client must agree to the arrangement (including the share each lawyer is to receive) in writing. That was not done here.

(B) is incorrect because even if the fee were divided in proportion to the services performed and/or the responsibilities assumed by each, Beta's association is improper, for the reasons stated in (A) above.

(C) looks to be correct, for the reasons stated in (A) above.

(D) is incorrect because even if a written statement is given Plaintiff at the close of the case Plaintiff was deprived of the opportunity to consent or not to Beta's representation when Beta was first brought into the case by Alpha.

Because (A), (B) and (D) are incorrect (C) must be the correct answer.

Question 55

The correct answer is C.

(A) is incorrect because the identity of Repo, a potential witness, is a matter of public record, and information contained in a public record is within the categories of extrajudicial statements that a lawyer involved in litigation may make without violating the disciplinary rules on pre-trial publicity.

(B) is incorrect because even if jurors learned of Attorney's remarks those remarks would not materially prejudice any trial; the statements are neutral regarding the witness's state of mind and concern (as mentioned in (A) above) a matter of public record.

(C) looks to be correct for the reasons stated in (A) and (B) above.

(D) is incorrect because **if** the statements made by Attorney were in violation of the rule against certain pre-trial publicity Attorney would be subject to discipline whether or not the trial had commenced.

Because (A), (B) and (D) are incorrect (C) must be the correct answer.

Question 56

The correct answer is D.

(A) is incorrect because Alpha, although employed in the district attorney's office during the investigation of Deft, acquired no knowledge of the facts through that employment. **If** Alpha had been involved personally and substantially in the investigation **or** had acquired confidential information about the investigation Alpha would not be able to represent Deft subsequently and Beta, now associated with Alpha, would be vicariously disqualified in the absence of adequate screening procedures. As it is, either Alpha or Beta may represent Deft.

(B) is incorrect for the reasons stated in (A) above. **If** either Alpha or Beta was disqualified from representing Deft that disqualification would be cured by the consent of the district attorney's office, but there is no disqualification of Alpha or Beta here.

(C) is incorrect because Alpha is not disqualified, as stated in (A) and (B) above. **If** Alpha was disqualified and screening procedures were necessary for Beta's being able to represent Deft, then Alpha's participation in the representation or sharing in the fee would defeat the screening and disqualify Beta; but there is no such disqualification here.

(D) Because (A), (B) and (C) are incorrect (D) must be the correct answer. Alpha is not disqualified and therefore no reason exists to disqualify Beta.

Question 57

The correct answer is D.

(A) is incorrect because, while Prosecutor does have the obligation to accurately state the testimony in the case, doing so does not excuse his express assertion of his personal beliefs about Wit's credibility. That assertion is a violation of a disciplinary rule and, therefore, cannot constitute proper behavior.

(B) is incorrect because even if he truly believed Wit was lying he was obligated to avoid stating that belief to the jury, as stated in (A) above.

(C) is incorrect because Prosecutor's ethical error was not in alluding to the beliefs of the jurors but rather alluding expressly to his own.

(D) Because (A), (B) and (C) are incorrect (D) must be the correct answer. No attorney, whether in a civil or criminal case, may expressly assert his or her personal opinion as to guilt, innocence, liability, justness of a cause or credibility of a witness.

Question 58

The correct answer is A.

(A) looks to be correct. Client told Attorney that he could be available any time during October, November and December, therefore refraining from indicating any preference as to month or date. Attorney may therefore properly schedule trial at any time within those months, unless it somehow appears that a particular date might prejudice Client. There is no such indication given in this question. It may be a better practice to first consult with Client to ensure that no prejudice exists, but that might not be feasible if Attorney is attempting to find a date acceptable to opposing counsel and court clerk, as well as to Client. We will feel more confident in choosing (A) if we can eliminate the other choices.

(B) is incorrect because the choice as to favoring the scheduling of a criminal trial over a civil trial is for the court to make, not the lawyer. Attorney has no right to favor one client over another; such favoring would constitute a conflict of interest.

(C) is incorrect because there is no indication here that Attorney is not managing her calendar in such a way as to ensure the prompt resolution of her cases.

(D) is incorrect because whether or not Attorney was court-appointed is immaterial; her ethical obligations to her clients and to the court system would be the same.

Because (B), (C) and (D) are incorrect (A) must be the correct choice.

Question 59

The correct answer is A.

(A) looks to be correct, because Attorney interviewed Able and Baker, heard confidential information from both and represented both. Now that those clients' interests have diverged Attorney can no longer represent them concurrently, even if they both consent, as one is making a claim against the other and no lawyer could **reasonably** believe that competent and diligent representation could be provided both of them. Attorney has entered an appearance on behalf of both Able and Baker and so must **request** the court to allow withdrawal.

(B) is incorrect because Able has consented to Attorney's withdrawal from representing him, but has not consented, in writing, to Attorney representing Baker in a case where Able and Baker have adverse interests. If Attorney continued to represent Baker he would have to be ready to impeach Able's testimony with his prior inconsistent statements to Attorney. Able would be a **former** client in the same case; Attorney is precluded, absent written consent, from representing anyone with interests adverse to Able. Additionally, if Able denied making those statements Attorney would have to testify to them, and thereupon become a witness as well as an advocate, itself a violation of disciplinary rules. If Attorney chose **not** to impeach Able Attorney would not be representing Baker with diligence and zeal.

(C) is incorrect because Baker has consented to Attorney's withdrawal from representing him, but has not consented, in writing, to Attorney representing Able in a case where Baker and Abel have adverse interests. (This situation is the mirror image of that presented in (B) above.)

(D) is incorrect because, whether or not Attorney called Able as a witness Attorney would be representing adverse interests.

Because (B), (C) and (D) are incorrect (A) must be the correct choice.

Question 60

The correct answer is C.

(A) is incorrect because Judge is not allowed to engage in ex parte communication with anyone other than court personnel whose function is to aid Judge, or with fellow judges, unless Judge, prior to deciding the case, communicates its contents to all counsel and gives them an opportunity to respond. Here Judge, although not responsible for initiating the communication, did engage in it and there is no indication that counsel were advised.

(B) is incorrect because the rule against ex parte communication does not exempt communication with a person disinterested in the outcome.

(C) looks to be correct as it gives the rule stated in (A) above.

(D) is incorrect because even if Attorney was on record as counsel in the case Judge cannot properly communicate with him or her ex parte.

Because (A), (B) and (D) are incorrect (C) must be the correct choice.

Question 61

The correct answer is D.

(A) is incorrect because Attorney advertised a $600 fee and is therefore bound to charge no more than that amount. The fact that the $2,000 he actually charged would have been reasonable if the advertisement had not been made does not change Attorney's obligation, given the broadcast of the advertisement.

(B) is incorrect because Attorney is bound by the terms of the advertisement whether or not the tax problems were anticipated, as stated in (A) above.

(C) is incorrect because Attorney is bound by the terms of the advertisement even if Client acquiesces in paying more than the advertised fee.

(D) Because (A), (B) and (C) are incorrect (D) must be the correct answer. As stated above, Attorney is bound by the terms of the advertisement.

iestion 62

The correct answer is A.

(A) looks to be correct because lawyers are not allowed to form a partnership with non-lawyers if any of the activities of the partnership will consist of the practice of law. Doing so assists the unauthorized practice of law and violates a disciplinary rule, even if no one but the lawyer performs any legal service.

(B) is incorrect because lawyers may receive fees paid for other than legal services, as long as they do not do so in a partnership formed with a non-lawyer when any of the partnership activities consist of the practice of law. A lawyer, for instance, could receive fees for real estate work in a real estate partnership that did not provide any legal services.

(C) is incorrect because Attorney is subject to discipline for forming the instant partnership with a non-lawyer even though the partnership would provide high-quality service.

(D) is incorrect because Attorney is subject to discipline for **forming** the instant partnership, not for allowing a non-lawyer to provide legal services, as stated in the second sentence of (A) above.

Because (B), (C) and (D) are incorrect (A) must be the correct answer.

Question 63

The correct answer is D.

(A) is incorrect because Attorney, although an officer of the court having the obligation to act within the bounds of the law and of the MRPC, does not have an obligation to disclose this information, given him in confidence by his client. In fact, Attorney **does** have the obligation to keep the information confidential, to ensure that it is **not** disclosed absent Client's consent.

(B) is incorrect because Attorney has an obligation to keep the information confidential in spite of the fact that doing so impedes the state from discovering significant evidence.

(C) is incorrect because the **reason** Attorney has no obligation to disclose is the confidential nature of the information imparted to him, not the fact that he did not represent or advise Client with respect to the prior crimes. Had Attorney advised Client with respect to how to commit the prior crimes, or to avoid detection for their commission, he would be subject to discipline (and criminal prosecution) for reasons independent of any obligation to disclose or withhold information.

(D) Because (A), (B) and (C) are incorrect (D) must be the correct answer. The information imparted to Attorney is confidential and must not be disclosed; if Attorney did disclose it without Client's consent he would then be subject to discipline.

Question 64

The correct answer is C.

(A) is incorrect because Beta, while a member of the bar and therefore licensed to practice law, is admittedly not competent to handle this particular case without assistance from another lawyer who is competent in the area.

(B) is incorrect. While Alpha may withdraw from a case if work on it would cause unreasonable financial hardship, any hardship here would not be "unreasonable" given the fact that Alpha willingly accepted Corp as a client, knowing what kind of work the representation would entail, prior to deciding to spend time on more remunerative cases.

(C) looks to be correct. If Beta continues representing Corp without adequate preparation or assistance, Beta is in violation of a disciplinary rule, and Alpha is also in violation of a disciplinary rule (and therefore acting improperly) because Alpha has directed Beta's violation of that disciplinary rule.

(D) is incorrect because the client need not give permission to Alpha to assign Beta, or any associate, to the case, **if** that assignment was appropriate. The assignment, for reasons stated in (A) and (C) above, is not appropriate here. If the client did give Alpha permission to assign Beta to work on this matter, in spite of the lack of adequate assistance and supervision, such permission would still not excuse the incompetent representation that would result; a client's consent to incompetent representation does not justify such representation.

Because (A), (B) and (D) are incorrect (C) must be the correct answer.

Question 65

The correct answer is A.

(A) looks to be the correct answer. Bank and Corp currently have interests that do not conflict. Their interests may conflict in the future, but under the circumstances outlined in the question Attorney has a reasonable belief that he can currently represent the interests of both clients adequately, and both have given informed consent (presumably in writing) to the representation.

(B) is incorrect because an arrangement being customary in the community would not save it **if** it was improper under the MRPC. As stated in (A) above, however, this arrangement is not improper.

(C) is incorrect because it is appropriate for a client to pay a lawyer for the services rendered. Here, Attorney provided services to Corp, a client, and Corp paid Attorney his fees. (**If** Corp was not a client and paid Attorney for services rendered to Bank, a client, such payment would be improper without Bank's consent.)

(D) is incorrect because, given the circumstances outlined in the question, Corp and Bank do **not** have differing interests.

Because (B), (C) and (D) are incorrect (A) must be the correct answer.

Question 66

The correct answer is C.

(A) is incorrect because Attorney is "advertising," not "soliciting." Solicitation (in person, live telephone or real-time electronic communication) is, with some exceptions, prohibited, but advertising, if presented appropriately (e.g., not misleading, not self-laudatory or extremely undignified) is generally permitted.

(B) is incorrect because the use of a coupon is not extremely undignified or otherwise inappropriate.

(C) looks to be correct because the advertisement appears appropriate, as long as it is accurate and as long as Attorney is actually willing to provide the services provided for the fee stated.

(D) is incorrect because even if Attorney seeks business from persons already represented by a lawyer that desire is legitimate. (The other lawyers may not provide representation in the areas in which Attorney practices.) What Attorney is **not** allowed to do is to contact a person represented by a lawyer in a particular matter (without that lawyer's permission and without independent legal authority) when Attorney is representing a client in the **same** matter.

Because (A), (B) and (D) are incorrect (C) must be the correct answer.

Question 67

The correct answer is D.

(A) is incorrect because Attorney **is** subject to discipline for contacting (in this case through another person) a person represented by a lawyer in a particular matter (without that lawyer's permission and without independent legal authority) when Attorney is representing a client in the **same** matter. The fact that Attorney was following Plaintiff's instructions does not avoid the violation of a disciplinary rule.

(B) is incorrect because the importance of the evidence obtained through the disciplinary violation stated in (A) above does not excuse that violation. Attorney is still subject to discipline.

(C) is incorrect because if Attorney had interviewed Defendant personally the disciplinary violation referred to above would be the same. Attorney is not allowed to make contact with Defendant, under the circumstances outlined in this question, either directly or indirectly.

(D) Because (A), (B) and (C) are incorrect (D) must be the correct answer.

Question 68

The correct answer is A.

(A) looks to be correct because a lawyer is subject to discipline for compensating another person for recommending the lawyer's legal services. The compensation is usually in the form of direct payment but, as here, it may be in the form of mutual recommendation.

(B) is incorrect because, although improper, the arrangement does not involve the practice of law with a non-lawyer; no partnership between Attorney and Broker has been formed, only an agreement to recommend one another.

(C) is incorrect because the arrangement is improper for the reasons stated in (A) above; the fact that neither party shares in the other's fees does not make the arrangement proper.

(D) is incorrect because the arrangement is improper for the reasons stated in (A) above; the fact that the fees are otherwise reasonable does not make the arrangement proper.

Because (B), (C) and (D) are incorrect (A) must be the correct answer.

Question 69

The correct answer is D.

(A) is incorrect because even though Judge no longer has a financial interest in the outcome of the cases handled by her former firm she was associated with the firm while those matters were pending, and ruling on those matters now that she is on the bench therefore would create an **appearance** of impropriety which she must avoid, according to her obligations under the CJC.

(B) is incorrect because the appearance of impropriety stated in (A) above would exist whether or not the fee requests are contested.

(C) is incorrect because the appearance of impropriety, although lessened somewhat by Judge's notations of her former association with Law Firm, would still exist.

(D) Because (A), (B) and (C) are incorrect (D) must be the correct answer. As stated in (A) above, Judge's ruling on fees to be awarded her former firm, even if scrupulously fair, would create the appearance of impropriety and therefore would not be proper.

Question 70

The correct answer is B.

Which of the numbered choices are proper?

I is proper because Client is entitled to a total of $42,000 (70% of the settlement). Attorney may therefore send Client the $30,000 previously deposited in the Clients' Trust Account and later send client $12,000 from that account, after Sureco's check for $30,000 is deposited therein.

II is proper because Client is entitled to a total of $42,000 (70%) of the settlement) but only half of the settlement has been received to date. Attorney may therefore send Client $21,000 of the $30,000 previously deposited in the Clients' Trust Account while retaining the remaining $9,000 in that account. The remaining $9,000 appears to belong to Attorney (30% of the amount received to date) but given Client's demand for the full $30,000 the $9,000 must be considered to be in dispute at the present time, so if not sent to Client must remain in the Clients' Trust Account (**not** transferred to Attorney's personal account) until the dispute is resolved (presumably when Sureco's check is deposited therein).

III is not proper for the reasons stated in II above.

Because only choices I and II are proper (B) is the correct answer.

Question 71

The correct answer is D.

(A) is incorrect because even though Attorney believed the position she advocated was in the public interest she should have disclosed the fact that she represented a private client in her appearance. What a client tells a lawyer is generally confidential but the **identity** of the client is generally not confidential; it should have been disclosed so that Congress could more accurately evaluate her testimony. Failure to disclose means that Attorney's action were improper.

(B) is incorrect because Congress, while interested in the content of the testimony, is also interested in the motivation of the person presenting that testimony. The identity of the person paying the witness is a strong clue to the witness's motivation.

(C) is incorrect because a lawyer may accept a fee for trying to influence legislative action; such an attempt is within the bounds of proper advocacy for a client. What makes Attorney's actions improper is not the attempt to influence Congress but rather her withholding of the identity of her private client, as stated in (A) above.

(D) Because (A), (B) and (C) are incorrect (D) must be the correct answer. As stated in (A) above, a lawyer appearing in a legislative hearing should identify the capacity in which she appears.

Question 72

The correct answer is C.

(A)   is incorrect because the information requested is confidential, even if it is not within the attorney-client privilege or attorney work product. Confidentiality is broader than privilege and work product, and, if disclosure is not consented to by Baker, Attorney is bound to avoid that disclosure.

(B)   is incorrect because confidentiality outlasts the attorney-client relationship. Baker is no longer Attorney's client but is a former client to whom the duty of confidentiality still applies.

(C)   looks to be correct. The information, being confidential, as stated in (A) above, may not be disclosed by Attorney without the consent of the former client and Baker has refused to consent.

(D)   is incorrect because if the former client has refused consent to disclose Attorney must abide by that refusal, even if Attorney believes that disclosure would be in Baker's best interests. It is Baker who has the right to make the decision as to disclosure or nondisclosure.

Because (A), (B) and (D) are incorrect (C) must be the correct answer.

Question 73

The correct answer is A.

(A)   looks to be correct because a lawyer is subject to discipline for attempting to deprive the court or a party of the opportunity to obtain evidence, including testimonial evidence. Attorney's encouragement of Witt to leave the country is such an attempt.

(B)   is incorrect because Attorney had no obligation to subpoena Witt, although knowing she was an eyewitness. Witt would testify against Attorney's client and so Attorney would be acting appropriately by **not** making any effort to have Witt testify and by hoping that the opponent would not learn of Witt's existence. Taking any affirmative steps to prevent the opponent from discovering Witt's existence, however, is improper, as stated in (A) above.

(C)   is incorrect because Attorney's encouragement of Witt to leave the country is a disciplinary violation, whether or not Witt had been subpoenaed by the opponent.

(D)   is incorrect because Attorney's encouragement of Witt to leave the country is a disciplinary violation, whether or not Attorney offered her any inducement to leave.

Because (B), (C) and (D) are incorrect (A) must be the correct answer.

Question 74

The correct answer is C.

(A)   is incorrect. It is true that Client is engaged in continuing illegal conduct, in remaining in hiding, but Attorney is not subject to discipline because he is not aiding Client in her illegal conduct and he is not counseling her to remain a fugitive. Attorney is acting appropriately in his representation of Client.

(B)   is incorrect because a lawyer cannot be disciplined for giving appropriate advice to a client merely because the client refuses to follow that advice.

(C)   looks to be correct for the reasons stated in (A) above.

(D)   is incorrect because Attorney would be acting appropriately in representing Client whether or not he believed the indictment is defective. The legitimacy of the indictment does not mean that Client has no right to legal representation.

Because (A), (B) and (D) are incorrect (C) must be the correct answer.

Question 75

The correct answer is B.

(A) is incorrect. While Attorney is subject to discipline for his actions it is not because he failed to obtain Husband's consent to the representation. Attorney had personal and substantial responsibility for aspects of this case as a governmental worker: an assistant county attorney. Even if he had left that governmental employment he would be disqualified from private employment on the same matter. Husband's consent would not prevent Attorney's disqualification.

(B) looks to be correct for the reasons stated in (A) above.

(C) is incorrect because Attorney is still employed by the government, but even if he had left that employment he would be precluded from representing Wife in this case, for the reasons stated in (A) above.

(D) is incorrect because Attorney **is** subject to discipline, for the reasons stated in (A) above.

Because (A), (C) and (D) are incorrect (B) must be the correct answer.

Question 76

The correct answer is A.

(A) looks to be correct because a lawyer, while representing a client, is subject to discipline for communicating about the subject of the representation with any person known to be represented by another lawyer in the matter, unless the other lawyer has consented to the communication or the communication is authorized by law or court order.

(B) is incorrect because it indicates that Attorney is subject to discipline only if the statement is later used to Claimant's disadvantage. Discipline is appropriate regardless of how the statement is used, as stated in (A) above.

(C) is incorrect because whether or not Claimant had filed suit at the time of the interview is immaterial.

(D) is incorrect because arranging for the interview constitutes the disciplinary violation, whether or not Attorney conducts any subsequent litigation.

Because (B), (C) and (D) are incorrect (A) must be the correct answer.

Question 77

The correct answer is A.

(A) looks to be correct because a lawyer is subject to discipline for practicing in a professional corporation or association authorized to practice law for a profit if a non-lawyer is a director or officer. Veep, a non-lawyer, is an officer of the corporation.

(B) is incorrect because a non-lawyer **may** hold stock as an executor of the will of a deceased member of the organization for a reasonable period of time.

(C) is incorrect because Delta, although a salaried employee and not a member or shareholder of the organization, is a lawyer and therefore bound by the disciplinary rules of the MRPC.

(D) is incorrect because Veep's position as officer of the corporation, not Veep's participation in any decision about a particular case, is what disqualifies that corporation from being a legitimate organization in which lawyers may practice.

Because (B), (C) and (D) are incorrect (A) must be the correct answer.

Question 78

The correct answer is B.

(A) is incorrect because it states the wrong reason for Attorney's being subject to discipline. While the amount received by Attorney would be contingent on the receipts from sale of media rights it would not be contingent on a finding of liability in this case or on the amount of damages recovered, assuming proof of liability.

(B) looks to be correct because a lawyer is subject to discipline for making an agreement, during the representation, that gives the lawyer media rights to portrayals based in substantial part on information relating to the representation. This representation is not yet concluded.

(C) is incorrect because Attorney **is** subject to discipline, for the reasons stated in (B) above. The civil nature of a paternity suit is immaterial.

(D) is incorrect because Attorney **is** subject to discipline, for the reasons stated in (B) above. The fact that Plaintiff received independent advice prior to entering the agreement is immaterial.

Because (A), (C) and (D) are incorrect (B) must be the correct answer.

Question 79

The correct answer is A.

(A) looks to be the correct answer because Attorney properly informed Husband and Wife of the potential dangers of the limited representation, secured their written consent to that representation and determined, with reason, that neither party would be materially prejudiced if no settlement was reached. A conflict situation could possibly arise in the future but none exists at the present time.

(B) is incorrect because Attorney's previous representation of Husband and Wife is immaterial to the propriety of the present representation.

(C) is incorrect because Attorney did **not** ask for or receive a waiver of client confidentiality; what Husband and Wife communicate to her and what she communicates to them is confidential as to the rest of the world. Because she represents both equally, however, what one tells her separately cannot be kept confidential from the other.

(D) is incorrect. Attorney **did** advise both Husband and Wife, in writing, that they might be better off with separate lawyers, but that advice was not an absolute prerequisite to the representation of both of them.

Because (B), (C) and (D) are incorrect (A) must be the correct answer.

Question 80

The correct answer is B.

(A) is incorrect because it indicates that Attorney may disclose the confidential information only if Client does not object. A lawyer may, however, disclose confidential information when necessary to establish a defense to a claim against the lawyer based upon conduct in which the client was involved, whether or not the client consents.

(B) looks to be correct, for the reasons stated in (A) above.

(C) is incorrect because Attorney may disclose the confidential information, as stated in (A) above, whether she does so to defend herself in a civil or a criminal proceeding.

(D) is incorrect because Attorney may disclose, when necessary to defend herself, even if disclosure is detrimental to Client.

Because (A), (C) and (D) are incorrect (B) must be the correct answer.

Question 81

The correct answer is A.

(A) looks to be the correct answer because lawyers are not allowed to lie, be deceitful or to engage in misrepresentation, even if they are doing those things in order to benefit a client. Attorney will be subject to discipline if she falsely tells Employee that she is not a suspect (because she is a suspect). Additionally, Attorney will be subject to discipline if she tells Employee her statements will be held confidential because Attorney represents Company, not Employee, and the statements will be disclosed to Company.

(B) is incorrect because even if Employee is advised to retain counsel Attorney plans to engage in the misrepresentation described in (A) above.

(C) is incorrect because misrepresentation is a disciplinary offense whether or not legal proceedings are pending.

(D) is incorrect because misrepresentation is a disciplinary offense whether or not the person to whom misrepresentations are made is a client.

Because (B), (C) and (D) are incorrect (A) must be the correct answer.

Question 82

The correct answer is C.

(A) is incorrect because Judge's conduct was improper. The fact that the judgment was supported by evidence at trial is immaterial; Judge has engaged in ex parte contact that might influence the outcome of the litigation. Only if Judge informed counsel for the parties of the contact and allowed them an opportunity to respond would the contact possibly be appropriate.

(B) is incorrect because Judge has the right to question witnesses and even to call witnesses to gather facts, but not to gather facts through ex parte communication without subsequent notice to counsel, as stated in (A) above.

(C) looks to be correct, for the reasons stated in (A) above. The fact that Judge acted through another person (Clerk) does not mitigate the impropriety.

(D) is incorrect because Judge's actions were improper whether or not Engineer testified.

Because (A), (B) and (D) are incorrect (C) must be the correct answer.

Question 83

The correct answer is B.

(A) seems to be incorrect. Attorney is subject to discipline but probably not for this reason, but rather for commingling; he put Client's money in his personal account to cover his personal check. The fact that Client was deprived of ten days of interest is probably insignificant, given that the amount of interest is likely too small to have gone to Client; it probably would have gone to fund indigent legal services under an IOLTA plan ("Interest on Lawyer's Trust Account") and Client, after having been informed of Attorney's actions, did not insist the ten days of interest be returned.

(B) looks to be correct because lawyers are not allowed to use clients' funds for personal purposes, even if all funds are replaced and the client approves of the lawyer's actions. Commingling is a very serious offense and, therefore, even if there is a slight possibility that (A) above is correct, (B) is definitely a stronger answer. We are instructed to choose the "best" of the four choices presented and choice (B), far stronger than choice (A), is "best," given that choices (C) and (D) below begin with the incorrect premise that the facts presented do **not** subject Attorney to discipline.

(C) is incorrect because Attorney is subject to discipline regardless of Client not being harmed and regardless of Attorney's (correct) surmise that Client would not object.

(D) is incorrect because Attorney is subject to discipline regardless of Client's approval.

Because (A), (C) and (D) are incorrect (B) must be the correct answer.

Question 84

The correct answer is A.

(A) looks to be correct because a lawyer is subject to discipline for entering into a contingent fee arrangement with a client represented in a criminal case, even if the fee seems otherwise reasonable. The retainer agreement here was contingent on the outcome of the case so violates the disciplinary rule.

(B) is incorrect because the disciplinary rule prohibiting a lawyer from acquiring a proprietary interest in the client's property pertains only to property that is the subject of the litigation for which the lawyer was retained. Here, the facts do not indicate that Deft's automobile was the subject of the litigation.

(C) is incorrect because a contingent fee in a criminal case is prohibited whether or not the charges are ultimately dismissed.

(D) is incorrect. Under the MRPC an otherwise legitimate contingent fee arrangement must be reduced to writing, but in this criminal case any contingent fee is illegitimate and therefore prohibited, whether or not it is reduced to writing.

Because (B), (C) and (D) are incorrect (A) must be the correct answer.

Question 85

The correct answer is D.

(A) is incorrect because Alpha **is** subject to discipline for communicating with Pres without her opponent's counsel's consent or independent legal authority to communicate. Agri is the corporate opponent of Alpha and that means that all persons currently employed by Agri whose actions may be imputed to it are within the prohibition, as are all persons who have the authority to obligate the organization with regard to the matter. Pres's actions and Pres's status were and are of that nature. Pres's personal liability to Agri is immaterial with regard to Alpha's prohibited actions.

(B) is incorrect because Alpha **is** subject to discipline, as stated in (A) above.

(C) is incorrect because Alpha has violated a disciplinary rule by improperly communicating with Pres whether Pres is called as a friendly or an adverse witness.

(D) Because (A), (B) and (C) are incorrect (D) must be the correct answer. Pres is the president of Agri and therefore has the authority to obligate the organization with regard to this matter.

Question 86

The correct answer is B.

(A) is incorrect because the fact that the opponent's lawyer is being aided by Attorney's lump sum payment does not subject Attorney to discipline for failing to represent his or her own clients diligently and zealously, as long as Attorney's own clients are benefited by that lump sum payment. It is not the case that every act by a lawyer that benefits an opponent thereby harms a client; often the nature of a settlement is that both sides benefit.

(B) looks to be correct because lawyers settling a case for multiple clients must secure the approval of every client as to the total amount and the amount that will be received by each of the clients. Each client must consent, therefore, not only to what he or she receives but also to what every other client receives. If Attorney does not reveal to every client what every other client is to receive, therefore, the required consent is absent and Attorney is in violation of a disciplinary rule.

(C) is incorrect because not revealing all the information necessary to secure the informed consent required is a disciplinary violation, even if the reason for not revealing the information is the desire to benefit all clients by ensuring that the settlement is accepted, and even if each client is satisfied with the amount that client received.

(D) is incorrect because Attorney **is** subject to discipline for not revealing all necessary information, regardless of client satisfaction, as stated in (C) above.

Because (A), (C) and (D) are incorrect (B) must be the correct answer.

Question 87

The correct answer is C.

(A) is incorrect. Alpha gained the information while representing Beta and it is therefore confidential, meaning not only that Alpha does not have to report the embezzlement to the disciplinary authorities but also that Alpha is **prohibited** from voluntarily disclosing it. The information did not come from Alpha's client so is not within the attorney-client privilege, but confidentiality is broader than privilege and covers this communication. If and when a court orders that this non-privileged information be revealed Alpha would have to reveal it, but until and unless that happens Alpha is bound to avoid disclosure.

(B) is incorrect because even if failure to report results in the continued concealment of Beta's breach of trust, Alpha is not "assisting" in that concealment by holding the information confidential, as Alpha is required to do, as stated in (A) above.

(C) looks to be correct, for the reasons stated in (A) above.

(D) is incorrect because it misstates the reason that Alpha has no obligation to report Beta's embezzlement. If Alpha had an obligation to report (which Alpha does not, as stated in (A) above) that obligation would not be discharged merely because the information would probably be disclosed by Bank.

Because (A), (B) and (D) are incorrect (C) must be the correct answer.

Question 88

The correct answer is B.

(A) seems to be incorrect. While it is true that Alpha and Beta are not subject to discipline for the advertisement, assuming that all statements in it are factually accurate and not otherwise misleading, the fact that law and medicine are licensed professions is, by itself, immaterial. If Alpha was, in fact, not the holder of an M.D. degree the lawyers here **would** be subject to discipline for false advertising in spite of the fact that medicine is a licensed profession.

(B) looks to be correct. If the lawyers possess the degrees stated the advertisement is not false or misleading. Lawyers are allowed to communicate, in their advertising, many kinds of information, if accurate, such as schools attended, **degrees awarded**, publications, foreign languages spoken, jurisdictions to which they are admitted to practice, etc. It is now even more apparent that (B) is a stronger answer than (A); if (C) and (D) are incorrect then (B) will be the "best" answer.

(C) is incorrect. Self-laudatory communication is considered misleading if it cannot be factually validated (e.g., "the finest matrimonial lawyer in the state"). But an M.D. degree can be factually validated.

(D) is incorrect because a degree is an educational attainment that can be advertised whether or not the lawyers' practice is limited to areas in which that degree is relevant.

Because (A) seems to be incorrect and (C) and (D) are definitely incorrect (B) is the "best" choice and must be the correct answer.

Question 89

The correct answer is D.

(A) is incorrect because it is generally proper for lawyers in the same firm to consult with one another regarding their cases. Only if Client had specifically requested that Alpha not discuss the case with anyone else, even other persons in Alpha's firm, **and** if Alpha accepted the representation with that limitation, would it be improper for Alpha to consult with Beta. Without that specific request communication within the firm is considered impliedly consented to by Client. If Beta provides some assistance in the case it would not be improper for the firm to charge Client for Beta's time, even if that increased the total fee.

(B) is incorrect because Client's consent, absent the specific request mentioned in (A) above, will be implied.

(C) is incorrect because Alpha's consulting Beta is proper whether or not Client is identified to Beta, given the implied consent by Client mentioned in (A) above.

(D) Because (A), (B) and (C) are incorrect (D) must be the correct answer. Client, by not making a specific request for non-disclosure by Alpha, has impliedly consented to Alpha communicating with other persons in the firm in order to provide better representation

Question 90

The correct answer is D.

(A) is incorrect because Judge's qualifications to hear the case, while strong, do not overcome the appearance of impropriety that would be created by hearing the case while Judge's brother owns a substantial interest in one of the parties.

(B) is incorrect because even though Judge believes he can be fair, and even if that belief is accurate, the **appearance** of impropriety stated in (A) above still remains.

(C) is incorrect because it misstates the reason that Judge's hearing the case is improper. In some instances disqualification based on a judge's financial interest, or those of a close family member, **can** be waived. Those instances are stated in (D) below.

(D) Because (A), (B) and (C) are incorrect (D) must be the correct answer. When financial interests are the reason for a judge to recuse himself the judge **may**, if he thinks he can be fair to all parties, disclose the financial interest to the parties and to their counsel, and then allow all of them to decide, outside of the judge's presence, whether to have the judge continue on the case. If all parties and counsel agree, in writing, to have the judge continue, he may do so.

Question 91

The correct answer is B.

(A) is incorrect. Attorney **is** subject to discipline if she calls Baker to testify because a lawyer is not allowed to knowingly present perjured testimony (or any false evidence), even if she does it in order to assist her client, and Attorney knows that Baker will lie on the stand. Choice (A), however, indicates that Attorney would not be subject to discipline for knowingly presenting perjured testimony as long as she informs the court of that fact prior to the testimony. That is wrong. Prior notice will not prevent the disciplinary violation.

(B) looks to be correct, for the reasons stated in (A) above.

(C) is incorrect because Attorney is in violation of a disciplinary rule for the reasons stated in (A) above regardless of what defense she relies on or what she argues to the jury.

(D) is incorrect because a client's insistence that a lawyer present perjured testimony does not excuse the lawyer's compliance with that demand.

Because (A), (C) and (D) are incorrect (B) must be the correct answer.

Question 92

The correct answer is C.

Which of the numbered choices are proper?

I is proper because it is accurate and factual; i.e., can be verified by public records.

II is proper for the same reason as (I) above.

III is proper for the same reason as in (I) and (II) above.

IV is **not** proper because of the second sentence. The first sentence is accurate and factual but the second, even if it reflects the truth, appears to commit the candidate with respect to the merits of cases or issues likely to come before the court. Judicial candidates for election are prohibited from doing so.

Because choices I, II and III are proper but choice IV is not, (C) is the correct answer.

Question 93

The correct answer is B.

(A) is incorrect because it is proper for Judge to accept an offer to speak at a bar association meeting, presumably devoted to the improvement of the law, and to accept free transportation and lodging for Judge and her husband, assuming that those costs are reasonably incurred. If costs in excess of $500 are reasonably incurred no impropriety exists.

(B) looks to be correct for the reasons stated in (A) above.

(C) is incorrect. The fact that bar association members regularly appear in Judge's court does not make Judge's acceptance of the costs of attending improper since the costs are paid by the association. No individual lawyer makes any payment directly to the judge.

(D) is incorrect because providing free transportation to Judge's husband does not transform a reasonable cost into an unreasonable one.

Because (A), (C) and (D) are incorrect (B) must be the correct answer.

Question 94

The correct answer is D.

Which of the numbered choices are proper?

I is proper because it is a neutral statement reflecting the reality of the postures of the adversaries: Agency has charged that Client acted wrongfully and Client has denied the charge. Attorney has made no attempt to improperly influence the decision-maker through these public statements.

II is proper because it explains the procedures to be followed by the adversaries. This is also a neutral statement, not one that attempts to improperly influence the decision-maker.

III is proper because it is a request for public assistance in the resolution of the matter, made in a neutral manner, not one that attempts to improperly influence members of the public to testify in any particular way. (An improper statement might be: "Client needs witnesses who know from their own observations and opinions that Client never did the things they've charged him with.")

Because choices I, II and II are all proper (D) is the correct answer.

Question 95

The correct answer is B.

(A) is incorrect because Attorney was acting for the client in an emergency situation, providing legal services reasonably necessary under the circumstances. No lawyer experienced in the drafting of wills was available. Even if Attorney omitted some formality that invalidated the will, therefore, no impropriety occurred; Attorney did the best he or she could.

(B) looks to be correct for the reasons stated in (A) above.

(C) is incorrect because Attorney acted properly under the circumstances, as stated in (A) above. If Attorney had **not** acted properly Doctor's waiver of Attorney's malpractice liability would not make those actions proper; prospective waiver is improper without the client's having been actually represented by other independent counsel with regard to making that waiver.

(D) is incorrect because, in spite of lacking the skill ordinarily required for the representation, Attorney acted properly under the circumstances, as stated in (A) above.

Because (A), (C) and (D) are incorrect (B) must be the correct answer.

Question 96

The correct answer is A.

(A) looks to be correct because the non-lawyer employee of Bank (the office manager) is assisting the law firm but not by practicing law in any manner. Only if confidential information of clients were disclosed to that employee would the arrangement with Bank be improper.

(B) is incorrect. While the arrangement is proper, as stated in (A) above, it is not proper **because** the employee is paid by Bank. It would still be proper if payment was made by the law firm, and it would be improper in spite of Bank being the payor if confidential information were disclosed.

(C) is incorrect because the arrangement **is** proper, for the reasons stated in (A) above. The fact that a non-lawyer advises lawyers on fees and time charges is not improper; that advice does not constitute the practice of law. Advising clients, drafting documents for them or representing them in legal proceedings would constitute the practice of law but Bank employee is not doing any of those things.

(D) is incorrect. Bank is involved, through its employee office manager, in the management of the law firm but that management does not constitute the practice of law, as stated in (C) above.

Because (A), (B) and (C) are incorrect (A) must be the correct answer.

Question 97

The correct answer is C.

(A) is incorrect because lawyers may advance the costs of litigation to clients they represent in that litigation. Guaranteeing payment to the bank that advanced the funds for those costs is an indirect method of advancing the client's litigation expenses, so is appropriate and not a violation of a disciplinary rule.

(B) is incorrect. While Attorney **is** helping to finance litigation by her guarantee to the bank that assistance is permitted by the MRPC.

(C) looks to be correct for the reasons stated in (A) and (B) above. Attorney is not subject to discipline.

(D) is incorrect. While Attorney is not subject to discipline for her actions the reason for that is not that she took the case on a contingent fee basis; whether she had a contingent fee, hourly fee or flat fee is immaterial; she may in any of those instances advance (or guarantee) the costs of the litigation.

Because (A), (B) and (D) are incorrect (C) must be the correct answer.

Question 98

The correct answer is A.

(A) looks to be the correct answer because a lawyer representing one party in any matter is prohibited from communicating about that matter with another party who is represented by counsel in the matter, unless counsel has consented or unless law or court order authorizes such communication. The motion served on Plaintiff here is, among other things, a form of communication about the subject matter of the case and, apparently, there has not been any consent by counsel for Plaintiff.

(B) is incorrect. While Alpha **is** subject to discipline for serving the motion and tender on Plaintiff personally (absent legal authorization), prior notice to Beta of the intention to serve Plaintiff would **not** have prevented the disciplinary violation unless Beta **consented** to such service.

(C) is incorrect because Alpha **is** subject to discipline, as stated in (A) and (B) above. While it is true that the decision to accept or reject a settlement offer rests with Plaintiff, not Beta, it is Beta's right, as Plaintiff's representative, to receive the offer and to present it to Plaintiff. Alpha cannot usurp that right.

(D) is incorrect because Alpha **is** subject to discipline, as stated in (A), (B) and (C) above. The fact that the motion and tender are public documents is immaterial; Alpha cannot serve them personally on Plaintiff without Beta's consent.

Because (B), (C) and (D) are incorrect (A) must be the correct answer.

Question 99

The correct answer is C.

(A) is incorrect because a lawyer may not participate in offering or accepting an agreement restricting the right of that lawyer or any other lawyer to practice law (except as a condition of maintaining retirement benefits). The disciplinary rule so stating also prohibits any agreement in which a restriction on the lawyer's right to practice is part of the settlement of a client controversy. Although the proposed agreement here is limited to subsequent proceedings in the same matter it is still a violation of the rule, and therefore improper.

(B) is incorrect. Even if Alpha believes the proposed settlement, with its restriction on Alpha's practice, is in the best interests of Wife, entering into that agreement is improper for the reasons stated in (A) above.

(C) looks to be correct for the reasons stated in (A) above. Alpha's agreement to not represent Wife in the future is improper.

(D) is incorrect. Alpha's agreement to restrict future practice is improper **even if** Wife's interests can be adequately protected by another lawyer in the future.

Because (A), (B) and (D) are incorrect (C) must be the correct answer.

Question 100

The correct answer is B.

Which of the numbered choices are proper?

I is improper because the dispute between Attorney and Plaintiff is whether Attorney is owed $5,000 or $3,000 of the $25,000 in the Clients' Trust Account. That means that Client is owed at least $20,000 and that amount must be promptly forwarded to Client. Withholding the money due Plaintiff by retaining the full $25,000 in the Clients' Trust Account is therefore improper.

II is proper. Plaintiff would be sent the $20,000 that is definitely due him or her and Attorney would receive the $3,000 that is definitely owed Attorney for legal fees. The remaining $2,000, which is in dispute, remains in the Clients' Trust Account, as is appropriate, until the dispute is resolved.

III is improper. Sending Plaintiff the $20,000 definitely due him or her is appropriate but transferring the remaining $5,000 to Attorney's office account is improper while $2,000 of that amount is in dispute.

Because only choice II is proper (B) is the correct answer.

Question 101

The correct answer is C.

(A) is incorrect. While it is true that Attorney complied with the requirement to speak truthfully and without intent to deceive the court, the closing argument was **not** proper because Attorney asserted personal knowledge of the facts in issue, and also expressed Attorney's personal opinion on negligence, an ultimate issue in the case.

(B) is incorrect because the closing argument was **improper**, for the reasons stated in (A) above. The rules of evidence, legally the same for trials to a judge and to a jury, are often **applied** more loosely in trials to a judge, but that does not excuse Attorney's **ethical** lapse in expressing personal knowledge and personal opinion.

(C) looks to be correct because of the reasons stated in (A) and (B) above.

(D) is incorrect because it does not matter whether or not there exists other evidence in the record about the facts asserted by Attorney. In either case Attorney acted improperly in asserting personal knowledge and personal opinion.

Because (A), (B) and (D) are incorrect (C) must be the correct answer.

Question 102

The correct answer is C.

(A) is incorrect because Plaintiff was not practicing law when he represented himself in small claims court. Every layperson as well as every lawyer has the right to self-representation. Only a lawyer has the right to represent **another** person; that representation is the practice of law. Plaintiff represented himself, so when Attorney assisted him he was not assisting the practice of law.

(B) is incorrect. A lawyer is generally allowed to offer unsolicited, in-person advice as long as the offer is not made to secure employment and as long as employment does not result. No employment was sought here and none ensued. (Even if Attorney had offered unsolicited, in-person legal advice for the purpose of securing employment by Plaintiff he would not be subject to discipline because the offer was made to a close friend. That is one of the exceptions to the rule generally prohibiting solicitation.)

(C) looks to be correct for the reasons stated in (A) above.

(D) is incorrect because Attorney, being a close friend of Plaintiff, **could** have given advice with the intent to secure compensated employment, as stated in (B) above.

Because (A), (B) and (D) are incorrect (C) must be the correct answer.

Question 103

The correct answer is D.

(A) is incorrect because a lawyer does not violate a disciplinary rule merely by representing a person who admits to a past crime.

(B) is incorrect because a person who has committed a crime has the right to representation, whether or not he admits his crime, and a lawyer has the right to represent him, whether or not he admits his crime.

(C) is incorrect because the perjury occurred in the past, and its disclosure to Attorney is confidential. (**If** the past perjury had occurred while Attorney was representing Client, **and** the proceeding in which it occurred had not yet concluded, Attorney would have the obligation to reveal it if the client would not, but that is not the case here.)

(D) Because (A), (B) and (C) are incorrect, (D) must be the correct answer. Attorney **would** be subject to discipline if she informed the authorities of the perjury because she would be revealing confidential information about a past crime without Client's consent.

Question 104

The correct answer is C.

(A)   is incorrect because Electco is Attorney's client, and therefore has the right to decide whether to accept settlement or not. A lawyer must comply with a client's decision as to whether to settle a matter, even if the lawyer's advice differs from the client's decision. That disagreement does not constitute a conflict of interest requiring the lawyer to withdraw.

(B)   is incorrect because although a lawyer must not engage in **frivolous** litigation a lawyer need not avoid non-frivolous litigation that is desired by a client, nor must the lawyer withdraw because the lawyer had advised settlement rather than litigation.

(C)   looks to be correct. If Electco has a defense supportable by a good faith argument the litigation raising that defense is not frivolous. If not, Attorney is not required to withdraw as counsel.

(D)   is incorrect because Attorney, although employed by Electco and under the supervision of the general counsel, is still responsible, individually, for any disciplinary violations Attorney commits. **If** a disciplinary rule required Attorney's withdrawal, Attorney would have to withdraw. As mentioned above, there is no such disciplinary rule.

Because (A), (B) and (D) are incorrect (C) must be the correct answer.

Question 105

The correct answer is D.

(A)   is incorrect because it is improper for a judge who has participated personally and substantially in any matter; i.e., on its merits, and then rejoined the private Bar, to then represent a party in connection with that matter. Alpha might be upholding the prior judicial decision but is still in violation of a disciplinary rule.

(B)   is incorrect because the disciplinary rule referred to in (A) above is violated whether or not Alpha's conduct of the first trial is in issue.

(C)   is incorrect because the disciplinary rule referred to in (A) above is violated whether or not the present suit is brought in bad faith.

(D)   Because (A), (B) and (C) are incorrect (D) must be the correct answer. Alpha is precluded from representation of either party in this matter because of the prior judicial participation.

Question 106

The correct answer is A.

(A)   looks to be correct because a lawyer representing a client in a case is generally prohibited from communicating with a represented opponent, unless the opponent's lawyer has consented. Since a lawyer is prohibited from violating a disciplinary rule through the actions of another, Alpha is guilty of misconduct by having Inv contact Defendant.

(B)   is incorrect because Inv was not engaging in the unauthorized practice of law by contacting Defendant. Alpha is subject to discipline for contacting Defendant through Inv, not for assisting unauthorized practice of law.

(C)   is incorrect because the fact that Inv is not a lawyer does not save Alpha from disciplinary action for having Inv contact Defendant.

(D)   is incorrect because Alpha violated a disciplinary rule by making contact with Defendant, whether or not Defendant's lawyer was doing an adequate job of representation.

Because (B), (C) and (D) are incorrect (A) must be the correct answer.

Question 107

The correct answer is C.

(A) is incorrect because direct mail is a legitimate form of lawyer advertising, provided it is not false or misleading. Advertising may be directed toward clients or non-clients (and is usually directed more toward non-clients, as is the case here).

(B) is incorrect because, even assuming that service as governor is unrelated to lawyerly ability, it is not prohibited from lawyer advertising unless false or misleading. He stated that he had been governor for eight years, and that statement was not false or misleading.

(C) looks to be correct. The announcement's information was true, therefore not false or misleading.

(D) is incorrect because information that is not false or misleading may be disseminated whether or not it is already in the public domain

Because (A), (B) and (D) are incorrect, (C) must be the correct answer.

Question 108

The correct answer is D.

(A) is incorrect because a lawyer with supervisory authority over another lawyer is obligated to supervise that subordinate lawyer in an adequate manner. Attorney failed to do that by assigning Associate to supervise paralegals in an area with which Associate was unfamiliar. If Attorney was willing to answer Associate's questions as Associate learned the area the supervision might have been adequate, but Attorney directed Associate "not to bother" him. The fact that the paralegals were experienced in the area does not suffice; even competent paralegals must be supervised by a member of the Bar who is able and willing to undertake that supervision.

(B) is incorrect. It is true that Attorney is ultimately liable for the accuracy of the title searches, but that civil liability does not excuse the lack of supervision required, as mentioned in (A) above.

(C) is incorrect because the lack of required supervision constitutes a disciplinary violation, whether or not it results in lower fees charged to clients.

(D) Because (A), (B) and (C) are incorrect (D) must be the correct answer. Attorney acted improperly in failing to adequately supervise the work of Associate.

Question 109

The correct answer is B.

(A) is incorrect because failing to put an entire fee agreement in writing, while definitely unadvisable, is not a disciplinary violation unless the fee is **contingent.** In this case Able and Baker charged an hourly fee, not a contingent fee.

(B) looks to be correct, because Able and Baker raised their hourly rates, thereby unilaterally altering the agreement they had with Client. Clients are liable only for the fees to which they agree. (Able and Baker could have notified Client of their proposed new rates. If Client agreed they would be acting properly in charging those rates. If Client disagreed Able and Baker could have refused to undertake representation of Client in new business matters.)

(C) is incorrect because imposing a new rate on clients without their assent is a disciplinary violation, even if the new rate is, objectively, a fair one.

(D) is incorrect because Client did **not** agree to pay Able and Baker's hourly rate, whatever it became, but rather agreed to pay $180/hour for partners' time and $110/hour for that of associates.

Because (A), (C) and (D) are incorrect (B) must be the correct answer.

Question 110

The correct answer is B.

Which of the numbered choices are proper?

I   is proper because it constitutes an argument that one witness's testimony is in direct contradiction to that of two other witnesses seen and heard by the jury. The jury can decide if the contradiction exists, and if so what significance it has. This is appropriate closing argument.

II   is proper because it constitutes an argument that one witness had motivation to lie while others did not. The jury saw and heard the witnesses and can decide whether they believe such motivation exists, and if so what significance it has. This is appropriate closing argument.

III is improper because Attorney is asserting a personal opinion about a witness's credibility. This is not appropriate closing argument and is, in fact, a disciplinary violation.

Because choices I and II are proper but choice III is not, (B) is the correct answer.

Question 111

The correct answer is D.

(A) is incorrect. While it is true that clients often prefer to pay a **contingent** fee to a lawyer, and may prefer to do so in **domestic relations** cases also, a lawyer who charges such a fee, or even offers to do so, is in violation of a disciplinary rule, if the fee is contingent on the securing of a divorce, or on the amount of alimony or support, or property settlement in lieu thereof.

(B) is incorrect because a contingent fee in a domestic relations case as described in (A) above is improper even if not "excessive."

(C) is incorrect because there are **some** instances in which a lawyer may acquire a proprietary interest in a cause of action: for instance, an attorney's lien, if authorized by law, to secure fees or expenses, or a reasonable contingent fee, in an **appropriate** civil case. This domestic relations case, however, is not an appropriate one for a contingent fee, as mentioned in (A) above.

(D) Because (A), (B) and (C) are incorrect (D) must be the correct answer. The retainer contract is improper because the fee is contingent.

Question 112

The correct answer is B.

(A) is incorrect because Alpha is subject to discipline for her failure to act with reasonable diligence and promptness in her representation. She knew that an answer had to be served ten days after Beta's demand, which could arrive at any time, yet left her office on a two-month vacation without making provision for someone, in her absence, to either answer or summon her if necessary.

(B) looks to be correct, for the reasons stated in (A) above.

(C) is incorrect because Alpha's neglect subjects her to discipline even if, as in this case, the neglect is not fatal to Client's case. The neglect **could** have been fatal. The question to be determined is whether Alpha has violated a disciplinary rule, not whether that violation eventually harms or does not harm Client.

(D) is incorrect. Even assuming that Alpha did not know of Beta's demand she did know that a demand could be made at any time and that an answer would then have to be served in ten days. Nonetheless, she put herself in a position in which she might very well be unable to serve that answer.

Because (A), (C) and (D) are incorrect (B) must be the correct answer.

Question 113

The correct answer is C.

Which of the numbered choices are proper?

I   is proper because the extrajudicial statement to the reporter merely repeats allegations in the pleadings. Since the pleadings are already part of the public record the statement is unlikely to materially prejudice the trial.

II   is improper because it refers to medical tests not yet in evidence (at the close of Plaintiff's case). The tests may never be admitted, yet their disclosure at this time could result in the jury hearing about them, thus possibly prejudicing the trial.

III is proper because lawyers are allowed to publicly request assistance in obtaining evidence for a trial.

Because choices I and III are proper but choice II is not, (C) is the correct answer.

Question 114

The correct answer is B.

(A)   is incorrect because Beta's comments are equally proper, or improper, whether or not Beta is also a judicial candidate.

(B)   looks to be correct because a lawyer is allowed to comment on the qualifications or integrity of a judicial candidate, as long as the comment is not made with knowing falsity or reckless disregard as to its truth or falsity. An honest and candid opinion contributes to the administration of justice.

(C)   is incorrect because the remarks do not bring the judiciary into disrepute; Alpha is not yet a judge. Even if Alpha were already on the bench and running for re-election, an honest and accurate assessment by Beta would be appropriate.

(D)   is incorrect because a lawyer's public comments on judicial candidates **are** appropriate, as mentioned in (B) and (C) above.

Because (A), (C) and (D) are incorrect (B) must be the correct answer.

Question 115

The correct answer is B.

(A)   is incorrect because a lawyer must have **good cause** to withdraw from representation, unless the client chooses to discharge the lawyer. The lawyer may not discontinue representation without good cause.

(B)   looks to be correct because Client's conduct is making the representation unreasonably difficult and that difficulty is one recognized kind of the good cause mentioned in (A) above.

(C)   is incorrect because, by stating "No," it denies Attorney's right to seek to withdraw, even in the face of unreasonable demands, as mentioned in (B) above.

(D)   is incorrect because it states that a lawyer may not withdraw without the client's consent, even in the face of unreasonable demands. That is untrue, as mentioned in (B) and (C) above.

Because (A), (C) and (D) are incorrect (B) must be the correct answer.

Question 116

The correct answer is D.

(A) is incorrect because Judge is **not** exercising the discretion allowed by the rule of the judicial district in which she sits. She does not attempt to determine if third postponement requests are "appropriate" but grants them absent any such determination. In so acting she violates her duty to dispose of all judicial matters promptly, efficiently and fairly.

(B) is incorrect because appellate courts generally refuse to review lower court determinations regarding postponements. Even in the rare instance where such review might be granted it would not excuse the failure of Judge to expedite the determination of the matter before her.

(C) is incorrect. While it is true that judges have no official obligation to encourage settlement (doing so, with the consent of the parties, is encouraged), that is not the reason Judge's actions are improper, as mentioned in (A) above.

(D) Because (A), (B) and (C) are incorrect (D) must be the correct answer. Judge's actions are improper for the reasons mentioned in (A) above.

Question 117

The correct answer is D.

(A) is incorrect because a lawyer may not represent a client without doing so competently, diligently, and with zeal in advocacy. If Attorney represented Owner and did not disclose the memorandum's information Attorney would not be delivering the full benefit of representation to which Owner is entitled and would be acting improperly. Since the memorandum was confidential to former client DOT, however, and confidentiality survives the termination of the attorney-client relationship, Attorney could not disclose the memorandum's information in representing Owner without acting improperly. The two conflicting obligations mean that any representation of Owner in this proceeding by Attorney would be improper. Attorney must, therefore, decline the representation.

(B) is incorrect for the reasons mentioned in (A) above. (Of course, the holder of confidential information has the right to waive confidentiality. If DOT did that here Attorney could represent Owner, but there is no reason to think that DOT would do so, and the question does not indicate any inclination on DOT's part to do so.)

(C) is incorrect because Attorney's obligation to hold the memorandum confidential, mentioned in (A) above, includes not disclosing the information to Owner, whether Attorney officially represents Owner or not.

(D) Because (A), (B) and (C) are incorrect (D) must be the correct answer. Representation of Owner must be refused; disclosure of the information must also be refused.

Question 118

The correct answer is A.

(A) looks to be correct because a lawyer, generally prohibited from acting as a witness in litigation for which the lawyer is employed, **is** allowed to testify in certain instances. One of them is a situation such as this, where Attorney's testimony will be on a matter of formality (the will's execution) that is uncontested. Additionally, Attorney's testimony is particularly necessary because the other subscribing witness has predeceased Testator. Attorney's acceptance of the representation is therefore proper, even though Attorney will also act as a witness.

(B) is incorrect because the Executor's beneficial interest, or lack of such interest, has nothing to do with Attorney's obligations in this case.

(C) is incorrect because Attorney, given the circumstances mentioned in (A) above, may represent Executor and act as witness in this case, even if Executor would not suffer substantial hardship in the absence of that representation.

(D) is incorrect for the reasons mentioned in (A) above.

Because (B), (C) and (D) are incorrect (A) must be the correct answer.

Question 119

The correct answer is B.

(A) is incorrect. Whether or not the prospective jurors investigated are actually selected to serve on the jury does not matter with regard to Attorney's conduct. The investigation is intended to harass prospective jurors and members of their families. It therefore violates disciplinary rules prohibiting lawyer conduct that is criminal and reflects adversely on trustworthiness and fitness to practice law, conduct prejudicial to the administration of justice, and conduct seeking to influence jurors or prospective jurors. A lawyer cannot avoid responsibility by acting through another person.

(B) looks to be correct for the reasons mentioned in (A) above.

(C) is incorrect because Attorney is subject to discipline for the reasons mentioned in (A) above, dealing with intended harassment of prospective jurors, even if the matters inquired into are relevant to jurors' qualifications.

(D) is incorrect because Attorney is subject to discipline for conduct intended to harass prospective jurors, even if that harassment is conducted indirectly; i.e.., without actually contacting any prospective juror.

Because (A), (C) and (D) are incorrect (B) must be the correct answer.

Question 120

The correct answer is D.

(A) is incorrect because a lawyer may not assert arguments that would be adverse to a will that the lawyer had drafted and, in this case, witnessed. Representing Son would therefore be improper.

(B) is incorrect because the fact that Son is a beneficiary in both wills does not excuse Attorney's conduct, as mentioned in (A) above.

(C) is incorrect because a lawyer does **not** guarantee the validity of a will he or she prepares. Nonetheless, Attorney may not represent Son, for the reasons mentioned in (A) above.

(D) Because (A), (B) and (C) are incorrect (D) must be the correct answer, as mentioned in (A) above.

Question 121

The correct answer is A.

(A) looks to be correct, because a lawyer must be diligent in representing a client, and failed that duty by neglecting to file a responsive pleading to the counterclaim. The fact that Plaintiff failed to honor an agreement to reimburse Attorney for expenses does not obviate the neglect. That failure might be sufficient reason for Attorney to seek to withdraw from the representation, but until such withdrawal is accomplished Attorney still has the obligation to represent Plaintiff diligently.

(B) is incorrect because even if Attorney had asked leave of court to withdraw the obligation of diligence remained on Attorney until withdrawal was accomplished, and that never occurred.

(C) is incorrect because Plaintiff's breach of **contractual** duty does not excuse Attorney's breach of the **ethical** duty of diligence; Attorney is subject to discipline.

(D) is incorrect because the absence of prejudice to Plaintiff, relevant to any damages in any **contractual** dispute between lawyer and client, does not excuse Attorney's breach of the **ethical** duty of diligence; Attorney is subject to discipline.

Because (B), (C) and (D) are incorrect (A) must be the correct answer.

Question 122

The correct answer is B.

(A) is incorrect because it indicates that Judge's duty to recuse herself so as to avoid her bias is obviated by the duty to hear the case if she is better qualified to do so than other available judges. This is untrue. Despite her greater expertise Judge must recuse herself for bias.

(B) looks to be correct, for the reason stated in (A) above.

(C) is incorrect because it indicates that recusal for bias is obviated when only legal, as opposed to factual issues, are involved in the case. This is untrue.

(D) is incorrect because Judge's duty to recuse herself is independent of any party's motion to do so. **Even if** all parties agreed to **waive** the recusal a judge must insist on recusing herself when she believes she cannot be impartial.

Because (A), (C) and (D) are incorrect (B) must be the correct answer.

Question 123

The correct answer is B.

(A) is incorrect. Attorney is subject to discipline, but not for accepting legal fees in advance of performing the work. Such conduct is permissible as long as the lawyer deposits all funds for work **not yet performed** in a clients' trust fund account.

(B) looks to be correct. $500 of the $5,000 given to Attorney belonged to Attorney because five hours of work had already been performed. The other $4,500 still belonged to Client because the work to earn it had not yet been performed. After the $5,000 check was deposited in the Client's Trust Account Attorney had the right to withdraw only $500, but he caused withdrawal of an extra $2,500, expecting to complete the 25 hours necessary to earn it the following week. Even if the full 25 hours of work were performed the following week the money was withdrawn too soon to comply with the disciplinary rule.

(C) is incorrect because it states Attorney is not subject to discipline, and that is wrong, for the reasons mentioned in (A) and (B) above. Transferring $200 to the Clients' Trust Account the following week was the right thing to do, at that time, and indicates Attorney's essential honesty, but does not negate the wrongful withdrawal of $2,500 the week before.

(D) is incorrect because it states Attorney is not subject to discipline, and that is wrong. The fact that Attorney actually believed that 25 hours would be earned the week subsequent to the withdrawal from the Clients' Trust Account, and that such belief was reasonable, does not negate the wrongful withdrawal, as mentioned in (C) above.

Because (A), (C) and (D) are incorrect (B) must be the correct answer.

Question 124

The correct answer is D.

(A) is incorrect because it indicates that Candidate is not subject to discipline, and that is wrong. Candidate personally solicited campaign funds in violation of the rule that **only a campaign committee** may solicit judicial campaign funds. The fact that the funds were later turned over to such a committee does not negate the earlier disciplinary violation.

(B) is incorrect because a legitimate campaign committee may include lawyers likely to practice before the candidate. Candidate is still subject to discipline, for the reason stated in (A) above.

(C) is incorrect because it states that a judicial candidate may solicit campaign funds personally rather than through a committee, as long as no contributor is a lawyer. That is wrong. Only a committee may solicit campaign funds for a judicial candidate, regardless of whether the contributors are members of the Bar, or not.

(D) Because (A), (B) and (C) are incorrect (D) must be the correct answer.

Question 125

The correct answer is C.

(A) is incorrect. Although Alpha acted officially and personally as a judge in the matter she is now asked to appear in as a lawyer, her official action was merely administrative, **not substantial,** and had nothing to do with the **merits** of the case. She will not be subject to discipline, therefore, for appearing in the case now as a lawyer.

(B) is incorrect because Alpha's former association with the court does not prevent her from appearing in that court as a lawyer without being subject to discipline. If her opponent suspects bias the opponent may move to recuse. If a judge who is a former associate of Alpha believes that bias might affect the case such motion might be granted, or the judge might recuse himself or herself even in the absence of a motion. In any case, Alpha's actions in taking the representation do not violate a disciplinary rule.

(C) looks to be correct for the reasons stated in (A) above.

(D) is incorrect because it states that the reason Alpha avoids discipline is that all information she acquired in the case was a matter of public record. That fact is not relevant. She avoids discipline for the reason stated in (A) above. If Alpha **had** participated personally and substantially as a judge in this matter she would then be subject to discipline for taking the case as a lawyer, regardless of the fact that the information she acquired was a matter of public record.

Because (A), (B) and (D) are incorrect (C) must be the correct answer.

Question 126

The correct answer is B.

(A) is incorrect because there is no disciplinary violation in pursuing a non-legal occupation while simultaneously maintaining one's status as a lawyer.

(B) looks to be correct because a lawyer is subject to discipline for any act of fraud, deceit or dishonesty in that lawyer's life, whether related to law, any other profession, business or occupation, or personal life.

(C) is incorrect for the reason stated in (B) above. The act need not be the subject of conviction; it need not even be criminal in nature.

(D) is incorrect because the standard of proof in any jurisdiction's disciplinary cases is independent of the standard in other civil or criminal cases. If the disciplinary authority is convinced by the appropriate disciplinary standard that the lawyer did the fraudulent act at issue a violation will be found.

Because (A), (C) and (D) are incorrect (B) must be the correct answer.

Question 127

The correct answer is D.

(A) is incorrect because a reasonable contingent fee in a non-matrimonial civil case (the fee proposed here), **is** appropriate even though it gives a lawyer a proprietary interest in the client's case. Attorney is therefore not subject to discipline.

(B) is incorrect because a contingent fee may well be reasonable even though the amount received by the lawyer is greater than his or her usual hourly fee; the lawyer is being "rewarded" for taking a chance that there would be no fee at all (if no damages were awarded) or only a fee reflecting less than what an hourly rate would have produced, if the damages were small.

(C) is incorrect because **if** a fee is **not** reasonable the lawyer is subject to discipline whether the lawyer or the client first proposed it.

(D) Because (A), (B) and (C) are incorrect (D) must be the correct answer.

Question 128

The correct answer is B.

(A) is incorrect because it indicates that the reason the lawyer **may** disclose the information about the prospective suicide attempt is that it constitutes a crime and is therefore not within the attorney-client evidentiary privilege. This is wrong for two reasons. First, the duty of confidentiality is broader than the evidentiary privilege and therefore exists in many instances where the privilege does not. Second, the mere fact that confidential information reveals a future crime does not necessarily remove it from attorney-client confidentiality. What gives Attorney discretion in this case to disclose confidential information regarding the imminent suicide attempt is the fact that disclosure seems necessary to prevent, in the words of the current version of the Model Rules of Professional Conduct, **reasonably certain death or substantial bodily harm,** whether or not that harm constitutes a crime.

(B) looks to be correct, on its face. It states that the information concerns a future crime (true in this particular jurisdiction) and that it is likely to result in Client's imminent death. As mentioned in (A) above, the prevention of reasonably certain death or substantial bodily harm (regardless of whether a crime is likely to be committed) gives a lawyer discretion to disclose the confidential information. There is no need today for the proposed answer to include the fact that the information concerns a "future crime," but under the version of the Model Rules of Professional Conduct that existed when this question was first released (i.e., prior to amendment of the rules in 2002) a lawyer would have discretion to reveal the information only if it concerned a future crime of the client that involved the likelihood of imminent death or substantial bodily harm.

(C) is incorrect because Attorney may disclose the information if she or he believes Client is likely to attempt suicide, for the reasons stated in (A) and (B) above, regardless of whether Client has attempted suicide in the past.

(D) is incorrect because Attorney may disclose the information necessary to prevent Client's possible death even if such revelation harms Client's defense against civil commitment; any disclosure of confidential information is likely to harm a client in some way but this instance is an exception to confidentiality.

Because (A), (C) and (D) are incorrect (B) must be the correct answer.

Question 129

The correct answer is B.

(A) is incorrect because Attorney is subject to discipline whether or not the trial judge rules in Baker's favor.

(B) looks to be correct. Attorney is subject to discipline for using her public position on the budget committee that funds courts, to attempt to influence the judge hearing a case involving the uncle of one of Attorney's financial contributors.

(C) is incorrect because a lawyer is subject to discipline for attempting to influence a judicial decision through her position as a legislator. A lawyer may not attempt to improperly influence a judicial decision whether or not that lawyer is representing a client at the time of the impropriety.

(D) is incorrect. Even if state law allows legislators to engage in part-time legal practice they are not allowed to attempt to improperly influence judicial decisions in that practice.

Because (A), (C) and (D) are incorrect (B) must be the correct answer.

Question 130

The correct answer is C.

(A) is incorrect because the retainer agreement is improper. Attorney is not allowed to prospectively limit his liability unless the client **is independently represented** in making the agreement. In this case independent representation was suggested by Attorney but not secured by the client; the agreement therefore subjects Attorney to discipline. "Fair consideration" for the client's agreement to limit liability does not alter the disciplinary rule.

(B) is incorrect because the retainer agreement is improper, and in fact subjects Attorney to discipline, as mentioned in (A) above. Reasonable belief in the agreement's fairness and the lawyer's competence does not alter the disciplinary rule.

(C) looks to be correct, for the reasons mentioned in (A) above.

(D) is incorrect because the **substance** of the retainer form is what is important, not the means by which it is applied to each new client. A preprinted form, if it were in accordance with Attorney's ethical obligations, would not be objectionable.

Because (A), (B) and (D) are incorrect (C) must be the correct answer.

Question 131

The correct answer is A.

(A) looks to be correct because causing a person to leave the jurisdiction to make her unavailable as a witness is a violation of the disciplinary rule prohibiting the obstruction of another party's access to evidence.

(B) is incorrect because violating the rule mentioned in (A) above subjects a lawyer to discipline whether or not the other party is aware of the witness, or of her views, or has had reasonable opportunity to become aware.

(C) is incorrect because violating the rule mentioned in (A) above subjects a lawyer to discipline even if other potential witnesses exist, and even if written evidence equivalent to the potential testimony of the witness exists.

(D) is incorrect because the disciplinary rule mentioned in (A) above is violated whether or not a request for the potential witness's testimony has been made.

Because (B), (C) and (D) are incorrect (A) must be the correct answer.

Question 132

The correct answer is D.

(A) is incorrect because Attorney is not subject to discipline if she follows Client's instructions. The money belongs to Client (less any sum due Attorney) and Client may do with it what he wants. The bank has no lien on the money, even assuming Client owes Bank the $900 claimed. Whether or not that amount is disputed is irrelevant.

(B) is incorrect for the reasons mentioned in (A) above. Attorney is not subject to discipline for following Client's instructions, even if she knew Client was planning to force Bank to sue him. That plan does not constitute any fraud in which Attorney gave assistance.

(C) is incorrect because it indicates that Attorney would be subject to discipline if she had reason to believe Client lacked the funds to pay any judgment subsequently obtained by Bank. Attorney is not responsible for assisting in the discharge of Client's debts.

(D) Because (A), (B) and (C) are incorrect (D) must be the correct answer.

Question 133

The correct answer is A.

(A) looks to be correct. Lawyer advertising and letterhead rules require that any information disseminated be accurate, not false or misleading. None of the information on this letterhead is false or misleading and the lawyers are therefore **not** subject to discipline.

(B) is incorrect because no rule requires that there be a particular jurisdiction where all partners are admitted to practice.

(C) is incorrect because a firm name in a particular jurisdiction may include the name of a lawyer not admitted in that jurisdiction, as long as that fact is clearly communicated, as was done in this case.

(D) is incorrect because a lawyer may make it known, by advertising or letterhead, that he or she is admitted in particular jurisdiction(s), even if the lawyer is not engaged in active practice there. There is no false or misleading information disseminated here.

Because (B), (C) and (D) are incorrect (A) must be the correct answer.

Question 134

The correct answer is C.

(A) is incorrect because the **identity** of a client (as opposed to information derived in or related to the representation) is usually not within a lawyer's obligation of confidentiality. Exception exist, but this case does not present any of them. Attorney's actions were improper because he attempted to mislead the congressional committee into believing he was testifying as an interested citizen, unbiased by any particular economic interest (other than his own), when he was actually presenting information designed to assist his client's economic interests. (It is legitimate to testify before legislative committees in an attempt to influence them, but not to engage in misrepresentation, as was done here.)

(B) is incorrect because the **identity** of a client is usually not part of attorney-client privilege (nor the broader concept of confidentiality), as mentioned in (A) above. Attorney acted improperly when he misled the congressional committee by not disclosing his representative posture.

(C) looks to be correct for the reasons stated in (A) above.

(D) is incorrect because Attorney's actions were improper, as mentioned in (A) above, whether or not he accepted compensation in return for his testimony.

Because (A), (B) and (D) are incorrect (C) must be the correct answer.

Question 135

The correct answer is A.

(A) looks to be correct because Judge, as trustee, is a fiduciary for her grandchildren and therefore not disinterested in the fortunes of Big Oil, a litigant in a case assigned to Judge for trial. Despite Judge's belief that she can be fair and impartial (a belief that may very well be accurate) her presiding over the case presents a situation in which her impartiality might be reasonably questioned by others, since the trust she administers has a substantial, not de minimus, stake in Big Oil. Judge **must** therefore disqualify herself, although such disqualification, once announced, might conceivably be **remitted**. That remittance, however, may be accomplished only if Judge discloses on the record the basis of her disqualification, requests the parties and lawyers, out of Judge's presence, to consider whether they all desire the disqualification to be waived, the parties and lawyers, without Judge's participation, all agree to waive the disqualification, Judge is then willing to participate, **and** the agreement is then incorporated into the record. Because none of the choices presented by this question mention the possibility of remittal, (A) appears to be correct in stating that Judge must disqualify herself.

(B) is incorrect because the disqualification is necessary to prevent the appearance of judicial impropriety since Judge's impartiality might be reasonably questioned even if the value of the stock is unlikely to be affected by the outcome of the litigation.

(C) is incorrect because disqualification is necessary whether Judge personally owns stock or is concerned because she is trustee who owns a legal interest in the stock while acting as a fiduciary for others with an equitable interest. In either instance there is an appearance of impropriety.

(D) is incorrect because the appearance of impropriety exists although Judge believes (even if accurately) that she can remain impartial. Unless remittal is effectuated (and the question does not allow us to assume it will be) Judge must disqualify herself.

Because (B), (C) and (D) are incorrect (A) must be the correct answer.

Question 136

The correct answer is A.

(A) looks to be correct because withdrawal from representation, which is **mandatory** when a lawyer **knows** that her client intends illegal or fraudulent activity, is instead **permissive** when the lawyer **reasonably believes** that her client will use her services **criminally or fraudulently.**

(B) is incorrect because Attorney does **not know** her client's actions will be criminal. Withdrawal is permissive, therefore, not mandatory, as mentioned in (A) above.

(C) is incorrect because the client's fear that Attorney's withdrawal would "send a signal," even if the fear is justified, does not prevent Attorney from withdrawing, if she chooses to do so. A lawyer's withdrawal in this situation does not constitute a breach of confidentiality.

(D) is incorrect because the possibility that withdrawal might imperil the timeliness of the filing does not prevent Attorney from withdrawing, if she chooses to do so. A lawyer's withdrawal in this situation does not constitute a breach of competent or diligent representation.

Because (B), (C) and (D) are incorrect (A) must be the correct answer.

Question 137

The correct answer is D.

Which of the numbered choices are proper?

I   Is improper, because part of the check ($70) belongs to the client even though it was sent to Attorney and even though a portion of it ($30) belongs to Attorney. It must be deposited in a clients' trust fund account (**or** a separate trust fund account established solely for Client).

II is proper, because after the check is deposited in the trust fund account mentioned above one way for Attorney to obtain the $30 portion is to bill Client or request Client to pay.

III is proper, because after the check is deposited in the trust fund account mentioned above another way for Attorney to obtain the $30 portion is to write a check from the trust fund account to the order of Attorney for that portion, while writing another check to Client for $70.

Because choices II and III are proper but choice I is not, (D) is the correct answer.

Question 138

The correct answer is C.

(A) is incorrect because a lawyer is subject to discipline only for making a **knowingly** false statement of law or fact to a tribunal, and the fact pattern in this question states that Beta did **not** know it was false. (In real life, Beta would be in a precarious situation, because "knowledge" may be inferred from circumstances and the appellate court may infer that Beta was aware of the falsity of the statement. Even if the court did not make that inference it might very well believe that not being aware of the transcript indicated that Beta had not exercised the necessary degree of diligence on behalf of Plaintiff. The emergency nature of the situation in which Beta argued the case might possibly avoid a disciplinary charge.)

(B) is incorrect because if Beta did not know whether the statement was true the statement was not knowingly false, as mentioned in (A) above.

(C) looks to be correct for the reasons mentioned in (A) above.

(D) is incorrect because truthfully recounting the statement made by Alpha in the brief ("... as stated in our brief, it is uncontraverted that ....") would not, by itself, excuse Beta's statement **if Beta knew** that the statement in the brief was false. If Beta did know the statement was false an obligation would arise to correct that false statement, and failure to do so would subject Beta to discipline.

Because (A), (B) and (D) are incorrect, (C) must be the correct answer.

Question 139

The correct answer is D.

(A) is incorrect because a judge must not accept a gift, loan, favor, or bequest from anyone, unless it is from relatives or friends for a special occasion or a gift incident to a public testimonial . A judge may enter into a commercial loan agreement on the same terms offered to the public at large, but that is not the case here; this loan is a "favor."

(B) is incorrect because the fact that Bank is not likely to appear before Judge is irrelevant; accepting the favor is still improper.

(C) is incorrect because accepting the favor is improper whether the impropriety is committed by one judge or all judges.

(D) Because (A), (B) and (C) are incorrect (D) must be the correct answer, for the reasons mentioned in (A) above.

Question 140

The correct answer is B.

(A) is incorrect because it indicates that Attorney may not participate in Law Firm's use of Admin's services if Admin has access to client files. Admin's duties within the firm may well give access to client files, but that access, by itself, does not constitute impropriety. Admin must be informed, of course, of Law Firm's duty of confidentiality, as must be any non-lawyer employee. In addition, Admin, a non-lawyer, must not be allowed to control the professional judgment of any lawyer in the firm.

(B) looks to be correct, as mentioned in the last sentence in (A) above.

(C) is incorrect because, while lawyers are not generally allowed to share legal fees with non-lawyers, an exception exists for wages, compensation plans and retirement plans for non-lawyer employees of lawyers or a law firm.

(D) is incorrect because Admin's duties do not include anything that constitutes the practice of law. Admin does not advise clients or represent them in any proceeding, nor does Admin draft legal documents or perform legal research for the firm's clients. When the law firm assists Admin, therefore, it does not assist in the unauthorized practice of law.

Because (A), (C) and (D) are incorrect (B) must be the correct answer.

Question 141

The correct answer is C.

(A) is incorrect. A lawyer may withdraw when continued representation will result in an unreasonable financial burden on the lawyer, but the degree of that burden and its reasonableness should be determined at the time the lawyer seeks to withdraw from each individual case, not at the outset of the relationship when the client is asked to sign the stipulation. In this case Attorney has experienced several instances of clients' untimely payment of fees, but there is no indication that she is suffering an "unreasonable financial burden," even when the defaulting clients' cases are aggregated. There seems no need, therefore, to accelerate the decision to withdraw, if payments are late, to the beginning of the relationship. A lawyer also has the right to withdraw when the client fails to fulfill an obligation to the lawyer regarding the lawyer's services and has been given reasonable warning of the impending withdrawal. The stipulation of consent the lawyer has the client sign at the outset of the relationship does not comport with the "reasonable warning" required prior to actual withdrawal.

(B) is incorrect because the duty to weigh the need to withdraw for "unreasonable financial burden" is on the lawyer, at the time of withdrawal, not on the client at the outset of the relationship, as mentioned in (A) above. In addition, consent by the client at the outset does not satisfy the requirement of "reasonable warning," as mentioned in (A) above.

(C) looks to be correct because, in addition to the client's failure to pay fees when due, withdrawal requires either "unreasonable financial burden" to be shown, or "reasonable warning" of the impending withdrawal, as mentioned in (A) above.

(D) is incorrect because clients need not be provided an opportunity for independent advice prior to signing a fee agreement with a lawyer at the outset of the representation. (**Note** the possible confusion here with the requirement of actual independent representation prior to making an agreement that limits the lawyer's prospective liability to the client.)

Because (A), (B) and (D) are incorrect (C) must be the correct answer.

Question 142

The correct answer is D.

(A) is incorrect because a lawyer must not accept payment for representing a client from a person other than the client unless the client gives informed consent, there is no interference with the lawyer's professional judgment, and lawyer-client confidentiality is preserved. In this instance there is no indication that Aunt is interfering in the case or demanding access to confidential information, but she has insisted that Defendant not be told of her payment. If he is not, there can be **no consent.**

(B) is incorrect because the fact that the overall fee will not be excessive does not excuse the lack of consent, as mentioned in (A) above.

(C) is incorrect because it is permissible for persons to finance litigation to which they are not parties, but not without consent, which does not exist here, as mentioned in (A) above.

(D) Because (A), (B) and (C) are incorrect (D) must be the correct answer, for the reasons mentioned in (A) above.

Question 143

The correct answer is C.

(A) is incorrect. It is true that Attorney **is subject to civil liability** for the negligence of the paraprofessional legal assistant, even if Attorney generally exercised appropriate supervision over the paraprofessionals and had no specific knowledge of this particular lapse. It is **not** the case, however, that Attorney is subject to discipline given such facts (even though a **lawyer** might be subjected to discipline for failing to act diligently had the lawyer missed the statute of limitations). **Discipline** will be imposed on a lawyer for the acts of another **only when the lawyer acts wrongfully**; e.g., orders or ratifies improper conduct, or knows of it at a time when its consequences could be avoided or mitigated but fails to take reasonable remedial action.

(B) is incorrect because the client does not have the right to decide if a lawyer should be disciplined. A client only has the right to make a complaint to the disciplinary authorities. If the client does complain the possibility of recovery from a civil suit is not thereby abrogated. The two remedies are independent.

(C) looks to be correct for the reasons mentioned in (A) above.

(D) is incorrect because Attorney **is** subject to civil liability, as mentioned in (A) above.

Because (A), (B) and (D) are incorrect (C) must be the correct answer.

Question 144

The correct answer is B.

Which of the numbered choices subject Attorney to discipline?

I does not subject Attorney to discipline because Attorney had a good faith belief, based upon Wit's prior statements, that Deft had been drinking heavily prior to the accident. That belief justified Attorney asking the question on cross examination, even if Attorney had no independent evidence available.

II subjects Attorney to discipline because statements by lawyers of their personal knowledge of the facts in the case are prohibited, even when the lawyer is telling the truth.

III subjects Attorney to discipline because statements by lawyers of their personal beliefs about the case or the credibility of the witnesses are prohibited, even when the lawyer is telling the truth.

Because choice I does not subject Attorney to discipline but choices II and III do, (B) is the correct answer.

The correct answer is B.

(A) is incorrect because it indicates that Pros is not subject to discipline for failure to disclose information negating guilt to Deft's counsel as long as the jury could make its own identification of Deft from the videotape. That proviso is relevant to the jury's determination in the case, but irrelevant to Pros's ethical duty to disclose. All evidence or information that negates the guilt of an accused (or that mitigates the offense or, if not privileged, might lessen the sentence) must be disclosed.

(B) looks to be correct, for the reasons mentioned in (A) above.

(C) is incorrect because the prosecutor's duty is not confined to situations in which the accused (whether through counsel or otherwise) makes a discovery request.

(D) is incorrect because the prosecutor's ethical duty to provide exculpatory information is independent of the degree to which that information might influence the jury, as mentioned in (A) above.

Because (A), (C) and (D) are incorrect (B) must be the correct answer.

Question 146

The correct answer is C.

(A) is incorrect. Attorney's initial conduct in depositing the $5,000 in her Client's Trust Account was proper, because her fees had not yet been earned. As indicated by her monthly statements, however, services were rendered and lawyer fees were therefore periodically earned. As soon as the fees were earned they became the property of Attorney, not Client, and should have been withdrawn from the Client's Trust Account, because clients' property and a lawyer's property must not be commingled. Because Attorney's earned fees were not withdrawn, therefore, her conduct was improper.

(B) is incorrect. Attorney's conduct in rendering periodic and accurate billing was proper, but her failure to withdraw her fees, as earned, was improper, as mentioned in (A) above.

(C) looks to be correct for the reasons mentioned in (A) above.

(D) is incorrect because advanced payments against a lawyer's fee are not necessarily excessive or unreasonable.

Because (A), (B) and (D) are incorrect (C) must be the correct answer.

Question 147

The correct answer is D.

Which of the numbered choices subject Alpha to discipline?

I does not subject Alpha to discipline because flyers are a legitimate form of advertising as long as they are not false or misleading. Since all factual information in them was correct they were not false, and there is no indication that they were misleading. (If the flyers were handed to the artists in the booth **in person** that solicitation would be prohibited conduct but that was not done here.)

II does not subject Alpha to discipline in the absence of any indication that the retainer agreement called for an illegal, excessive or unreasonable fee; e.g., an offer to represent artists in criminal traffic violation cases on a contingent fee basis. The retainer agreement on the back of the flyer is informational only; no prospective client need sign it now or in the future.

III does not subject Alpha to discipline because a law practice need not be conducted from an indoor office at all times. It may be conducted from a van, and the sign on the van complies with the rules: it is not false or misleading.

Because neither choice I, nor II, nor III subjects Alpha to discipline, (D) is the correct answer.

Question 148

The correct answer is C.

(A) is incorrect. Even though negative statements about the character and fitness of a sitting judge may lessen confidence in the legal system, lawyers have the right to criticize judges and judicial candidates as long as their statements are not knowingly false or made with reckless disregard for their truth or falsity. In this case Alpha "reasonably believed" Beta's actions as campaign manager for Alpha's opponent in a legislative race were unethical and illegal, said so, and now refers reporters back to those statements. Alpha is not subject to discipline for doing so.

(B) is incorrect because Alpha's current complaints about Beta need not be limited to those concerning legal knowledge; they may (and do) make reference to Alpha's reasonable belief that Beta lacks character and fitness generally. This is not a disciplinary violation, as mentioned in (A) above.

(C) looks to be correct, for the reasons mentioned in (A) above.

(D) is incorrect because Alpha's comments must be evaluated on their own ground; the fact that Beta either does or does not have equal access to the press is irrelevant to Alpha's conduct.

Because (A), (B) and (D) are incorrect (C) must be the correct answer.

Question 149

The correct answer is B.

(A) is incorrect. It is proper for Judge to undertake this guardianship because it involves a close family member and will not interfere with the performance of her judicial duties. The propriety of the undertaking is **not** destroyed by her receiving the compensation ordinarily incident to such guardianships. Judges must avoid financial dealings that might reasonably be perceived to exploit the judicial position or involve the judge in frequent transactions with lawyers or other persons likely to come before them; neither is likely here.

(B) looks to be correct, for the reasons mentioned in (A) above.

(C) is incorrect because there is nothing wrong with a judge who acts, incidentally, as a guardian for a member of her family, to appear periodically in court as that guardian, or, for that matter, to prepare and sign pleadings, motions, and other papers.

(D) is incorrect for the reasons mentioned in (A) and (C) above.

Because (A), (C) and (D) are incorrect the correct answer must be (B).

Question 150

The correct answer is C.

(A) is incorrect. Alpha is not subject to litigation sanction for reasons to be mentioned in (C) below. **If Alpha were subject** to litigation sanction for filing a claim not based on existing law or a non-frivolous argument for its extension or reversal, **discussing** the adverse authority **with Client** would **not** have prevented the imposition of such sanction.

(B) is incorrect. Alpha is not subject to litigation sanction for reasons to be mentioned in (C) below. If the third ground was not withdrawn, and Beta never cited the U.S. Supreme Court decision that is directly adverse to that third ground, Alpha would have an affirmative obligation to cite it (and then try to distinguish it), but that cannot happen now because the third claim **was** withdrawn. Adverse law does **not** have to be cited until the opponent has had the chance to cite it and has missed that chance.

(C) looks to be correct. Alpha is not subject to litigation sanction because the third ground, based on law recently eliminated by the U.S. Supreme Court, was withdrawn within ten days of the filing of the complaint, subsequent to Alpha's reception of Beta's motion that cited the Supreme Court decision. Rule 11 of the Federal Rules of Civil Procedure states that a lawyer, by signing and submitting a pleading or other paper, certifies that to the best of the lawyer's knowledge the claims made are warranted by existing law or the extension, modification or reversal of that law. Rule 11 also states that violations of the lawyer's obligations under the rule may lead to litigation sanctions against the offending lawyer, **unless, within 21 days after service of the motion** to sanction the lawyer, the offending claim is corrected or withdrawn. No motion was made by Beta and no other action was taken by the court.

(D) is incorrect because Alpha is not subject to litigation sanction for the reasons mentioned in (C) above. The fact that Alpha knew or should have known of the recent decision at the time the complaint was filed would not change the situation as long as the third ground in that complaint was withdrawn within the appropriate period of time. Additionally, **if** Alpha knew of the recent decision the third ground might still have been included in the complaint (and might have remained there without subjecting Alpha to sanction) **if** Alpha also had a good faith basis for believing that the decision might be modified or reversed, or that he might be able to distinguish it.

Section 3

MPRE Practice Test
with Explanatory Answers

MPRE Practice Test
Questions

Question # 1

A business attorney entered into a partnership with a certified public accountant. The partnership provided legal and other assistance to clients in connection with business and tax planning, tax filings, and other personal and corporate business matters. The accountant performed only work that she was authorized to perform as a certified public accountant. The attorney made reasonable efforts to ensure that the accountant did not interfere with the attorney's compliance with his professional obligations as a lawyer.

Is the attorney subject to discipline?

A) Yes, because some of the activities of the partnership consisted of the practice of law.

B) Yes, because lawyers may not form partnerships with nonlawyers.

C) No, because the accountant performed only work that she was authorized to perform as a certified public accountant.

D) No, because the attorney made reasonable efforts to ensure that the accountant did not interfere with the attorney's compliance with his professional obligations as a lawyer.

Question # 2

An attorney is widely regarded as an exceptionally competent practitioner in the field of criminal law. A client of the attorney became the subject of a grand jury investigation in a matter that could result in a felony indictment. The client lacked sufficient funds to pay for the attorney's services beyond the grand jury stage. He asked the attorney to provide limited representation for a flat fee. Under the arrangement he proposed, the attorney would advise the client concerning the grand jury investigation, but the representation would end when an indictment was returned or the grand jury decided not to indict. The attorney fully advised the client of the practical and legal aspects of the client's proposal.

Is it proper for the attorney to accept this limited representation?

A) Yes, because the client and not the attorney suggested this arrangement.

B) Yes, because the attorney and the client may agree to limit the scope of the representation so long as the limitation is reasonable under the circumstances.

C) No, because the attorney should not limit the scope of the representation based on the client's ability to pay.

D) No, because the scope of the representation may not be limited in a criminal case.

Question # 3

An attorney represents a client who is under indictment for homicide. In the course of the representation, the client told the attorney that she had previously killed two other people. These murders are completely unrelated to the murder indictment for which the attorney is providing representation. With the client's consent, the attorney made a tape recording of the client's confession regarding the unrelated homicides. At the attorney's request, the client also drew a map of the remote locations of the victims' graves from the unrelated killings. Those bodies have not been found by the police, and the client is not a suspect in either crime, both of which remain unsolved.

Is the attorney subject to discipline if he fails to voluntarily disclose to the authorities his knowledge of the two prior murders and the locations of the victims' bodies?

A) Yes, because as an officer of the court, the attorney must disclose any knowledge that he has, whether privileged or not, concerning the commission of the prior crimes by his client.

B) Yes, because the attorney is impeding the state's access to significant evidence.

C) No, because the attorney did not represent or advise his client with respect to the prior crimes.

D) No, because the information was obtained by the attorney in the course of the representation.

Question # 4

A woman has asked an attorney to represent her in obtaining compensation for a tract of land that is being condemned by the state department of transportation to build a new highway. Two years ago, the attorney had been employed by the department and had been assigned to search title on several tracts of land, including the one owned by the woman. The attorney remembers a department engineer had drafted a confidential memorandum advising against running a new highway across the woman's land because of a potential adverse environmental impact. Because of this information, the attorney believes it is possible to prevent the condemnation of the woman's land or to increase the settlement amount.

What is the proper action for the attorney to take?

A) Represent the woman on the issue of damages only and not disclose the information that might prevent the condemnation.

B) Represent the woman and attempt to prevent the condemnation by using the information about the adverse environmental impact.

C) Refuse to represent the woman but disclose to her the information about the adverse environmental impact.

D) Refuse to represent the woman and not disclose the information about the adverse environmental impact.

Question # 5

An attorney who is a sole practitioner limits his practice to personal injury cases. He regularly places advertisements in local newspapers, stating that his practice is limited to personal injury cases, including medical malpractice. After seeing one of the attorney's ads, a man approached the attorney for representation in a medical malpractice case. After a 30-minute interview, the attorney told the man that he was too busy to take his case because it appeared quite complicated. He further offered to refer the man to another lawyer who regularly practiced in the field. He reminded the man that he should see another lawyer promptly before the statute of limitations expired and he lost his right to sue.

Although the attorney did not charge the man for the interview, the man was upset at wasting 30 minutes of his time. The man did not contact another lawyer until eight months later, when he learned that the statute of limitations on his claim had expired six months after his interview with the attorney. In fact, the man had a meritorious medical malpractice claim.

Is the attorney subject to civil liability?

A) Yes, because the attorney falsely advertised his availability for medical malpractice cases.

B) Yes, because the attorney did not advise the man as to the date the statute of limitations would expire.

C) No, because the attorney did not violate any duty owed to the man.

D) No, because the attorney offered to refer the man to another medical malpractice lawyer.

Question # 6

An attorney is employed by a client who is a fugitive from justice under indictment for armed robbery. The attorney, after thorough legal research and investigation of the facts furnished by the client, reasonably believes the indictment is fatally defective and should be dismissed as a matter of law. The attorney advised the client of his opinion and urged the client to surrender. The client told the attorney that she would not surrender.

The attorney informed the district attorney that he represented the client and that he had counseled her to surrender but that she refused to follow his advice. The attorney has not advised his client on how to avoid arrest and prosecution and does not know where she is hiding.

Is the attorney subject to discipline if he continues to represent the client?

A) Yes, because the client is engaging in continuing illegal conduct.

B) Yes, because the client refused to accept the attorney's advice and surrender.

C) No, because the attorney is not counseling the client to avoid arrest and prosecution.

D) No, because the attorney reasonably believes the indictment is defective.

Question # 7

An attorney represented a real estate developer who was trying to buy several properties. The attorney arranged a meeting with an owner of two large parcels of land, hoping to arrange a sale to the developer. When the attorney scheduled this meeting, he neither knew nor asked whether the owner was represented by counsel in the matter. Shortly after the meeting began, the owner disclosed that he had retained counsel to assist in the sale of the two parcels of land, but that his lawyer could not be present that day. He further stated that he would be meeting with his lawyer the next day. The attorney asked the owner if they could talk anyway, and stated that he wouldn't ask the owner to sign anything until his lawyer had a chance to look over anything they discussed.

The owner, an experienced businessman and negotiator, agreed to continue as suggested, and a tentative agreement was soon worked out.

Was the attorney's conduct proper?

A) Yes, because the owner knowingly agreed to continue the discussions without his own lawyer being present.

B) Yes, because the attorney did not present the owner with any documents to sign during the meeting.

C) No, because the attorney negotiated with the owner after learning that the owner was represented by a lawyer in the matter.

D) No, because the attorney failed to ascertain whether the owner was represented by a lawyer before beginning the negotiation session.

Question # 8

An attorney represented a seller in negotiating the sale of his ice cream parlor. The seller told the attorney in confidence that, although the business had once been very profitable, recent profits had been stable but modest. As the negotiations proceeded, the buyer appeared to be losing interest in the deal. Hoping to restore the buyer's interest, the attorney stated, "The ice cream business is every American's dream: happy kids, steady profits, and a clear conscience." The buyer bought the ice cream parlor but was disappointed when his own profits proved to be modest.

Is the attorney subject to discipline?

A) Yes, because the attorney made a false statement of fact to the buyer.

B) Yes, because the attorney exaggerated the profitability of the business.

C) No, because the attorney represented the seller, not the buyer.

D) No, because the attorney's statement constitutes acceptable puffing in negotiations.

Question # 9

An attorney represented a client as a plaintiff in a personal injury matter under a standard contingent fee contract. The client agreed to settle the case for $1,000,000, from which funds the attorney would receive $250,000. The client informed the attorney that she planned to take $25,000 of the settlement funds and spend the money purchasing lottery tickets. The attorney told the client that he disagreed with this plan and encouraged the client to take some classes on investing money. The client agreed to take the classes, but still insisted on playing the lottery.

The attorney received the check for $1,000,000 three days before the client was to attend the investing classes. The attorney held the check for one week, giving the client at least a few days of classes. The attorney then informed the client of the receipt of the funds, disbursed the funds according to the agreement, and also furnished the client with an accounting. The attorney told the client that he had delayed notice to allow time for the client to come to her senses. The client laughed and said, "I guess your plan worked, because these classes have convinced me to invest my money in the stock market instead of playing the lottery."

Is the attorney subject to discipline?

A) Yes, because the attorney had a duty to promptly notify the client of the receipt of the $1,000,000.

B) Yes, because the attorney gave unsolicited advice about nonlegal matters.

C) No, because the client did not object to the withholding of the notice and funds.

D) No, because the attorney acted in the client's best interest.

Question # 10

An attorney served two four-year terms as the state's governor immediately prior to reopening his law office in the state. The attorney printed and mailed an announcement of his return to private practice to members of the bar, previous clients, and personal friends whom he had never represented. The printed announcement stated that the attorney had reopened his law office, gave his address and telephone number, and added that he had been the state's governor for the past eight years.

Is the attorney subject to discipline for the announcement?

A) Yes, because the mailing included persons who had not been his clients.

B) Yes, because his service as governor is unrelated to his ability as a lawyer.

C) No, because the information in the announcement was true.

D) No, because all of the information was already in the public domain.

Question # 11

An attorney practices law in the same community as a lawyer who is running for election as a state judge. The attorney has frequently observed the judicial candidate's courtroom demeanor in litigated cases. Based on those experiences, the attorney believes that the judicial candidate does not have a proper judicial temperament. A local news reporter asked the attorney how he would rate the candidate, and the attorney responded in good faith that he believed the candidate was unsuited for the bench and lacked the proper judicial temperament for a judge. A local newspaper with a wide circulation quoted the attorney's remarks.

Were the attorney's remarks proper?

A) Yes, because the attorney was not seeking judicial office.

B) Yes, because the attorney believed the candidate was unsuited for the bench.

C) No, because the remarks serve to bring the judiciary into disrepute.

D) No, because a lawyer should not publicly comment on candidates for judicial office.

Question # 12

Under a state law, the court's appointment of lawyers as special masters in certain proceedings is discretionary with the court. A judge decided to appoint special masters in all such proceedings, regardless of their nature and complexity, and decided that compensation for such appointees would be at a reasonable hourly rate. The judge believed that this practice would ensure competent and impartial handling of every proceeding. The judge further decided to use published law directories to compile a list of qualified prospective appointees.

Is the judge's proposed practice proper?

A) Yes, because it results in competent and impartial handling of the proceedings.

B) Yes, because the appointees will be compensated at a reasonable hourly rate.

C) No, because the practice may result in unnecessary appointments.

D) No, because the judge cannot use law directories to compile a list of qualified prospective appointees.

Question # 13

An attorney is a member of the bar and a salaried employee of a bank's trust department. As part of his duties, he prepares a monthly newsletter concerning wills, trusts, estates, and taxes that the bank sends to all of its customers. The newsletter contains a recommendation to the customer to review his or her will in light of the information contained and, if the customer has any questions, to bring the will to the bank, where the attorney will review the customer's will and answer the customer's legal questions. The bank provides the attorney's services to its customers for no charge.

Is the attorney subject to discipline for the foregoing?

A) Yes, because by sending out the newsletter the attorney is giving legal advice to persons who are not his clients.

B) Yes, because the attorney is assisting the bank in the unauthorized practice of law.

C) No, because no charge is made for the attorney's advice.

D) No, because the attorney is a member of the bar.

Question # 14

A client retained an attorney to recover for a personal injury. In the retainer agreement signed by the client and the attorney, the client agreed to cooperate fully and pay the attorney a contingent fee computed as a percentage of the amount of recovery after expenses: 25 percent if settled before trial, 30 percent if settled before verdict, 35 percent after verdict, and 40 percent after appeal.

The attorney's representation of the client in the matter extended over a three-year period during which the attorney advanced a large amount for litigation expenses. After trial, the client obtained a jury verdict for an amount larger than either the attorney or the client had anticipated. However, the defendant filed an appeal based on questions of evidence and the measure of damages. Meanwhile, the defendant made an offer of settlement for approximately the amount the attorney had originally projected as reasonable to expect. The client, who was hard pressed financially, directed the attorney to accept the offer and settle. The attorney refused, because she was confident that there was no reversible error in the trial and that the appeal was without merit. The attorney reasonably believed that the appeal was filed solely to gain negotiating advantage in settlement negotiations.

Is the attorney subject to discipline?

A) Yes, because the attorney's percentage under the fee contract increased after appeal.

B) Yes, because the client directed the attorney to accept the settlement offer.

C) No, because the decision whether to settle or defend an appeal is a tactical matter for the attorney to determine.

D) No, because evaluation of the merits of an appeal requires the exercise of independent professional judgment.

Question # 15

An attorney represented both the owner of an art gallery and a publisher. The gallery owner and the publisher each made a practice of paying the attorney's fees in cash. The attorney received separate cash payments from the gallery owner and the publisher on the same day. Each payment consisted of ten $100 bills, which the attorney immediately deposited in her bank account. One week later, the attorney was contacted by United States Treasury agents, who informed her that four of the bills had been identified as counterfeit. The agents did not accuse the attorney of knowingly passing the counterfeit money but asked her who had given her the bills. The attorney was subpoenaed to testify before a grand jury and was asked who could have given her the counterfeit money.

Is it proper for the attorney to provide the grand jury with the names of the gallery owner and the publisher?

A) Yes, because negotiation of a counterfeit bill is a criminal act.

B) Yes, because under the circumstances neither client's identity is privileged.

C) No, because counterfeiting is not a crime that involves an imminent threat of death or serious bodily harm.

D) No, because the attorney has no way of knowing which of the two clients gave her the counterfeit bills.

Question # 16

A corporation has applied to a bank for a $900,000 loan to be secured by a lien on the corporation's inventory. The inventory, consisting of small items, constantly turns over. The security documents are complex and if improperly drawn they could result in an invalid lien. The bank has approved the loan on the condition that the corporation and the bank jointly retain an attorney to prepare the necessary security instruments and that the corporation pay the attorney's fees. Both the corporation and the bank gave informed consent in writing to the attorney's representation of both parties. This arrangement is customary in the city in which the attorney's law office and the bank are located. It is obvious to the attorney that he can adequately represent the interests of both the corporation and the bank.

Is it proper for the attorney to prepare the security documents under these circumstances?

A) Yes, because both the bank and the corporation have given their informed consent to the arrangement.

B) Yes, because the arrangement is customary in the community.

C) No, because the attorney's fees are being paid by the corporation, not the bank.

D) No, because the corporation and the bank have differing interests.

Question # 17

An attorney represented a plaintiff in a civil suit against a defendant who was represented by other counsel. In the course of developing the plaintiff's case, the attorney discovered evidence that she reasonably believed showed that the defendant had committed a crime. The attorney felt that the defendant's crime should be reported to local prosecutorial authorities. After full disclosure, the plaintiff consented to the attorney's doing so. Without advising the defendant's counsel, the attorney informed the local prosecutor of her findings, but she sought no advantage in the civil suit from her actions. The defendant was subsequently indicted, tried, and acquitted of the offense.

Was the attorney's disclosure to prosecutorial authorities proper?

A) Yes, because the attorney reasonably believed the defendant was guilty of a crime.

B) Yes, because the attorney was required to report knowledge of criminal conduct when that knowledge was obtained through unprivileged sources.

C) No, because the attorney did not advise the other counsel of her disclosure before making it.

D) No, because the plaintiff's civil suit against the defendant was still pending.

Question # 18

An attorney hired a recent law school graduate as an associate. For the first six months, the associate was assigned to draft legal documents that the attorney carefully reviewed and revised before filing. However, shortly after the associate was admitted to the bar, the attorney told the associate that he would be going on vacation the following week and was assigning her the representation of the landlord in a housing case that was going to trial while he was away. The associate had never conducted or observed a trial before and, because she had not previously worked on any housing cases, she was unfamiliar with the relevant law and procedure. She did not believe that she would have enough time to learn everything that she needed to know, but she was reluctant to decline the assignment. Before the trial began, she met with the landlord and disclosed that this would be her first trial, but the landlord did not object. Although the associate prepared diligently, the landlord lost the trial.

Is the attorney subject to discipline?

A) Yes, because the attorney did not ensure that the associate was competent to conduct the trial on her own..

B) Yes, because the landlord lost the trial.

C) No, because the attorney could reasonably assume that, having been admitted to the bar, the associate was capable of conducting the trial.

D) No, because the landlord did not object to the associate's representation.

Question # 19

An attorney represented the plaintiff in an automobile accident case. Two weeks before the date set for trial, the attorney discovered that there was an eyewitness to the accident. The attorney interviewed the witness. Her version of the accident was contrary to that of the plaintiff and, if believed by the trier of fact, would establish that the plaintiff was at fault. The witness told the attorney that she had not been interviewed by defense counsel.

The witness also told the attorney that she was uncomfortable with testifying and that she had been thinking about taking a vacation to Europe the following week. The attorney told the witness that, since no one had subpoenaed her yet, she had no obligation to appear. He told her that trials were very difficult for witnesses and suggested that she take the vacation so that she would be unavailable to testify.

Is the attorney subject to discipline?

A) Yes, because the attorney asked the witness to leave the jurisdiction.

B) Yes, because the attorney did not subpoena the witness knowing she was an eyewitness.

C) No, because the witness had not been subpoenaed by the defense.

D) No, because the attorney did not offer the witness any inducement not to appear at the trial.

Question # 20

An attorney represented the plaintiff in a personal injury matter. The attorney had heard that the defendant in the matter was anxious to settle the case and reasonably believed that the defendant's lawyer had not informed the defendant about the attorney's recent offer of settlement. The attorney instructed her nonlawyer investigator to tell the defendant about the settlement offer so that the attorney could be sure that the defendant's lawyer did not force the case to trial merely to increase the defendant's lawyer's fee.

Is the attorney subject to discipline?

A) Yes, because the defendant was represented by counsel.

B) Yes, because the attorney was assisting the investigator in the unauthorized practice of law.

C) No, because the investigator is not a lawyer.

D) No, because the attorney reasonably believed that the defendant's lawyer was not keeping the defendant informed.

Question # 21

An attorney was approached by a husband and a wife who had decided to dissolve their marriage. They had no children and had worked out a tentative mutual property settlement. They did not want to retain separate lawyers because they hoped to save money and believed that working with one attorney was more likely to result in a reasonably amicable dissolution. Before coming to the attorney, they had drafted and each had signed a written agreement not to run up the costs and increase the adversarial nature of the dissolution by retaining separate lawyers.

The attorney believed that he was able to provide competent and diligent representation to both the husband and the wife. The attorney consulted with both independently concerning the implications of the common representation, including the advantages and risks involved and the effect on their respective attorney-client privileges. The attorney reduced the disclosures to writing in the form of a written retainer agreement and gave them each several days to consult independent legal counsel if they so desired. The husband and the wife each chose not to consult independent counsel.

After six months of reasonably amicable negotiations, the wife announced that she had changed her mind about the representation and had decided to retain her own lawyer. However, after the husband and the attorney insisted that she was obligated to adhere to her prior written agreement, she reluctantly agreed to abide by it. The attorney was then able to draft a property settlement agreement satisfactory to both parties.

Is the attorney subject to discipline for his conduct in the representation?

A) Yes, because the attorney should not have undertaken to represent both the husband and the wife in the first place.

B) Yes, because the attorney insisted that the wife not hire another lawyer.

C) No, because both the husband and the wife initially consented to all aspects of the representation.

D) No, because the husband and the wife independently made the agreement that neither would retain separate counsel.

Question # 22

An attorney is a well-known tax lawyer and author. During congressional hearings on tax reform, the attorney testified to her personal belief and expert opinion on the pending reform package. She failed to disclose in her testimony that she was being compensated by a private client for her appearance. In her testimony, the attorney took the position favored by her client, but the position was also one that the attorney believed was in the public interest.

Was it proper for the attorney to present this testimony without identifying her private client?

A) Yes, because the attorney believed that the position she advocated was in the public interest.

B) Yes, because Congress is interested in the content of the testimony and not who is paying the witness.

C) No, because a lawyer may not accept a fee for trying to influence legislative action.

D) No, because a lawyer who appears in a legislative hearing should identify the capacity in which the lawyer appears.

Question # 23

An attorney closed her law practice when she became a state senator. A bank, one of the senator's former private clients, asked her as its senator to try to persuade a state agency to grant the bank a license to open a new branch bank. While the bank's request was pending before the agency, the senator wrote a letter on her legislative letterhead to the agency's chair, asserting that the branch would satisfy a local business need and urging that the bank's application be granted. The senator neither sought nor received any compensation from the bank for her efforts. Eventually the agency granted the bank's application, in part because of the senator's efforts.

Is the senator subject to discipline?

A) Yes, because the senator used her public position to attempt to influence the agency on behalf of the bank.

B) Yes, because the agency granted the bank's application in part due to the senator's efforts.

C) No, because the senator's letter to the agency's chair did not express an opinion about the law.

D) No, because the senator acted on behalf of the bank as a constituent and not as a client.

Question # 24

A county law prohibits stores from selling alcoholic beverages before noon on Sundays. Failure to comply is a misdemeanor punishable by a fine of $150.

An attorney was hired by a client who owns several liquor stores. The client asked the attorney whether any store owners had been prosecuted for violating the law and whether the fine could be imposed for every sale on a Sunday before noon or only for every Sunday on which alcohol was sold before noon. The client also asked what he could do to minimize the risk that he would be detected.

The attorney accurately told the client that the fine could only be imposed for each Sunday on which he sold alcoholic beverages before noon, not for each transaction, and that no one had been prosecuted under the law as yet. She also told him that she thought it would be improper to advise him about how to avoid detection. The client thanked the attorney for the information and hung up. Several weeks later, the attorney learned that the client had begun to open his store for business on Sundays at 9 a.m.

Is the attorney subject to discipline?

A) Yes, because the attorney reasonably should have known that the information she gave the client would encourage him to violate the law.

B) Yes, because the attorney did not discourage her client from breaking the law.

C) No, because the attorney merely gave the client her honest opinion about the consequences that were likely to result if he violated the law.

D) No, because the lawyer and the client could have discussed the best way to avoid detection under the criminal law.

Question # 25

A judge has served on a trial court of general jurisdiction for almost three years. During that time, he was assigned criminal cases almost exclusively. Several months ago, however, the judge was assigned an interesting case involving a constitutional challenge to a statute recently passed by the state legislature. The statute permitted any local public school district with an overcrowding problem to purchase educational services for its students in any other public or private school within fifteen miles.

Although the briefs submitted by the parties were excellent, the judge was not confident that he had a good grasp of the issues in the case. Accordingly, he took one of his more experienced colleagues on the trial court out to lunch and discussed the case with her in great detail. The colleague was far more conservative than the judge, but he agreed with her and eventually ruled in accord with her views. The case is now on appeal.

Is the judge subject to discipline?

A) Yes, because the judge sought an ex parte communication on the merits of a case pending before him.

B) Yes, because the judge initiated a discussion with a colleague that may have influenced his judgment in the case.

C) No, because the judge is permitted to obtain the advice of a disinterested expert on the law.

D) No, because the judge was permitted to consult about a pending case with another judge.

Question # 26

An attorney is a senior partner at a law firm in which there are 50 lawyers. The firm pays each of its lawyers a fixed annual salary. In addition, at year's end, each lawyer receives a bonus from the profits of the firm in the proportion that the annual salary of each bears to the total of the fixed annual salaries of all lawyers.

The attorney plans to introduce a new management plan under which the firm's nonlawyer office administrator would have general charge of all business matters but would not participate in any decisions involving legal judgment. The administrator would be paid a fixed annual salary and would be included as a participant in the firm's bonus plan on the same basis as the lawyers in the firm. This would usually yield a bonus of approximately one-fourth to one-third of the administrator's total annual compensation. The amount paid to the administrator will not exceed the compensation commonly paid to law office administrators within the local legal community.

Is it proper for the attorney to institute such a plan?

A) Yes, because the amount paid to the administrator does not exceed the compensation commonly paid to law office administrators within the local legal community.

B) Yes, because an employee of the firm may be compensated based on the profits of the firm.

C) No, because the administrator's bonus is computed on the same basis as those of the lawyers in the firm.

D) No, because the administrator's compensation is derived from the legal fees of the firm's lawyers.

Question # 27

An attorney represented a client in an action against the client's former partner to recover damages for breach of contract. During the representation, the client presented the attorney with incontrovertible proof that the former partner had committed perjury in a prior action which was resolved in the partner's favor. Neither the attorney nor the client was involved in any way in the prior action. The attorney believes that it would be detrimental to the client's best interests to reveal the perjury because of the implication that might be drawn from the former close personal and business relationship between the client and the former partner.

Would it be proper for the attorney to fail to disclose the perjury to the tribunal?

A) No, because the information is unprivileged.

B) No, because the attorney has knowledge that the former partner perpetrated a fraud on the tribunal.

C) Yes, because neither the client nor the attorney was involved in the prior action.

D) Yes, because the attorney believes that the disclosure would be detrimental to the client's best interests.

Question # 28

An attorney represented ten plaintiffs in a case against a railroad in which the plaintiffs were injured when a train derailed. The railroad offered the attorney a $500,000 lump sum settlement for the ten plaintiffs. The attorney allocated the $500,000 among the ten plaintiffs with the amount paid each plaintiff dependent on the nature and extent of that plaintiff's injuries. The attorney reasonably believed the division was fair to each plaintiff.

The railroad would not settle any of the claims unless all were settled. The attorney told each plaintiff the total amount the railroad was prepared to pay, the amount that the individual would receive, and the basis on which that amount was calculated. The attorney did not tell any plaintiff the amount to be received by any other plaintiff. The attorney believed that if she revealed to each plaintiff the amount of each individual settlement, it might jeopardize the settlement.

Each of the plaintiffs agreed to his or her settlement amount and was satisfied with that amount.

Is the attorney subject to discipline for entering into this settlement?

A) Yes, because the attorney was aiding the lawyer for the railroad in making a lump sum settlement.

B) Yes, because no individual plaintiff knew the amount to be received by any other plaintiff.

C) No, because disclosing all settlements to each plaintiff might have jeopardized the entire settlement.

D) No, because the attorney reasonably believed that the division was fair and each plaintiff agreed to his or her settlement and was satisfied with the amount.

Question # 29

An attorney was recently admitted to practice and was hired as a new associate of a large law firm. The attorney was working late one night when he received a telephone call from his cousin. The cousin said that he was calling from the police station because he had just been arrested for possession of cocaine with intent to distribute. He was permitted to make only one phone call, and the attorney was the only one he knew. The attorney responded that he had no criminal law experience and that his firm did not handle criminal cases. Nevertheless, the cousin pleaded with the attorney to come to the police station and see what he could do to get him out on bail. The attorney replied that he would do what he could.

The attorney went to the police station and used what information he recalled from his criminal law and procedure courses to attempt to get his cousin released on bail. However, as a result of his inexperience, the attorney was unable to secure his cousin's release that night. The next morning, the attorney found an experienced criminal lawyer for his cousin, who obtained his release within one hour.

Was the attorney's conduct proper?

A) Yes, because neither referral to another lawyer nor consultation with another lawyer was practical under the circumstances.

B) Yes, because the attorney was a close relative.

C) No, because the attorney had no special training or experience in criminal cases.

D) No, because the attorney did not have the requisite level of competence to accept representation in the case.

Question # 30

An attorney represents a client in commercial litigation that is scheduled to go to trial in two months. Over the past several weeks, the client has disagreed with almost every tactical decision that the attorney has made. Frustrated, the attorney finally said to the client that if she didn't like the way he was handling the lawsuit, perhaps she should get another lawyer. The client was upset at the suggestion and accused the attorney of trying to get out of the case. Reasonably believing that he could no longer work effectively with the client, the attorney sought the client's permission to withdraw from the representation, and the client reluctantly agreed. After giving the client sufficient notice to obtain replacement counsel, the attorney requested the court's permission to withdraw from the litigation, but the court denied the request.

May the attorney withdraw from the representation?

A) Yes, because the client agreed, and the attorney gave the client sufficient notice to obtain replacement counsel.

B) Yes, because the client had made it unreasonably difficult for the attorney to carry out the representation effectively.

C) No, because the court denied the attorney's request to withdraw.

D) No, because the attorney's withdrawal would cause material prejudice to the client, and the client's agreement was not voluntary.

Question # 31

An attorney is employed in the legal department of a public utility company and represents that company in litigation. The company has been sued by a consumer group that has accused the company of various acts in violation of its charter. Through its general counsel, the company has instructed the attorney not to negotiate a settlement but to go to trial under any circumstances because a precedent needs to be established. The attorney believes the defense can be supported by a good faith argument, but also believes the case should be settled if possible.

Must the attorney withdraw as counsel in this case?

A) Yes, because the company is controlling the attorney's judgment in refusing to settle the case.

B) Yes, because a lawyer should endeavor to avoid litigation.

C) No, because the company's defense can be supported by a good faith argument.

D) No, because, as an employee, the attorney is bound by the instructions of the general counsel.

Question # 32

An attorney was retained by a woman to advise her in negotiating a separation agreement with her husband. The husband, who was not a lawyer, had decided to act on his own behalf in the matter. The attorney never met or communicated with the husband during the negotiations. After several months, the woman advised the attorney that the parties had reached agreement and presented him with the terms. The attorney prepared a proposed agreement that contained all of the agreed-upon terms. The attorney mailed the proposed agreement to the husband, with a cover letter stating:

"As you know, I represent your wife in this matter and I do not represent your interests. I enclose two copies of the separation agreement that I have drafted in accordance with my client's directions. Please read the agreement and, if it meets with your approval, sign both copies before a notary and return them to me. I will then have your wife sign them and will furnish you with a fully executed copy."

Is the attorney subject to discipline?

A) Yes, because the attorney did not suggest that the husband seek the advice of independent counsel before signing the agreement.

B) Yes, because the attorney directly communicated with an unrepresented person.

C) No, because the attorney acted only as a scrivener.

D) No, because the attorney's letter did not imply that the attorney was disinterested and the attorney did not give legal advice to the husband.

Question # 33

An attorney's law firm regularly represented a large company in its international business transactions. The company became involved in a contractual dispute with a foreign government. The company invoked a mandatory arbitration procedure contained in the contract. Under the arbitration clause, each party was allowed to choose a partisan arbitrator and the partisan arbitrators were to choose an additional arbitrator to sit on the panel. The company selected the attorney to be on the arbitration panel. Neither the attorney nor his law firm had represented the company in connection with the contract with the foreign government. The arbitration was completed, and the company was awarded the sum of $100,000. The company then hired the attorney to enforce the award. The attorney obtained the consent of the other arbitrators before accepting the representation. He was successful in enforcing the award.

Is the attorney subject to discipline?

A) Yes, because the attorney should not have represented the company in a matter in which the attorney had been an arbitrator.

B) Yes, because the attorney should have declined the arbitration assignment in view of his law firm's regular representation of the company.

C) No, because the attorney obtained the consent of the other arbitrators before accepting the representation.

D) No, because the attorney was appointed to the arbitration panel as a partisan arbitrator.

Question # 34

An attorney represented a client who was injured when the television antenna he was attempting to erect in his yard came in contact with a power line. As part of its defense, the manufacturer of the antenna claimed that the antenna came with a warning label advising against erecting the antenna near power lines. The client told the attorney that he had not seen a warning label. The client's wife told the attorney that she had kept the antenna and the box it came in and that she saw no warning label anywhere.

When called by the attorney as witnesses, both the client and his wife testified that they had never seen a warning label. After their testimony, but while the trial was still in progress, the attorney learned from the wife's sister that there indeed had been a warning label on the box, but that the wife had removed and destroyed it. When the attorney confronted the wife with her sister's statement, the wife admitted destroying the label but insisted that her husband knew nothing about it. The attorney continued the trial, but made no reference to the absence of a warning label in his summation to the jury. Instead, the attorney argued that the warning label, even if seen, was insufficient to advise his client of the serious consequences that would ensue if the warning was not heeded. The jury found in favor of the manufacturer.

Is the attorney subject to discipline?

A) Yes, because the attorney called the wife as a witness and she gave perjured testimony.

B) Yes, because the attorney failed to take reasonable remedial action after he realized that the wife had given perjured testimony.

C) No, because the jury apparently disbelieved the wife's testimony.

D) No, because the attorney did not rely on the wife's testimony once he discovered the perjury.

Question # 35

An attorney represented a respondent in proceedings instituted by a child protection services agency to establish the paternity of a child and to recover past-due child support. The mother of the child had refused to file a complaint, had refused to retain a lawyer, and in fact had asked that the agency not file any action whatsoever. However, state law permitted the agency to commence paternity and support proceedings in its own name in such circumstances.

The attorney contacted the mother without the knowledge or consent of the agency or its lawyers. The attorney identified himself to the mother as "an officer of the court" and told the mother that he was investigating the matter. Based upon what she told him, the attorney prepared and the mother signed an affidavit truthfully stating that the respondent was not the father of the child.

Is the attorney subject to discipline?

A) Yes, because the attorney acted without the knowledge or consent of the agency or its lawyers.

B) Yes, because the attorney implied that he was disinterested in the matter.

C) No, because all of the attorney's statements to the mother were true.

D) No, because the attorney did not give the mother legal advice.

Question # 36

A recently graduated attorney began a plaintiffs' personal injury practice, but was having a difficult time attracting clients. The attorney hired an advertising agency to prepare a television commercial in which the attorney appeared to be arguing a case before a jury. In the commercial, the jury brought back a large award for the attorney's client. The voice-over stated that results would vary depending upon particular legal and factual circumstances. The attorney's only experience at the time the commercial was filmed was in moot court. As a result of airing the commercial, the attorney received several significant cases.

Is the attorney subject to discipline?

A) Yes, because the commercial created an unjustified expectation about the results that could be achieved in court.

B) Yes, because the commercial implied that the attorney had successfully argued a case to a jury.

C) No, because commercial speech is protected under the First Amendment.

D) No, because the commercial contained an express disclaimer about the results a client could expect.

Question # 37

An attorney regularly appears before a trial court judge who is running for reelection in six months. Over the past year, the attorney has noticed that the judge has become increasingly ill-tempered on the bench. Not only is the judge abrupt and critical of lawyers appearing before him, he is also rude and abusive to litigants. On more than one occasion, the judge has thrown his gavel across the courtroom in a fit of temper. The judge's conduct on the bench is often the subject of discussion whenever a group of lawyers meets. Some lawyers are automatically filing requests for judicial substitution whenever a case in which they are to appear is assigned to the judge.

The attorney discussed the matter with her law partners, who rarely make court appearances. The attorney's law partners suggested that she, too, file a request for judicial substitution whenever one of her cases is assigned to the judge. In addition, the attorney and her law partners discussed the possibility of reporting the judge to the appropriate disciplinary authority but are concerned that this would alienate the other judges to whom their cases are assigned. The attorney has reluctantly started filing for substitution of the judge in every one of her cases to which the judge is assigned, but she has taken no further action.

Is the attorney subject to discipline?

A) Yes, because the attorney failed to inform the appropriate authorities about the judge's conduct.

B) Yes, because, by filing automatic requests for substitution of the judge, the attorney undermined public confidence in the administration of justice.

C) No, because the attorney has a duty to represent her clients zealously.

D) No, because the judge is running for reelection and may not be reelected.

Question # 38

A company's president telephoned his city's best-known employment attorney and asked her to represent the company in a dispute that had just arisen with the company's chief financial officer. The attorney, who had never previously represented the company, agreed. At the president's insistence, she immediately commenced the representation. A few days later, during a meeting with the president, the attorney first revealed the amount of her customary hourly fee and then explained that the company would also be responsible for reimbursing her expenses. The president responded that her fee was higher than he had expected but that he would be happy for the company to pay it, given her excellent work to date. Although the attorney intended to follow up with a confirming letter, she never did so. For several more months, she assisted the company in resolving its employment dispute. Afterward, she sent the company a bill accurately reflecting her hourly fee and expenses, which were reasonable.

Is the attorney subject to discipline?

A) Yes, because she did not disclose the basis of her fee before commencing the representation.

B) Yes, because she did not confirm her fee agreement in writing.

C) No, because she disclosed the basis of her fee within a reasonable time after commencing the representation.

D) No, because she was not required to advise the client of her customary hourly fee, unless requested to do so.

Question # 39

Attorney Alpha, a sole practitioner, recently suffered a heart attack and was advised that she could not return to work for six months. Alpha delivered all of her clients' files to Attorney Beta, who is also a sole practitioner. Beta agreed to review each client's file promptly, take any action necessary to protect each client's interests, and treat the information in the files as confidential. Alpha then wrote her clients, advising each client that the client's file had been delivered to Beta for review and for any action necessary to protect the client's interest, and that the client was free to select another lawyer.

Alpha knows that Beta is a competent attorney. Beta did not accept the file of any person whose interests were, or could be, adverse to the interests of any of Beta's own clients.

Was it proper for Alpha to deliver the files to Beta for review?

A) Yes, because Alpha knows that Beta is competent to protect the clients' interests.

B) Yes, because Beta agreed to treat the information in the files as confidential.

C) Yes, because given her medical condition, Alpha's delivery of the files was necessary to protect the clients' interests.

D) No, because Alpha did not obtain the prior consent of each client whose file was delivered to Beta.

Question # 40

An attorney decided to obtain a master's degree in taxation, but lacked the funds required for tuition and expenses. The attorney consulted one of his clients, a wealthy banker, for advice about obtaining a loan. To the attorney's surprise, the client offered the attorney a personal loan of $10,000. The attorney told the client that he would prepare the required note without charge.

Without further consultation with the client, the attorney prepared and signed a promissory note bearing interest at the current bank rate. The note provided for repayment in the form of legal services to be rendered by the attorney to the client without charge until the value of the attorney's services equaled the principal and interest due. The note further provided that if the client died before the note was fully repaid, any remaining principal and interest would be forgiven as a gift.

The attorney mailed the executed note to the client with a transmittal letter encouraging the client to look it over and call with any questions. The client accepted the note and sent the attorney a personal check for $10,000, which the attorney used to obtain his master's degree. A month after the degree was awarded, the client was killed in a car accident. The attorney had not rendered any legal services to the client from the date of the note's execution to the date of the client's death. Thereafter, in an action brought by the client's estate to recover on the note, the court ruled that the note was discharged as a gift.

Was the attorney's conduct proper?

A) Yes, because the client, without having been requested by the attorney to do so, voluntarily made the loan.

B) Yes, because the court ruled that the note had been discharged as a gift.

C) No, because a lawyer may never accept a loan from a client.

D) No, because the attorney did not comply with the requirements for entering into a business transaction with a client.

Question # 41

A sole practitioner was appointed to represent a criminal defendant on appeal. A recently admitted lawyer who shared office space with the sole practitioner agreed to write the brief if the sole practitioner would pay him one-half of the statutory fee. The defendant agreed to the arrangement in writing, after full consultation. The recently admitted lawyer entered an appearance as co-counsel for the defendant and, with the sole practitioner's knowledge, applied for and received several extensions of time to file the brief. Subsequently, the appellate court dismissed the appeal for failure to pursue the appeal. A third lawyer was later appointed to represent the defendant, whose conviction was affirmed after the appeal was reinstated.

Is the sole practitioner subject to discipline?

A) Yes, because he neglected the defendant's case.

B) Yes, because he shared fees with the recently admitted lawyer.

C) No, because the defendant agreed in writing to the co-counsel arrangement.

D) No, because the affirmance by the appellate court indicated that the defendant's appeal was without merit.

Question # 42

After both parties had completed the presentation of evidence and arguments, the judge took under advisement a case tried without a jury. The case involved a difficult fact issue of causation and a difficult issue of law.

After the case was under advisement for several weeks, the plaintiff's attorney heard rumors that the judge was having difficulty determining the issue of factual causation and was uncertain about the applicable law. Immediately after hearing these rumors, the attorney telephoned the judge, told her of the rumors he had heard, and asked the judge if she would like to reopen the case for additional evidence and briefing from both parties. Thereafter the judge reopened the case for further testimony and requested supplementary briefs from both parties.

Was it proper for the attorney to communicate with the judge?

A) Yes, because both parties were given full opportunity to present their views on the issues in the case.

B) Yes, because the attorney did not make any suggestion as to how the judge should decide the matter.

C) No, because the attorney communicated with the judge on a pending matter without advising opposing counsel.

D) No, because the attorney caused the judge to reopen a case that had been taken under advisement.

Question # 43

An attorney represents the plaintiff in a defamation lawsuit. Both the plaintiff and the defendant are well-known public figures, and the lawsuit has attracted much publicity. The attorney has been billing the plaintiff at an agreed-upon hourly fee for his services. Recently the plaintiff suggested that, rather than paying hourly, she would like to assign the attorney the media rights to a book and movie based on her lawsuit as full payment of services rendered from that point until the end of the litigation. The attorney responded that he would consider it, but that the plaintiff should first seek independent advice as to whether such an arrangement would be in her best interest. The attorney knew that, in the unlikely event that the lawsuit was settled quickly, the media rights might be worth more than he would have earned on an hourly fee basis.

Is the attorney subject to discipline if he agrees to the plaintiff's offer?

A) Yes, because the attorney knew that, in the unlikely event that the lawsuit was settled quickly, the media rights might be worth more than he would have earned on an hourly fee basis.

B) Yes, because the attorney has not concluded the representation of the plaintiff.

C) No, because the defamation lawsuit is a civil and not a criminal matter.

D) No, because the attorney recommended that the plaintiff first seek independent advice before entering into the arrangement.

Question # 44

An attorney represented a plaintiff in an action against a manufacturer of a drain cleaner. The plaintiff's complaint alleged that the manufacturer's product exploded in use and caused her serious and permanent injuries. The jury agreed and awarded the plaintiff $5,000,000 in actual damages and an additional $5,000,000 in punitive damages. The manufacturer paid the judgment.

The attorney made this recovery the cornerstone of an aggressive television advertising campaign for his law practice. In those ads, a voice-over discussed the $10,000,000 recovery obtained in the plaintiff's case. The plaintiff praised the attorney's legal skills in an on-camera statement, saying that no one would work harder on a case than the attorney.

The plaintiff prepared her on-camera statement in response to the attorney's request, but without any further involvement by the attorney, and she believed it to be entirely true.

Is the attorney subject to discipline for using the television advertisement described above?

A) Yes, because the advertisement is likely to create an unjustified expectation about the results the attorney will be able to achieve and is therefore misleading.

B) Yes, because the attorney's advertisement contains a client testimonial.

C) No, because the plaintiff prepared the entire statement without any involvement by the attorney.

D) No, because the result obtained in the plaintiff's case was reported accurately, and the plaintiff believed that everything she said about the attorney was true.

Question # 45

A client telephoned an attorney who had previously represented him. The client described a problem on which he needed advice and made an appointment for the following week to discuss the matter with the attorney. Prior to the appointment, the attorney performed five hours of preliminary research on the client's problem. At the end of the appointment the client agreed that the attorney should pursue the matter and agreed to a fee of $100 per hour. The client then gave the attorney a check for $5,000 to cover the five hours already worked and as an advance on additional fees and expenses.

The attorney gave the check to the office bookkeeper with directions to deposit the check into the client trust account and immediately transfer $3,000 to the general office account to cover the five hours of research already conducted plus the 25 additional hours she would spend on the matter the following week. At that time, the attorney reasonably believed that she would spend 25 additional hours on the case.

The bookkeeper followed these directions. The next week, the attorney worked diligently on the matter for 23 hours. Reasonably believing that no significant work remained to be done on the matter, the attorney directed the bookkeeper to transfer $200 from the general office account to the client trust account. The attorney then called the client and made an appointment to discuss the status of the matter.

Is the attorney subject to discipline?

A) Yes, because the attorney accepted legal fees in advance of performing the work.

B) Yes, because the attorney transferred funds for unearned fees to the general office account.

C) No, because the attorney transferred the $200 owed to the client from the general office account to the client trust account.

D) No, because the attorney reasonably believed that she would spend 25 additional hours on the case.

Question # 46

An attorney agreed to represent a plaintiff in a personal injury matter. The original agreement between the attorney and the plaintiff specified a 30% contingent fee, which was a reasonable fee for the type of cases the attorney handled. One year into the litigation, the attorney noted that he was extremely busy and that many potential clients sought his services. As a result, the attorney raised his standard fee to a 35% contingent fee, which was also a reasonable fee. The attorney's agreement with the plaintiff was silent on the possibility of a fee increase. He approached the plaintiff and proposed that she agree to modify the contingent fee percentage from 30% to 35%. The attorney informed the plaintiff that if she did not agree, the attorney would find her another experienced personal injury lawyer at the original fee, but that the attorney was unwilling to continue the representation unless the fee was modified. The plaintiff reluctantly agreed to modify the fee agreement as the attorney proposed.

Subsequently, the plaintiff's case was settled. The plaintiff, however, refused to pay the attorney more than a 30% contingent fee, and the attorney sued the plaintiff to recover under the modified fee agreement.

Is the attorney likely to prevail?

A) Yes, because the attorney offered to find the plaintiff another experienced personal injury lawyer at the original rate.

B) Yes, because a contingent fee of 35% constituted a reasonable fee.

C) No, because the attorney did not suggest that the plaintiff seek the advice of independent counsel before accepting the increased fee.

D) No, because there were no special circumstances justifying the attorney's insistence on a fee increase.

Question # 47

An attorney represented a man in a case set for a jury trial. After the list of potential jurors was made available, the attorney hired a private investigator to interview the potential jurors and their family members concerning their relevant past experiences related to the subject matter of the action. The investigator did not inform the jurors or their family members that he was working on behalf of the attorney. The interviews were entirely voluntary and were not harassing.

The attorney did not provide the report of the interviews to opposing counsel. He used the report to make decisions regarding jury selection.

Is the attorney subject to discipline?

A) Yes, because the attorney did not provide the report of the interviews to opposing counsel.

B) Yes, because the investigator, at the attorney's direction, communicated with potential jurors prior to trial.

C) Yes, because the investigator did not inform the jurors or their family members that he was working on behalf of the attorney.

D) No, because the interviews were entirely voluntary and not harassing.

Question # 48

Able, Baker, and Carter had been indicted for the armed robbery of a cashier at a grocery store. Together, Able and Baker met with an attorney and asked her to represent them. The attorney then interviewed Able and Baker separately. Each told the attorney that the robbery had been committed by Carter while Able and Baker sat in Carter's car outside the store. They each said that Carter had said he needed some cigarettes and that they knew nothing of his plan to rob the cashier. The attorney agreed to represent both Able and Baker. One week before the trial, Able told the attorney that he wanted to plea bargain and that he was prepared to testify that Baker had loaned Carter the gun Carter used in the robbery. Able also said that he and Baker had shared in the proceeds of the robbery with Carter.

What is the proper course of action for the attorney to take?

A) Request court approval to withdraw as the attorney for both Able and Baker.

B) Continue to represent Baker and, with Able's consent and court approval, withdraw as Able's lawyer.

C) Continue to represent Able and, with Baker's consent and court approval, withdraw as Baker's lawyer.

D) Continue to represent Able and Baker, but not call Able as a witness.

Question # 49

A seller was engaged in negotiations to sell his interest in a large tract of land to a buyer who was unrepresented in the transaction. Before the seller went out of town for a few days, he told the buyer to call his attorney if the buyer had any questions about the property. The buyer called the seller's attorney, asked certain questions about the size of the tract, and expressed hesitations concerning the high asking price for the tract. The attorney responded that, based on his experience handling real estate transactions in the neighborhood, the buyer would be getting a lot of property for the price. At the time the attorney spoke to the buyer, the attorney knew that there was a defect in the title and that the buyer's attempt to purchase the seller's interest in the tract would not result in the buyer's acquisition of any interest in the property.

Relying on the attorney's assurance, the buyer agreed to make the purchase. Shortly after the sale closed, the buyer discovered that his acquisition was worthless.

Is the attorney subject to civil liability to the buyer?

A) Yes, because the attorney knowingly made false representations of fact to the buyer.

B) Yes, because the attorney implied that his opinion regarding the value of the property was a disinterested opinion.

C) No, because the attorney's statement that the buyer would be getting a lot of property for the money was a statement of opinion regarding the value of the property.

D) No, because the buyer was not a client of the attorney.

Question # 50

An attorney represents a famous politician in an action against a newspaper for libel. The case has attracted much publicity, and a jury trial has been demanded. After one of the pretrial hearings, as the attorney left the courthouse, news reporters interviewed her. In responding to the questions, the attorney truthfully stated that the judge upheld their right to subpoena the reporter involved and question the reporter on her mental impressions when she prepared the article. The attorney named the reporter involved.

Is the attorney subject to discipline for making this statement?

A) Yes, because the attorney identified a prospective witness in the case.

B) Yes, because prospective jurors might learn of the attorney's remarks.

C) No, because the statement relates to a matter of public record.

D) No, because the trial has not commenced.

Question # 51

An attorney regularly represents a certain client. When the client planned to leave on a world tour, she delivered to the attorney sufficient money to pay her property taxes when they became due. The attorney placed the money in his clients' trust account. When the tax payment date arrived, the attorney was in need of a temporary loan to close the purchase of a new personal residence. Because the penalty for late payment of taxes was only 2 percent while the rate for a personal loan was 6 percent, the attorney withdrew the client's funds from the clients' trust account to cover his personal check for the closing. The attorney was confident that the client would not object. Ten days later, after the receipt of a large fee previously earned, the attorney paid the client's property taxes and the 2 percent penalty, fully satisfying the client's tax obligation. After the client returned, the attorney told her what he had done, and the client approved the attorney's conduct.

Is the attorney subject to discipline?

A) Yes, because the attorney failed to pay the client the 10 days of interest at the fair market rate.

B) Yes, because the attorney used the client's funds for a personal purpose.

C) No, because the client was not harmed and the attorney reasonably believed at the time he withdrew the money that the client would not object.

D) No, because when the attorney told the client what he had done, the client approved his conduct.

Question # 52

Alpha and Beta practiced law under the firm name of Alpha & Beta. When Beta died, Alpha did not change the firm name. Thereafter, Alpha entered into an arrangement with another attorney, Gamma. Gamma pays Alpha a certain sum each month for office space, for use of Alpha's law library, and for secretarial services. Alpha and Gamma each have their own clients, and neither participates in the representation of the other's clients or shares in fees paid. On the entrance to the suite of offices shared by Alpha and Gamma are the words "Law Firm of Alpha, Beta & Gamma."

Is Alpha subject to discipline?

A) Yes, because Beta was deceased when Alpha made the arrangement with Gamma.

B) Yes, because Gamma is not a partner of Alpha.

C) No, because Alpha and Beta were partners at the time of Beta's death.

D) No, because Gamma is paying a share of the rent and office expenses.

Question # 53

A trial court judge had instructed his court clerk and his secretary that one of them should be present in the office during working hours to answer the telephone. One day, however, the secretary was out sick. The judge was in his office when his court clerk was at lunch, and when the telephone rang, the judge answered it. The call was from a lawyer in a case presently pending before the judge. The lawyer was calling to attempt to reschedule a pretrial conference set for the next day because of a sudden family emergency. The lawyer had tried to call opposing counsel on the case, but she was not answering his calls. The judge agreed to reschedule the pretrial conference for the following week. When the judge's court clerk returned from lunch, the judge instructed the clerk to contact opposing counsel to inform her of the telephone call and the fact that the pretrial conference had been rescheduled.

Did the judge act properly?

A) No, because the judge participated in an ex parte communication.

B) No, because there was still time for the calling lawyer to notify opposing counsel in order to reach agreement on rescheduling the pretrial conference.

C) Yes, because the ex parte communication was for scheduling purposes only and did not deal with substantive matters or issues.

D) Yes, because there was no one else in the office to take the lawyer's call.

Question # 54

An attorney who had represented a client for many years prepared the client's will and acted as one of the two subscribing witnesses to its execution. The will gave 10 percent of the client's estate to her housekeeper, 10 percent to her son and sole heir, and the residue to charity. Upon the client's death one year later, the executor named in the will asked the attorney to represent him in probating the will and administering the estate. At that time the executor informed the attorney that the son had notified him that he would contest the probate of the will on the grounds that the client lacked the required mental capacity at the time the will was executed. The attorney believes that the client was fully competent at all times and will so testify, if called as a witness. The other subscribing witness to the client's will predeceased the client.

Is it proper for the attorney to represent the executor in the probate of the will?

A) Yes, because the attorney is the sole surviving witness to the execution of the will.

B) Yes, because the attorney's testimony will support the validity of the will.

C) No, because the attorney will be called to testify on a contested issue of fact.

D) No, because the attorney will be representing an interest adverse to the client's heir at law.

Question # 55

An attorney entered into a written retainer agreement with a defendant in a criminal case. The defendant agreed in writing to transfer title to her automobile to the attorney if the attorney successfully prevented her from going to prison. Later, the charges against the defendant were dismissed.

Is the attorney subject to discipline for entering into this retainer agreement?

A) Yes, because the attorney agreed to a fee contingent on the outcome of a criminal case.

B) Yes, because a lawyer may not acquire a proprietary interest in a client's property.

C) No, because the charges against the defendant were dismissed.

D) No, because the retainer agreement was in writing.

Question # 56

A corporation hired a law firm to handle all of its corporate work. The firm had not previously represented a corporation on an ongoing basis, but decided that it wanted to attract additional corporate clients. Accordingly, the partners handling the corporation's work began a practice of giving to all lawyers in the firm, on a monthly basis, detailed descriptions of the work they were doing for the corporation for the purpose of illustrating what the firm could do for corporate clients. One of the partners mentioned this practice to the corporation's management, and the corporation complained that its confidences had been violated.

Was it proper for the partners to give detailed descriptions of the work being done for the corporation to other lawyers in the firm?

A) Yes, because, absent client instructions to the contrary, lawyers may discuss client information with other lawyers in the firm.

B) Yes, because lawyers may discuss client information with other lawyers in the firm, regardless of client instructions to the contrary, so long as the disclosure does not disadvantage the client.

C) No, because sharing the information increased the risk that it might be improperly disclosed to third parties outside the firm.

D) No, because lawyers may not disclose client information, even to other firm lawyers, unless the disclosure is in furtherance of the representation.

Question # 57

A judge has recently resigned from the state trial court bench. When she was a judge, she supervised activity in cases pending before another judge while he was on vacation. In one pending case, she entered an administrative order changing the courtroom in which a particular case was to be tried. After trial and appeal, the case was remanded for a new trial. The plaintiff in that case decided to change lawyers and has asked the recently resigned judge to try the case.

Will the judge be subject to discipline if she tries this case on behalf of the plaintiff?

A) Yes, because the judge acted officially as a judge with respect to an aspect of the case.

B) Yes, because the judge would try the case before a judge of the court on which she previously sat.

C) No, because the judge did not act as a judge with respect to a substantial matter in or the merits of the case.

D) No, because any information that the judge learned about the case while acting as a judge was a matter of public record.

Question # 58

An attorney agreed to represent a client in a lawsuit. The attorney and the client executed the attorney's preprinted retainer form that provides, in part:

"The client agrees to pay promptly the attorney's fee for services. In addition, the client and the attorney agree to release each other from any and all liability arising from the representation. The client agrees that the attorney need not return the client's file prior to receiving the client's executed release. Upon full payment, the attorney will return the file to the client."

Although the attorney recommended that the client consult independent counsel before signing the retainer agreement, the client chose not to do so. The attorney reasonably believes that his fee is fair and that the quality of his work will be competent.

Is the attorney's retainer agreement with the client proper?

A) Yes, because the attorney furnished consideration by agreeing to return the client's file.

B) Yes, because the attorney reasonably believes that his fee is fair and that the quality of his work will be competent.

C) No, because the attorney is attempting to limit his liability for malpractice.

D) No, because the attorney uses a preprinted form for all retainers.

Question # 59

A client retained an attorney to appeal his criminal conviction and to seek bail pending appeal. The agreed-upon fee for the appearance on the bail hearing was $100 per hour. The attorney received $1,600 from the client, of which $600 was a deposit to secure the attorney's fee and $1,000 was for bail costs in the event that bail was obtained. The attorney maintained two office bank accounts: a fee account, in which all fees collected from clients were deposited and from which all office expenses were paid, and a clients' trust account. The attorney deposited the $1,600 in the clients' trust account the week before the bail hearing. She expended six hours of her time preparing for and appearing at the hearing. The effort to obtain bail was unsuccessful. Dissatisfied, the client immediately demanded return of the $1,600.

What should the attorney do with the $1,600?

A) Transfer the $1,600 to the fee account.

B) Transfer the $600 to the fee account and leave $1,000 in the clients' trust account until the attorney's fee for the final appeal is determined.

C) Transfer $600 to the fee account and send the client a $1,000 check on the clients' trust account.

D) Send the client a $1,000 check and leave $600 in the clients' trust account until the matter is resolved with the client.

Question # 60

An attorney and a restaurant owner entered into a reciprocal referral arrangement. The attorney agreed to prominently display ads for the restaurant in her office, and to mention the restaurant to all of her clients who requested a recommendation of a nearby place to eat. In return, the owner agreed to prominently display ads for the attorney's firm in the restaurant and to recommend the attorney to any of his customers who indicated a need for the services provided by the attorney. The reciprocal referral agreement was not exclusive, and the clients and customers would be informed of the existence and nature of the agreement.

Is the attorney subject to discipline for entering into this agreement?

A) Yes, because she asked the owner to place ads for the firm in the restaurant.

B) Yes, because the agreement provided something of value to the restaurant owner in return for recommending the attorney's services.

C) No, because she did not pay the restaurant owner for the referrals.

D) No, because the agreement is not exclusive, and the clients and customers will be informed of the existence and nature of the agreement.

MPRE Practice Test
Explanatory Answers

Question # 1

(A)   Correct. This fact pattern presents the classic multidisciplinary practice of law issue. Lawyers and nonlawyers may not practice together in a single entity co-owned by the two professionals or sets of professionals if the entity delivers legal services. This answer is correct because it zeroes in on the fact that the partnership delivers legal services.

(B)   Incorrect. There is no absolute ban on lawyer and nonlawyer partnerships. The rule prohibits only those partnerships in which all or part of the services delivered are legal services. The lawyer could own part of this entity with the accountant if, for example, the partnership delivered only accounting services.

(C)   Incorrect. The accountant is a partner with the lawyer in the partnership, and that fact gives the accountant a portion of the profits of the entity and control over the law aspects of the business. What the accountant does in terms of work is not determinative.

(D)   Incorrect. It is true that the accountant should not interfere with the judgment of the lawyer. But that is not enough. The accountant as a partner in the partnership has legal and managerial control over the attorney's practice of law, which is prohibited behavior. So the lawyer would be subject to discipline.

Question # 2

(A)   Incorrect. Limitations on the scope of a representation will not be judged based upon whether they were suggested by the lawyer or the client.

(B)   Correct. A lawyer and client may agree to limit the scope of the lawyer's representation as long as the client has been fully informed. The limitation on the representation must be reasonable. In this case, it is entirely permissible for the client and the lawyer to agree to a limited representation that covers only the client's involvement in the grand jury proceeding.

(C)   Incorrect. Lawyers do not have an obligation to provide free legal services to everyone. The ability to pay is clearly one permissible factor in crafting a limited representation and, in this case, it puts the client in a better position than if he were not represented by the lawyer at all.

(D)   Incorrect. The law of lawyering does not prohibit limited representations in criminal cases.

Question # 3

(A)   Incorrect. There is no exception to Rule 1.6(a), the confidentiality rule, permitting or requiring a lawyer to disclose information relating to a client's representation when the information concerns the client's past crimes of violence. There are exceptions allowing the lawyer to disclose client confidences in certain circumstances—e.g., to prevent a future death or to prevent or rectify financial harm caused by a crime or fraud involving the lawyer's services—but these exceptions do not apply here.

(B)   Incorrect. Criminal laws involving obstruction of justice, as well as judicial opinions, require a lawyer under certain circumstances to disclose physical evidence of a crime when the lawyer possesses that evidence. But the laws and opinions regarding obstruction of justice do not require disclosure of the client's confidential information in this case.

(C)   Incorrect. The attorney's knowledge is information "relating to the representation" of the client in the homicide case, and therefore must be kept confidential under Rule 1.6(a), even though the information relates to murders other than the one for which the client is on trial. The information about the undiscovered homicides would potentially be relevant to the attorney in representing the client competently with regard to the crime charged. For example, the lawyer's knowledge of this information might influence the lawyer's advice to the client about whether to plead guilty or whether to testify at trial, and the information might influence the lawyer's strategic decisions.

(D)   Correct. In general, Rule 1.6(a) provides that "[a] lawyer shall not reveal information relating to the representation of a client unless the client gives informed consent." Further, no exception to the confidentiality rule allows or requires the attorney to disclose the information.

Question # 4

(A)   Incorrect. Under Rule 1.11(a)(1), a lawyer who was formerly employed by a government agency may not later represent a client "in connection with a matter in which the lawyer participated personally and substantially" as a public employee, unless the government agency consents. Having participated personally and substantially in an early stage of the condemnation matter by conducting a title search on the woman's property, the attorney may not now represent the woman in opposing or seeking additional damages for the condemnation.

(B)   Incorrect. Under Rule 1.11(a)(1), a lawyer who was formerly employed by a government agency may not later represent a client "in connection with a matter in which the lawyer participated personally and substantially" as a public employee, unless the government agency consents. Having participated personally and substantially in an early stage of the condemnation matter by conducting a title search on the woman's property, the attorney may not now represent the woman in opposing or seeking additional damages for the condemnation.

(C)   Incorrect. The attorney may not disclose information learned while working at the department because, under Rule 1.11(a)(2) and Rule 1.9(c), a lawyer who was formerly employed by the government must not reveal information relating to a former representation.

(D)   Correct. Rule 1.11(a)(1) provides that a lawyer who was formerly employed by a government agency may not later represent a client "in connection with a matter in which the lawyer participated personally and substantially" as a public employee, unless the government agency consents. Having participated personally and substantially in an early stage of the condemnation matter by conducting a title search on the woman's property, the attorney may not now represent the woman in opposing or seeking additional damages for the condemnation. Further, the attorney may not disclose the information learned while working at the department because, under Rule 1.11(a)(2) and Rule 1.9(c), a lawyer who was formerly employed by the government must not reveal information relating to a former representation.

Question # 5

(A)   Incorrect. Advertising in and of itself does not create an attorney-client relationship. The fact that the attorney advertised in this manner did not require that he be available for all medical malpractice cases.

(B)   Incorrect. The attorney declined to accept the matter and gave the man information about another lawyer and about the need to see that lawyer on a timely basis. The attorney did not have a duty to give the man the exact date the statute would run, unless that date happened to be in a very short time, such as within the next day or two.

(C)   Correct. The attorney talked to the prospective client, declined the representation, gave the man another lawyer's name, and urged him to contact that lawyer on a timely basis. Under Model Rule 1.18, the attorney did not owe the man any other duty.

(D)   Incorrect. The referral was not necessary under the rules, so that is not the reason why the attorney is not subject to civil liability. After he declined to accept the matter, the attorney told the man that he should see another lawyer on a timely basis. Under Model Rule 1.18, the attorney did not owe the man any other duty.

Question # 6

(A)   Incorrect. Although it is true that the client is engaging in continuing illegal conduct, the client is nevertheless entitled to the advice of a lawyer. So long as the lawyer does not knowingly counsel or assist the client in the illegal conduct (Model Rule 1.2(d)), the lawyer may continue to represent the client.

(B)   Incorrect. Although Model Rule 1.16(b)(4) grants a lawyer permission to withdraw if the client insists on action that the lawyer believes is repugnant or with which the lawyer fundamentally disagrees, the lawyer is not required to do so.

(C)   Correct. Under Rule 1.2(d), a lawyer may not knowingly counsel or assist a client in illegal conduct, but in this case, the lawyer has not done so.

(D)   Incorrect. Even if the indictment is defective, the client's conduct would still be illegal. Nevertheless, the lawyer may continue to represent the client so long as the lawyer does not knowingly counsel or assist the client in the illegal conduct.

Question # 7

(A)   Incorrect. Model Rule 4.2 prohibits a lawyer from communicating about a matter with a person known to be represented in the matter unless the person's lawyer consents to the communication. The Rule applies even if the represented person initiates or consents to the communication.

(B)   Incorrect. Model Rule 4.2 prohibits a lawyer from communicating about a matter with a person known to be represented in the matter unless the person's lawyer consents to the communication.

(C)   Correct. Model Rule 4.2 prohibits a lawyer from communicating about a matter with a person known to be represented in the matter unless the person's lawyer consents to the communication.

(D)   Incorrect. Model Rule 4.2 prohibits a lawyer from communicating about a matter with a person known to be represented in the matter unless the person's lawyer consents to the communication. The communication is prohibited, however, only when the lawyer knows that the person is represented. The rule imposes no duty to investigate.

Question # 8

(A) Incorrect. Model Rule 4.1 prohibits lawyers from making false statements of material facts in negotiations. According to the Comment, generally accepted conventions in negotiation, including certain types of statements such as estimates of price or value, ordinarily are not taken as statements of material facts. In this case, to the extent that the attorney may have exaggerated the value of his client's business, this exaggeration would not be considered a statement of material fact.

(B) Incorrect. An exaggeration such as the one made by the attorney in this case is not ordinarily considered a statement of material fact. Model Rule 4.1 prohibits lawyers from making false statements of material facts in negotiations.

(C) Incorrect. Model Rule 4.1 prohibits lawyers from making false statements of material facts in negotiations. It is irrelevant which party the attorney represents.

(D) Correct. Model Rule 4.1 prohibits lawyers from making false statements of material facts in negotiations. However, according to the Comment to this rule, estimates of price or value are generally not considered to be statements of material facts.

Question # 9

(A) Correct. Rule 1.15(d) requires the lawyer to "promptly notify the client" upon receiving funds in which the client has an interest. Here, the attorney deliberately delayed notifying the client for a week, until the client had been to classes in investing.

(B) Incorrect. The lawyer was permitted to give this unsolicited advice. Rule 2.1 permits a lawyer who is advising a client to "refer not only to law but to other considerations such as moral, economic, social, and political factors that may be relevant to the client's situation.".

(C) Incorrect. The lawyer's failure to promptly notify the client of the lawyer's receipt of client funds and to promptly deliver the funds to the client, as required by Rule 1.15(d), is not excused by the client's later failure to object..

(D) Incorrect. Rule 1.15(d) provides that the lawyer must promptly notify the client when the lawyer receives funds belonging to the client. There is no exception when the lawyer thinks it would be best for the client to delay notification.

Question # 10

(A)   Incorrect. Model Rule 7.3 prohibits lawyers from making in-person, live telephone, or real-time electronic contact to solicit for pecuniary gain, but this communication does not fall within the banned behavior. It is an advertisement governed by Model Rules 7.1 and 7.2. As a result, the communication is permissible so long as it does not contain any false or misleading statements, which this announcement did not.

(B)   Incorrect. Model Rule 7.1 forbids only false or misleading communications in lawyer advertising. A truthful statement about the attorney's prior service as governor is not likely to create any unjustified expectations and is therefore not misleading.

(C)   Correct. The communication is an advertisement. Model Rule 7.1, which covers lawyer advertising, forbids only false or misleading communications, and this communication was neither false nor misleading.

(D)   Incorrect. Information in the public domain can still be either false or misleading. As such, communication of that information might be prohibited under Model Rule 7.1, which forbids false or misleading communications in lawyer advertising.

Question # 11

(A)   Incorrect. It would have been proper for the attorney to provide good faith opinions about the judicial candidate's qualifications even if the attorney had also been seeking judicial office, since such opinions promote the administration of justice by assisting the voters in making informed electoral decisions. *See* Rule 8.2, cmt. [1]. As a candidate for public office, the attorney would have been required to comply with applicable provisions of the Code of Judicial Conduct, but that code would not have forbidden the attorney's comments.

(B)   Correct. The attorney's expression of good faith views about a judicial candidate's qualifications was proper, because "[e]xpressing honest and candid opinions on such matters contributes to improving the administration of justice." Rule 8.2, cmt. [1].

(C)   Incorrect. Although false statements about judicial candidates can unfairly undermine public confidence in the administration of justice, a lawyer's good faith expressions of opinion about the judicial candidate's temperament, based on the lawyer's experience, promote the administration of justice by enabling voters to make informed decisions and are encouraged under Rule 8.2.

(D)   Incorrect. False public statements about a judicial candidate's qualifications are improper, but not all public statements about judicial candidates are improper. On the contrary, honest and candid opinions are encouraged under Rule 8.2.

Question # 12

(A)   Incorrect. Achieving competence and impartiality does not justify making special master appointments in all cases before a judge. 2007 CJC 2.13(A)(2) requires that a judge avoid making unnecessary appointments.

(B)   Incorrect. Even if a special master charges a reasonable rate, the judge may not make unnecessary appointments. 2007 CJC 2.13(A)(2) requires that a judge avoid making unnecessary appointments.

(C)   Correct. The practice of making appointments without reference to need will result in unnecessary appointments and is therefore prohibited by 2007 CJC 2.13(A)(2).

(D)   Incorrect. Nothing in the code prohibits a judge from using a law directory to make appointments.

Question # 13

(A)   Incorrect. A newsletter does not provide legal advice about a particular client's problem, but just provides generalized legal information.

(B)   Correct. A bank may not provide legal services to its customers through a salaried lawyer because banks are not authorized to practice law. By providing these services, the attorney is assisting the bank in the unauthorized practice of law.

(C)   Incorrect. A bank may not provide legal services to its customers through a salaried lawyer because banks are not authorized to practice law. By providing these services, the attorney is assisting the bank in the unauthorized practice of law, whether or not the customer is charged for the work.

(D)   Incorrect. A bank may not provide legal services to its customers through a salaried lawyer because banks are not authorized to practice law. The attorney may do legal work for the bank, but may not do legal work for bank clients.

Question # 14

(A)   Incorrect. Although the percentage increase gives the attorney an incentive to favor going through the appeal, this incentive does not create an impermissible conflict of interest.

(B)   Correct. Under Model Rule 1.2(a), a lawyer must abide by a client's decision as to whether to settle a matter.

(C)   Incorrect. Under Model Rule 1.2(a), a lawyer must abide by a client's decision whether to settle a matter, regardless of the procedural status.

(D)   Incorrect. Although it is true that evaluating the merits of an appeal requires the exercise of independent professional judgment, Model Rule 1.2(a) confers upon the client the ultimate authority to determine the objectives of the representation and to make certain decisions, including a decision as to whether to settle a matter.

Question # 15

(A)   Incorrect. Under Rule 1.6(B)(6), the attorney may provide client confidences in response to a grand jury subpoena unless the information may be protected by the attorney-client privilege, in which case the attorney must assert the privilege unless the client waives it. In this case, the clients' names are confidential under Rule 1.6 but are not protected by the attorney-client privilege. The privilege covers only confidential communications between a client and a lawyer. It does not cover clients' identities unless disclosing their identities will implicitly reveal their confidential communications, which is not the case here. It is irrelevant that negotiating a counterfeit bill is a crime. If the attorney's information in this case was privileged, the attorney could not disclose it under the "crime-fraud" exception, even though passing counterfeit money is a crime, because the attorney does not know which client paid with counterfeit bills and also does not know whether the client who did so was aware that the bills were counterfeit.

(B)   Correct. Under Rule 1.6(B)(6), the attorney may provide client confidences in response to a grand jury subpoena unless the information may be protected by the attorney-client privilege, in which case the attorney must assert the privilege unless the client waives it. In this case, the clients' names are confidential under Rule 1.6 but are not protected by the attorney-client privilege. The privilege covers only confidential communications between a client and a lawyer. It does not cover clients' identities unless disclosing their identities will implicitly reveal their confidential communications, which is not the case here.

(C)   Incorrect. Under Rule 1.6(B)(6), the attorney may provide client confidences in response to a grand jury subpoena unless the information may be protected by the attorney-client privilege, in which case the attorney must assert the privilege unless the client waives it. In this case, the clients' names are not protected by the attorney-client privilege, so the attorney may reveal their names. The privilege covers only confidential communications between a client and a lawyer. It does not cover clients' identities unless disclosing their identities will implicitly reveal their confidential communications, which is not the case here. Therefore, it is irrelevant that the information is confidential under Rule 1.6(a) and that it is not subject to the exception under Rule 1.6(b)(1) that allows the disclosure of confidences to prevent reasonably certain death or substantial bodily harm.

(D)   Incorrect. Under Rule 1.6(B)(6), the attorney may provide client confidences in response to a grand jury subpoena unless the information may be protected by the attorney-client privilege, in which case the attorney must assert the privilege unless the client waives it. In this case, the clients' names are not protected by the attorney-client privilege, so the attorney may reveal their names. The privilege covers only confidential communications between a client and a lawyer. It does not cover clients' identities unless disclosing their identities will implicitly reveal their confidential communications, which is not the case here.

If, on the other hand, the attorney's information in this case were privileged (which it isn't), then the attorney could not disclose it under the "crime-fraud" exception because the attorney does not know which client paid with counterfeit bills and also does not know whether the client who did so was aware that the bills were counterfeit. But because the information is not privileged, the crime-fraud exception is inapplicable.

Question # 16

(A)   Correct. The attorney has a conflict of interest under Rule 1.7(a) arising out of the representation of two clients in the same transaction—the bank, which is the lender, and the corporation, which is the borrower. But Rule 1.7(b) allows the attorney to represent both clients with informed consent, confirmed in writing, because the attorney reasonably believes that he can competently and diligently represent them both.

(B)   Incorrect. The fact that the arrangement is customary in the community is irrelevant. The attorney has a conflict of interest under Rule 1.7(a) arising out of the representation of two clients in the same transaction—the bank, which is the lender, and the corporation, which is the borrower. However, the joint representation would be permissible in this situation under Rule 1.7(b).

(C)   Incorrect. In a joint representation such as this one, there is no restriction against the payment of legal fees by one of the two clients with informed consent, as required by Model Rule 1.8(f).

(D)   Incorrect. Although the clients have differing interests, and there is therefore a conflict of interest under Rule 1.7(a), Rule 1.7(b) allows the attorney to represent both clients with informed consent, confirmed in writing, because the attorney reasonably believes he can competently and diligently represent them both.

Question # 17

(A)   Correct. If a lawyer identifies criminal behavior on the part of an opposing party, upon consent of the client, the lawyer may disclose such information to the prosecutor. Once the lawyer has the client's consent, disclosure of the information would be permissive and not mandatory.

(B)   Incorrect. The lawyer is not required to report an opposing party's criminal activity to the prosecutor. Also, the decision to report the defendant to the criminal authorities does not depend on whether the information discovered is privileged or not.

(C)   Incorrect. There is no duty to inform the defendant's lawyer before reporting the information.

(D)   Incorrect. It was permissible to report even though the civil suit was pending because the attorney was not trying to get an advantage in the civil proceeding by making a complaint to the prosecutor. Had she been seeking an advantage, it might have been impermissible under the law and therefore under Rule 3.4.

Question # 18

(A)   Correct. Under Model Rule 5.1, a newly admitted lawyer in a firm must have his or her work properly supervised by a more experienced lawyer. Under Model Rule 1.1, a law firm owes a client a duty of competence, and when the firm uses less experienced lawyers to perform client work the partners must supervise that work. In this case, the associate, who had never conducted or observed a trial and had not worked on landlord-tenant cases before, needed supervision. There was not enough time for the associate to become familiar with the relevant law and procedure, nor did she have the experience to competently handle the case. The attorney did not take the proper precautions to make sure that the lawyer was adequately prepared to carry out the assignment.

(B)   Incorrect. The outcome of the trial is not relevant to whether the associate was properly supervised as required by Model Rules 1.1 and 5.1.

(C)   Incorrect. The associate's admission to the bar did not relieve the attorney of the responsibility to properly supervise and train her.

(D)   Incorrect. The consent of the landlord to this representation would not mitigate the violation of Model Rules 1.1 and 5.1, which impose a responsibility to properly train and supervise less experienced attorneys.

Question # 19

(A)   Correct. Model Rule 3.4(f) prohibits a lawyer from asking a person other than a client to refrain from voluntarily giving relevant information to another party unless the person is a relative or an employee or other agent of the client.

(B)   Incorrect. A lawyer is under no obligation to subpoena a witness that the lawyer does not intend to call at trial.

(C)   Incorrect. Even though the witness had not been subpoenaed by the defense, Model Rule 3.4(f) prohibited the attorney from asking the witness to refrain from voluntarily giving relevant information to another party.

(D)   Incorrect. Although the attorney did not offer the witness any inducement not to appear at trial, Model Rule 3.4(f) prohibited the attorney from asking the witness to refrain from voluntarily giving relevant information to another party.

Question # 20

(A)   Correct. Model Rule 4.2 prohibits a lawyer from communicating about a matter with a person known to be represented in the matter unless the person's lawyer consents to the communication or the communication is authorized by law. Under Rule 8.4(a), a lawyer may not violate the rules directly or through the acts of another. Here, the attorney used a nonlawyer agent to violate the anticontact rule.

(B)   Incorrect. The investigator merely relayed a communication from the attorney to the defendant and did not thereby engage in the unauthorized practice of law.

(C)   Incorrect. Model Rule 4.2 prohibits a lawyer from communicating about a matter with a person known to be represented in the matter unless the person's lawyer consents to the communication or the communication is authorized by law. Such communication is impermissible regardless of whether it is done by the attorney or by an agent of the attorney.

(D)   Incorrect. Model Rule 4.2 prohibits a lawyer from communicating about a matter with a person known to be represented in the matter unless the person's lawyer consents to the communication or the communication is authorized by law. The defendant's lawyer did not consent to the communication, and the fact that the defendant's lawyer was not relaying settlement offers did not otherwise justify the communication.

Question # 21

(A)   Incorrect. Under Rule 1.7, the initial representation was proper because it was reasonable for the attorney to believe that he was able to provide competent and diligent representation to both the husband and the wife, and the clients' consent was informed and in writing.

(B)   Correct. A client who has given consent to a potential conflict of interest may revoke the consent and may, like any other client, terminate the lawyer's representation at any time. It was improper for the attorney to insist that the wife adhere to her prior agreement in derogation of her absolute right to terminate the joint representation.

(C)   Incorrect. Even though the clients initially consented to the joint representation, each had an absolute right at any time to revoke the consent and, like any other client, to terminate the attorney's representation. It was improper for the attorney to insist that the wife had given up that right.

(D)   Incorrect. Even though the clients initially agreed between themselves to be jointly represented, each had an absolute right at any time to revoke the consent and, like any other client, to terminate the attorney's representation. It was improper for the attorney to insist that the wife had given up that right.

Question # 22

(A)   Incorrect. The attorney's conduct was improper because Model Rule 3.9 requires a lawyer representing a client before a legislative body to disclose that the appearance is in a representative capacity.

(B)   Incorrect. The congressional members at the hearing would be very interested in knowing whether a witness is possibly biased in his or her testimony; therefore, Model Rule 3.9 requires a lawyer appearing in a representative capacity to disclose that fact to the legislative body.

(C)   Incorrect. Lawyers frequently serve as paid lobbyists. This activity is permissible so long as the lawyer-lobbyist complies with applicable rules, such as the requirement to disclose his or her representative capacity when appearing before a legislative body.

(D)   Correct. Model Rule 3.9 requires a lawyer representing a client before a legislative body to disclose that the appearance is in a representative capacity.

Question # 23

(A)   Incorrect. The senator was not assisting the bank as a client but as a constituent. Therefore, she did not misuse her official position.

(B)   Incorrect. The senator's efforts as a legislator on behalf of a constituent were proper, since she was no longer practicing law and was not seeking to assist the bank as a private client. Therefore, it does not matter that the attorney influenced the agency.

(C)   Incorrect. In acting in her legislative capacity, a legislator who is a lawyer may express opinions about the law.

(D)   Correct. A practicing lawyer who is also a legislator may not use her official authority for the benefit of a private client. But that is not what occurred here. As in this case, a legislator who is a lawyer but who is no longer practicing law may assist a constituent in its dealings with a state agency.

Question # 24

(A)   Incorrect. The Model Rules do not ask lawyers to speculate as to whether their advice about the scope and enforcement of the law will ultimately be used to violate the law. The lawyer, by giving her opinion, did not assist the client in violating the law.

(B)   Incorrect. The lawyer told the client that she would not tell him how to avoid detection. She told him about the law and its history. Discouraging a client from violating the law might have been the best practice, but failing to discourage him is not cause for discipline.

(C)   Correct. Under Model Rule 1.2(d), a lawyer is permitted to delineate the law for a client but is not allowed to counsel or assist a client in violation of the law.

(D)   Incorrect. Lawyers may not give clients information on how to best avoid compliance with the law.

Question # 25

(A)   Incorrect. A conversation with another judge about a pending matter is not an ex parte communication.

(B)   Incorrect. A judge may consult with another judge in the court about a case as long as the judge to whom the case is assigned does not abrogate his or her responsibilities.

(C)   Incorrect. Under the 2007 CJC 2.9(A)(2), a judge may obtain written advice from a disinterested expert provided that the judge gives advance notice to the parties about details of the consultation and the opportunity to object and respond to the advice. This rule, however, is not applicable to a situation in which a judge consults with another judge in the court.

(D)   Correct. Judges are permitted to consult with other judges in the court about pending cases as long as they do not abrogate their responsibilities to decide the matters and as long as they make reasonable efforts to avoid receiving factual information not part of the record. 2007 CJC 2.9(A)(3).

Question # 26

(A)   Incorrect. The plan is proper, but the reason why it is proper has nothing to do with the compensation paid to other law office administrators in the community. This answer erroneously refers to Model Rule 1.5(a)'s guidelines on reasonable fees for lawyers, which list as one factor fees paid to other similarly situated lawyers in the community.

(B)   Correct. The plan for part of the administrator's compensation is based upon the net profits of the firm and this arrangement is expressly permitted in Model Rule 5.4(a) as long as the nonlawyer is an employee. The other aspects of the arrangement do not give the administrator an ownership interest in the firm nor any right to control the legal work done in the law firm, thus avoiding any violation of the rule.

(C)   Incorrect. The Model Rules do not address the basis on which net profits may be divided and distributed to nonlawyer employees. That decision is for the firm.

(D)   Incorrect. Lawyers may not share legal fees with nonlawyers, but Model Rule 5.4(a) contains an exception for the sharing of net profits with nonlawyer employees.

Question # 27

(A)   Incorrect. The lawyer's duty to protect client information under Rule 1.6(a) covers more than just privileged information. It covers all "information relating to the representation of a client."

(B)   Incorrect. A lawyer has a duty under Rule 3.3(b) to take remedial measures when the lawyer knows that a person engaged in criminal conduct related to a proceeding in which the lawyer represents a client. But that duty does not apply here, because the attorney did not represent the client in the proceeding in which the client's former partner committed perjury. Therefore, the duty to maintain confidentiality applies to this information.

(C)   Incorrect. A lawyer has a duty under Rule 3.3(b) to take remedial measures when the lawyer knows that a person engaged in criminal conduct related to a proceeding in which the lawyer represents a client. But the duty continues only to the end of that proceeding. Here, the proceeding in which the former partner committed perjury is over. Therefore, even if the lawyer had represented the client in that proceeding, the lawyer would have no duty at this time to disclose the former partner's perjury.

(D)   Correct. The information about perjury committed by the client's former partner is "information relating to the representation" which generally may not be disclosed without client consent. Confidential information may be disclosed under Rule 1.6(a) when "the disclosure is impliedly authorized in order to carry out the representation," but there would not be implied authorization where, as here, the disclosure would be likely to prejudice the client, not advance the client's objectives.

Question # 28

(A)   Incorrect. Rule 1.8(g) allows a lawyer to participate in an aggregate settlement of civil claims, as in this case, as long as the lawyer complies with the requirement of informed consent by all clients, which the attorney failed to do here.

(B)   Correct. Because this is an aggregate settlement of the clients' claims, Rule 1.8(g) requires the attorney to obtain the clients' informed consent, after disclosing "the existence and nature of all the claims" and "the participation of each person in the settlement." Comment [13] states that the necessary disclosure includes information about "all the material terms of the settlement, including what the other clients will receive."

(C)   Incorrect. Rule 1.8(g) and Comment [13] to the rule require disclosure of the material terms of the settlement regardless of whether the settlement will thereby be jeopardized, because all of the clients are entitled to material information regarding their decision on whether to accept the settlement offer, and each must give informed consent.

(D)   Incorrect. Whether or not the lawyer regards the aggregate settlement offer as fair, Rule 1.8(g) requires a lawyer to make full disclosure to the clients so that they can each make an informed decision as to whether to accept the offer. According to Comment [13] to Rule 1.8, the attorney did not make the required disclosure because she did not disclose "all the material terms of the settlement, including what the other clients will receive."

Question # 29

(A)   Correct. Under Rule 1.1, a lawyer may give advice on an emergency basis when referral or consultation with another lawyer is not possible. An emergency phone call from jail is one of those kinds of cases in which a lawyer may give advice even though the lawyer does not know criminal law. But for any additional work, the lawyer must become competent or find another lawyer to take on the matter, which the attorney did in this case.

(B)   Incorrect. Nothing in the rules makes conduct proper because the services are performed for relatives. That is, the work would have been acceptable even if the attorney was unrelated to the client since this was an emergency situation.

(C)   Incorrect. It is true that the attorney did not have experience in criminal law, but because this was an emergency case, the attorney was permitted to give advice.

(D)   Incorrect. The attorney did not take on the case, but only gave limited legal advice in an emergency situation, which is permitted by the rules.

Question # 30

(A)   Incorrect. In all court proceedings, the judge must consent to the withdrawal and substitution of counsel. Sufficient notice and client consent are not enough for withdrawal if the court does not agree. Rule 1.16(c) states that the lawyer must continue the case if ordered to do so by the court.

(B)   Incorrect. The client conduct is a reason for the lawyer to move for withdrawal, but the lawyer must get the court's permission before withdrawal would be proper. Rule 1.16(c) states that the lawyer must continue the case if ordered to do so by the court.

(C)   Correct. Rule 1.16(c) states that the lawyer must continue the case if ordered to do so by the court.

(D)   Incorrect. There is no evidence that the client would be prejudiced by the withdrawal. Withdrawal is improper because the court refused to grant permission to withdraw. Rule 1.16(c) states that the lawyer must continue the case if ordered to do so by the court.

Question # 31

(A)   Incorrect. Although the attorney had an obligation to use independent judgment in advising the client, Model Rule 1.2(a) provides that a lawyer must abide by a client's decision concerning the objectives of the representation.

(B)   Incorrect. Litigation is often necessary to vindicate a client's rights under law, and, as a result, nothing in the text or comments of the Model Rules suggests that lawyers should as a general matter endeavor to avoid litigation that is not frivolous.

(C)   Correct. Under Model Rule 3.1, it is not frivolous to begin a lawsuit or assert a defense if there is a good faith argument that will support the prosecution or defense.

(D)   No, because, as an employee, the attorney is bound by the instructions of the general counsel.

Question # 32

(A)   Incorrect. Model Rule 4.3 applies to a lawyer's dealings with an unrepresented person. It requires that the lawyer not state or imply that the lawyer is disinterested and that the lawyer not give legal advice to the unrepresented person. The attorney did neither here. Although the rule permits the lawyer to advise the unrepresented person to confer with counsel, it does not require the lawyer to do so.

(B)   Incorrect. Model Rule 4.3 expressly permits lawyers to contact unrepresented persons, so long as they follow certain requirements in dealing with those persons.

(C)   Incorrect. The attorney did not act as a scrivener or otherwise on behalf of the husband. As the attorney clearly stated, the attorney was acting solely on behalf of the wife in this matter. Whether the attorney acted as drafter or scrivener with respect to the proposed agreement is not relevant to the question of whether his contact with the husband was proper. Model Rule 4.3 permits a lawyer to contact an unrepresented person so long as the lawyer does not state or imply that the lawyer is disinterested. By clearly identifying the wife as his client, the attorney complied with this rule.

(D)   Correct. Model Rule 4.3 permits a lawyer to contact an unrepresented person so long as the lawyer does not state or imply that the lawyer is disinterested. By clearly identifying the wife as his client, the attorney complied with this rule.

Question # 33

(A)   Incorrect. Under Model Rule 1.12(d), an arbitrator selected as a partisan of a party in a multimember arbitration is not prohibited from subsequently representing that party in the same matter.

(B)   Incorrect. There is no rule that prohibits a party from choosing as a partisan arbitrator a member of the law firm that regularly represents the company in matters other than the subject of the arbitration.

(C)   Incorrect. Model Rule 1.12(d) does not require a lawyer who has served as a partisan arbitrator to obtain the consent of the other arbitrators before representing one of the parties to the arbitration. Moreover, if the representation was otherwise prohibited, as when a lawyer who served as a neutral arbitrator subsequently represents one of the parties in the same matter, the consent of the arbitrators would not cure the conflict.

(D)   Correct. Although a lawyer who served as a neutral arbitrator would be prohibited from undertaking the representation, Model Rule 1.12(d) expressly permits a lawyer selected as a partisan of a party in a multimember arbitration panel to subsequently represent that party in the same matter.

Question # 34

(A)   Incorrect. Model Rule 3.3(a)(3) prohibits a lawyer from knowingly offering evidence that the lawyer knows to be false, but the attorney did not know that the wife's testimony would be perjured when the attorney called her as a witness.

(B)   Correct. Model Rule 3.3(a)(3) requires that when a lawyer learns that a witness called by the lawyer has offered material evidence that is false, the lawyer must take reasonable remedial measures. That duty continues to the conclusion of the proceeding. Model Rule 3.3(c). Because the proceeding was not yet concluded when the attorney learned that the wife's testimony was false, the attorney had a duty to take reasonable remedial measures. Such measures would include meeting with the client and informing him of the attorney's obligation of candor to the court and asking the client to correct the fraud. If the client refused and if the attorney could not undo the prejudicial effect of the fraud, the attorney would need to disclose the fraud to the court.

(C)   Incorrect. Model Rule 3.3(a)(3) requires the lawyer to take reasonable remedial measures when the lawyer learns that the testimony was false, because the lawyer cannot know at that time the effect the false testimony will have on the fact finder.

(D)   Incorrect. It is insufficient for the attorney to refuse to rely on the false testimony in summation. Model Rule 3.3(a)(3) requires the lawyer to take reasonable remedial measures, including, if needed, disclosure to the tribunal.

Question # 35

(A)   Incorrect. Model Rule 4.2 prohibits a lawyer from communicating about the subject of the representation with a person the lawyer knows to be represented by another lawyer in the matter unless that lawyer consents; however, in this case, the mother was not represented by the agency or its lawyers or by any other lawyer.

(B)   Correct. Model Rule 4.3, which governs the conduct of lawyers dealing with unrepresented persons, prohibits a lawyer from stating or implying that the lawyer is disinterested in a matter in which the lawyer represents an interested party. The mother was an unrepresented person in this case.

(C)   Incorrect. Although it may be true that all lawyers are "officers of the court" in some sense, in this context such a statement clearly implied that the lawyer was disinterested in the outcome of the case, and such statements are prohibited by Model Rule 4.3.

(D)   Incorrect. Model Rule 4.3 prohibits a lawyer from giving an unrepresented person legal advice, but it also prohibits a lawyer from stating or implying that he or she is disinterested in a matter in which the lawyer represents an interested party, which is what the attorney did here.

Question # 36

(A)   Incorrect. Model Rule 7.1 prohibits false or misleading statements in lawyer advertising. An advertisement may truthfully report a lawyer's achievement on behalf of a former client unless it would lead a reasonable person to form an unjustified expectation that the same results could be obtained for other clients. The use of a prominent disclaimer, such as the voice-over in the ad, avoids such an expectation.

(B)   Correct. Although the advertisement does not expressly state that the attorney has successfully tried a case, the communication would lead a reasonable person to believe that. As a result, the communication is misleading and is prohibited by Model Rule 7.1.

(C)   Incorrect. It is true that commercial speech is protected under the First Amendment, but the First Amendment does not prohibit states from banning false or misleading communications in advertisements by professionals such as lawyers. Model Rule 7.1 prohibits false or misleading statements in lawyer advertising.

(D)   Incorrect. The voice-over disclaimer avoids unjustified expectations regarding the results a client could expect, but it does not avoid the misleading implication that the attorney had successfully argued a case to a jury. Model Rule 7.1 prohibits false or misleading statements in lawyer advertising.

Question # 37

(A)   Correct. Under Model Rule 8.3, a lawyer who has actual knowledge that a judge has committed a violation of the rules of judicial conduct that raises a substantial question as to that person's fitness for judicial office must inform the appropriate authority. In this fact pattern, the judge has on more than one occasion thrown a gavel across the courtroom and has been critical of lawyers and rude to litigants. Such behavior crosses the line into conduct that raises a substantial question as to his ability to judge.

(B)   Incorrect. Under Model Rule 8.3, a lawyer who has actual knowledge that a judge has committed a violation of the rules of judicial conduct that raises a substantial question as to that person's fitness for judicial office must inform the appropriate authority. Filing requests for substitution of the judge does not excuse the duty to report, but it really has nothing to do with public confidence in the judiciary. Failing to report the judge's behavior does affect public confidence.

(C)   Incorrect. Under Model Rule 8.3, a lawyer who has actual knowledge that a judge has committed a violation of the rules of judicial conduct that raises a substantial question as to that person's fitness for judicial office must inform the appropriate authority. Zealous representation of the attorney's clients does not relieve her of the duty to report the judge.

(D)   Incorrect. Under Model Rule 8.3, a lawyer who has actual knowledge that a judge has committed a violation of the rules of judicial conduct that raises a substantial question as to that person's fitness for judicial office must inform the appropriate authority. Whether or not the judge will be reelected does not affect the attorney's duty to report this matter to the appropriate authority.

Question # 38

(A)   Incorrect. Model Rule 1.5(b) says that the lawyer's basis for the fee must be disclosed before commencing *or within a reasonable time after commencing* a representation.

(B)   Incorrect. Model Rule 1.5(b) states that a fee arrangement shall be communicated to the client, preferably in writing, but written confirmation is not mandatory.

(C)   Correct. As required by the Model Rules, the lawyer disclosed the basis of the fee within a reasonable time after commencing the representation.

(D)   Incorrect. Because she was taking on a new representation in this case, the lawyer was required by the Model Rules to inform the client about the basis for her fee.

Question # 39

(A)   Incorrect. Even if Beta is competent, Alpha needs a client's consent to engage Beta in the representation and disclose the client's confidences to Beta. Rule 1.6(a) generally prohibits a lawyer from revealing information relating to the representation of a client without client consent. The disclosure to Beta was not "impliedly authorized in order to carry out the representation," because a client would not anticipate that his or her lawyer, who is a sole practitioner, would transfer the client's matters to a different lawyer.

(B)   Incorrect. Even if Beta agrees to keep the client's information confidential, the client's consent is needed to engage Beta and share the client's confidences with Beta. Subject to exception, Rule 1.6(a) generally prohibits a lawyer from revealing information relating to the representation of a client without client consent. No exception applies here.

(C)   Incorrect. If Alpha had first secured the clients' consent it would have been permissible to deliver the files to Beta. But absent client consent, the disclosure of clients' confidences to Beta was prohibited by Rule 1.6(a), since there was no applicable exception to the confidentiality duty expressed in that rule.

(D)   Correct. In general, Rule 1.6(a) prohibits a lawyer from revealing information relating to the representation of a client without client consent. A lawyer practicing in a law firm is impliedly authorized to disclose client confidences to other lawyers within the law firm, *see* Rule 1.6, cmt. [5], but not to lawyers outside the firm. There is an exception when a lawyer seeks legal advice from another lawyer about how to comply with the ethics rules, but that exception does not apply here. Therefore, the lawyer needed client consent.

Question # 40

(A)   Incorrect. The lawyer failed to comply with the procedural requirements of Rule 1.8(a) regarding business transactions with clients, and was required to do so even if the client initiated the transaction by offering to make the loan.

(B)   Incorrect. At the time of the transaction, the client was making a loan, not giving a gift, and therefore the lawyer was obligated, but failed, to comply with the procedural requirements of Rule 1.8(a) regarding business transactions with clients. Had this been a gift, not a loan, the lawyer's conduct would have been improper under Rule 1.8(c), because a lawyer may not prepare an instrument on behalf of a client that gives the lawyer a substantial gift, unless the lawyer and client are relatives.

(C)   Incorrect. A lawyer may accept a loan from a client as long as the lawyer complies with the requirements of Rule 1.8(a). In this case, the attorney violated Rule 1.8(a), which provides that a lawyer may not enter into a business transaction with a client unless the transaction is fair and reasonable, and unless the lawyer complies with procedural requirements, such as giving written advice about the desirability of seeking independent legal advice, and obtaining informed consent.

(D)   Correct. The attorney violated Rule 1.8(a), which provides that a lawyer may not enter into a business transaction with a client unless the transaction is fair and reasonable, and unless the lawyer complies with procedural requirements, such as giving written advice about the desirability of seeking independent legal advice, and obtaining informed consent.

Question # 41

(A)   Correct. A lawyer who is appointed to represent a criminal defendant must competently discharge his work or associate with someone who will perform the work competently with the consent of the client. The lawyer neglected the case because he referred the case to an inexperienced attorney and was aware that the attorney was not competently representing the defendant.

(B)   Incorrect. The client consented to the arrangement with full information and in writing, which is allowed under the rules.

(C)   Incorrect. The defendant's consent to the agreement did not relieve the sole practitioner of the responsibility of making sure that the appeal was timely filed.

(D)   Incorrect. The end result in the court did not relieve the sole practitioner of his responsibility to make sure that the first appeal was done properly.

Question # 42

(A)   Incorrect. The communication was improper. Model Rule 3.5 prohibits a lawyer from communicating ex parte with a judge unless authorized to do so by law or court order, neither of which occurred here.

(B)   Incorrect. The communication was improper. Model Rule 3.5 prohibits a lawyer from communicating ex parte with a judge unless authorized to do so by law or court order, neither of which occurred here.

(C)   Correct. Ex parte communications with the judge are prohibited by Model Rule 3.5. The attorney should have approached the judge jointly with opposing counsel or through a formal submission to the court with a copy to opposing counsel.

(D)   Incorrect. The content of the attorney's communication was unobjectionable. However, Model Rule 3.5 prohibits a lawyer from communicating ex parte with a judge unless authorized to do so by law or court order, neither of which occurred here. In this case, the lawyer participated in an unauthorized ex parte communication concerning the subject of the litigation.

Question # 43

(A)   Incorrect. The possibility that the media rights may turn out to be worth more than the attorney's hourly fee does not make the agreement improper. The attorney would not be entering an agreement for an "unreasonable fee" under Rule 1.5(a) because it was not likely that the media rights would in fact be worth more than his usual hourly fee. The agreement is improper, however, under Rule 1.8(d) because, prior to the conclusion of a representation, a lawyer may not make an agreement with the client giving the lawyer media rights to an account based in substantial part on information relating to the representation.

(B)   Correct. Under Rule 1.8(d), prior to the conclusion of a representation, a lawyer may not make an agreement with the client giving the lawyer media rights to an account based in substantial part on information relating to the representation.

(C)   Incorrect. The agreement would violate Rule 1.8(d), which prohibits a lawyer, prior to the conclusion of a representation, from acquiring media rights to the client's account, which would be based in substantial part on information relating to the representation. The rule applies in civil as well as criminal matters.

(D)   Incorrect. Under Rule 1.8(d), prior to the conclusion of a representation, a lawyer may not make an agreement with the client giving the lawyer media rights to an account based in substantial part on information relating to the representation. Even if the client is advised to first obtain independent legal advice, this conduct is forbidden, because it creates an unwaivable conflict while the representation is being conducted.

Question # 44

(A)   Correct. Model Rule 7.1 prohibits false or misleading statements in lawyer advertising. The Comment to the Rule notes that an advertisement truthfully reporting a lawyer's achievement on behalf of a client may be misleading if presented so as to lead a reasonable person to form an unjustified expectation that the same results can be obtained for other clients in similar matters without reference to the specific factual and legal circumstances of each client's case. An express and prominent disclaimer would be necessary to avoid such unjustified expectations here.

(B)   Incorrect. There is no per se ban on client testimonials in Model Rule 7.1 or any of the other advertising rules. Such testimonials are prohibited only when they include false or misleading communications. Here, the misleading communication is the voice-over discussion of the result in the plaintiff's case, not the plaintiff's own statements.

(C)   Incorrect. The attorney is responsible for the entire content of the advertisement, regardless of the lack of the attorney's involvement in creating the ad or the testimonial.

(D)   Incorrect. Model Rule 7.1 prohibits false or misleading statements in lawyer advertising. It is true that the advertisement does not contain any false statements; however, the report of the attorney's achievement on the plaintiff's behalf is misleading because it could lead a reasonable person to form an unjustified expectation that the same results could be achieved for other clients.

Question # 45

(A)   Incorrect. An attorney may accept legal fees in advance of performing legal work, as long as the lawyer complies with the requirement of Rule 1.15(c) that the advance fees be deposited in a client trust account until earned.

(B)   Correct. Rule 1.15(c) requires a lawyer to "deposit into a client trust account legal fees and expenses that have been paid in advance, to be withdrawn by the lawyer only as fees are earned or expenses incurred." Since the attorney had earned only $500, for five hours of work, at the time of receiving the client's check, only $500 should have been withdrawn from the trust account and placed in the general office account.

(C)   Incorrect. Under Rule 1.15(c), a lawyer may not hold fees paid in advance in the lawyer's general office account and later transfer unearned portions to the client trust account, as the attorney did here. Rather, the lawyer must deposit the advance payment in the client trust account and withdraw the payment for fees as they are earned.

(D)   Incorrect. Regardless of whether a lawyer expects to earn fees paid in advance, Rule 1.15(c) requires the lawyer to deposit the advance payment in the client trust account until the fees are actually earned.

Question # 46

(A)   Incorrect. All modifications of a fee agreement in an existing representation are subject to special scrutiny. The lawyer, who has the burden of proof in any dispute about the fees, must justify the proposed modification by showing special circumstances. Note that the only reasons given for the proposed fee increase were that the lawyer was busy and was in demand, neither of them valid reasons for raising a fee. The fact that the lawyer offered to find another lawyer who would charge the original fee does not excuse his behavior.

(B)   Incorrect. All modifications of a fee agreement in an existing representation are subject to special scrutiny. The lawyer, who has the burden of proof in any dispute about the fees, must justify the proposed modification by showing special circumstances, none of which are present here. The fact that the proposed fee was reasonable is not relevant to whether the lawyer acted properly in insisting on the modification of the fee agreement.

(C)   Incorrect. The Model Rules and the law of lawyering do not state a need to get independent counsel in such a case. They do require, however, that the lawyer justify any proposed modification to the fee agreement by showing special circumstances, which the lawyer is unable to do in this case. Independent counsel would not have excused the lawyer's behavior.

(D)   Correct. The Model Rules and the law of lawyering require that the lawyer justify any proposed modification to the fee agreement by showing special circumstances. Special circumstances that would justify a modification to the agreement would include, for example, a change in the nature of the case, a need to add more defendants, or an unanticipated need to expend much more capital in advance to fund the case. No special circumstances were present in this case.

Question # 47

(A)   Incorrect. Model Rule 3.5(b) prohibits a lawyer from communicating ex parte with prospective jurors during the proceeding unless authorized to do so by law or court order. Providing a report of the interviews to opposing counsel would not have cured the violation here.

(B)   Correct. Model Rule 3.5(b) prohibits a lawyer from communicating ex parte with prospective jurors during the proceeding unless authorized to do so by law or court order. The attorney could not use a private investigator to do what the attorney could not do directly. Model Rule 8.4(a).

(C)   Incorrect. Model Rule 3.5(b) prohibits a lawyer from communicating ex parte with prospective jurors during the proceeding unless authorized to do so by law or court order. The attorney's conduct in this case was clearly prohibited by the rule, and informing the jurors or their family members that the contact was being made on behalf of the attorney would not cure the violation.

(D)   Incorrect. Model Rule 3.5(b) prohibits a lawyer from communicating ex parte with prospective jurors during the proceeding unless authorized to do so by law or court order. The attorney's conduct in this case was clearly prohibited by the rule even if the interviews were entirely voluntary and not harassing.

Question # 48

(A)   Correct. Attorney has a conflict of interest under Rule 1.7 and may not continue to represent both clients. If the attorney negotiates a plea bargain for Able, she will be prejudicing Baker, whereas if she fails to negotiate the plea bargain, she will be prejudicing Able. Under Rule 1.16(a)(1), the attorney must seek judicial permission to withdraw from the representation to avoid violating Rule 1.7.

(B)   Incorrect. If the attorney withdrew from representing Able, she would still have a conflict of interest under Rule 1.7 because of the duty to protect Able's confidences. There would be a risk that, in trying to avoid abusing Able's confidences, the attorney would fail to represent Baker competently, especially when the time came to cross-examine Able.

(C)   Incorrect. If the attorney withdrew from representing Baker but continued to represent Able, the attorney would have a conflict of interest under Rule 1.9(a), which concerns representations adverse to a former client. By continuing the representation of Able and negotiating an agreement whereby Able would testify against Baker, the attorney would be representing Able adversely to Baker, now a former client, in the same matter in which the attorney formerly represented Baker.

(D)   Incorrect. The attorney has a conflict of interest under Rule 1.7 and may not continue to represent both clients. If the attorney fails to negotiate the plea bargain for Able, she will be prejudicing Able. If Able does not enter into the plea bargain, the attorney will still have a conflict because it may be in Able's best interest to call Able as a witness, even though his testimony would prejudice Baker.

Question # 49

(A)   Correct. Normally, lawyers do not owe a duty to the opposing side of a transaction. But a lawyer may not make intentional or negligent misrepresentations to a third person. In this case, the attorney made a misrepresentation when he falsely told the buyer that he would be getting a lot of property for the price, because he knew that the buyer's attempt to purchase the seller's interest would not result in the buyer's acquisition of any interest in the property.

(B)   Incorrect. Whether the attorney was or was not disinterested does not change the fact that the attorney made a misrepresentation to the buyer.

(C)   Incorrect. The attorney's statement could not be construed as an "opinion." The attorney told the buyer that he would be getting a lot of property for the price, knowing that the buyer's investment would be compromised because of the title issue.

(D)   Incorrect. Normally, attorneys do not owe a duty to the opposing side of a transaction. In this case, however, the attorney made a statement to the buyer that was patently false, exposing himself to civil liability.

Question # 50

(A)   Incorrect. Model Rule 3.6 prohibits making public communications that have a substantial likelihood of materially prejudicing an adjudicative proceeding. There is no indication that the attorney's communication in this case would be materially prejudicial. In any event, Model Rule 3.6(b)(4) specifically permits statements concerning information obtained in a public record.

(B)   Incorrect. Model Rule 3.6 prohibits making public communications that have a substantial likelihood of materially prejudicing an adjudicative proceeding. There is no indication that this communication would be materially prejudicial, and Model Rule 3.6(b)(4) specifically permits statements concerning information obtained in a public record.

(C)   Correct. Such statements are permitted by Model Rule 3.6(b)(4).

(D)   Incorrect. Model Rule 3.6 prohibits making public communications that have a substantial likelihood of materially prejudicing an adjudicative proceeding. The prohibition in that rule against making prejudicial extrajudicial statements is not limited to statements regarding trials that have commenced.

Question # 51

(A)   Incorrect. Even if the lawyer had paid the higher rate of interest to the client, the lawyer's personal use of the client's funds and his failure to carry out the client's instructions would have been improper.

(B)   Correct. Client funds must be held for safekeeping in an account that is separate from the lawyer's funds and may be used only in accordance with the client's instructions, not for the lawyer's personal benefit. Further, the attorney was required to use the funds for the client's designated purpose, that is, for payment of the taxes when they became due, and for no other purpose.

(C)   Incorrect. Whether or not the client might be expected to acquiesce, a lawyer may not violate the client's instructions about how to use funds given to the lawyer for safekeeping, nor may the lawyer use those funds for personal purposes.

(D)   Incorrect. A client's later approval of the action does not excuse a lawyer's unethical use of client funds for personal purposes.

Question # 52

(A)   Incorrect. Model Rule 7.5 and its Comment permit a lawyer to use the name of a deceased member of a firm where there has been a continuing succession in the firm's identity, regardless of whether the deceased partner had given permission for the continuing use.

(B)   Correct. Model Rule 7.5(d) prohibits lawyers from stating or implying that they practice in a partnership or other organization when that is not the fact. The sign at the entrance to the suite of offices represents to the public that Alpha and Gamma practice together in a single law firm and is therefore prohibited by Rule 7.5(d), as well as by Model Rule 7.1, which prohibits false or misleading communications about a lawyer's practice.

(C)   Incorrect. Alpha was indeed permitted to continue to use Beta's name in his firm's name under Model Rule 7.5, but Rule 7.5(d) prohibits him from stating or implying that he and Gamma practice together in a single law firm.

(D)   Incorrect. Paying a share of the rent and other office expenses does not make Gamma a partner of Alpha, and Model Rule 7.5(d) prohibits Alpha from stating or implying that he and Gamma practice together in a single law firm.

Question # 53

(A)   Incorrect. The judge did speak ex parte with one of the lawyers, but this specific type of communication is expressly permitted by CJC 2.9(a)(1).

(B)   Incorrect. The ex parte communication was either proper or it was not. A determination as to whether there was time remaining to notify opposing counsel will not affect the propriety of the conduct.

(C)   Correct. Under CJC 2.9(a)(1), a judge or court official may speak ex parte with one of the litigants or a lawyer on a matter of scheduling or any other administrative issue.

(D)   Incorrect. The availability of others to take the call does not affect the propriety of the ex parte communication.

Question # 54

(A)   Incorrect. The fact that the attorney is the sole surviving witness to the will's execution means that the attorney is likely to be a necessary witness regarding the client's mental capacity when she executed the will. The attorney, therefore, may not also represent the executor in connection with the will contest, since Rule 3.7(a) provides that a lawyer may not serve as an advocate at a trial in which the lawyer is likely to be a necessary witness regarding a contested issue.

(B)   Incorrect. Under Rule 3.7(a), a lawyer may not represent a party at a trial in which the lawyer is likely to be a necessary witness relating to a contested issue, even if the testimony supports the party's position.

(C)   Correct. Rule 3.7(a) states that a lawyer may not serve as an advocate at a trial in which the lawyer is likely to be a necessary witness relating to a contested issue.

(D)   Incorrect. The fact that the attorney would be representing a party (the executor) who is adverse to the deceased client's heir is irrelevant. But for the fact that the attorney is a likely witness, the representation would be proper. However, Rule 3.7(a) provides that a lawyer may not serve as an advocate at a trial in which the lawyer is likely to be a necessary witness relating to a contested issue. A lawyer may not represent a party who contests a will prepared by the lawyer, but that lawyer may represent the executor of the client's estate unless the lawyer is likely to become a witness.

Question # 55

(A)   Correct. Rule 1.5(d)(2) provides that a lawyer may not represent a defendant in a criminal case on a contingent fee basis. Here, the client's payment of a fee (title to an automobile) was contingent on a successful outcome in the criminal case.

(B)   Incorrect. Rule 1.8(i) provides that a lawyer may not obtain a proprietary interest in the cause of action or the subject of the litigation the lawyer is conducting for a client, but the attorney has not done so in this case because the automobile is not involved in the litigation. Rule 1.8(i) does not prohibit a lawyer in all cases from obtaining a proprietary interest in a client's property. The fee agreement, however, was impermissible under Rule 1.5(d)(2) because the lawyer's fee was contingent on the successful outcome in the criminal case.

(C)   Incorrect. The fee agreement was impermissible under Rule 1.5(d)(2) because the lawyer's fee was contingent on the successful outcome of a criminal case. Therefore, even though the lawyer achieved success, he is subject to discipline for entering into an impermissible fee agreement.

(D)   Incorrect. Although it is true that a contingent fee agreement must be in writing, this agreement was improper for a different reason. Rule 1.5(d)(2) forbids a contingent fee agreement in a criminal case.

Question # 56

(A)   Correct. Although the nature of the work done for clients of the firm is confidential under Rule 1.6 and generally may not be disclosed to third parties without client consent, "[l]awyers in a firm may, in the course of the firm's practice, disclose to each other information relating to a client of the firm, unless the client has instructed that particular information be confined to specified lawyers." Rule 1.6, cmt. [5].

(B)   Incorrect. If the client instructs that particular confidential information be disclosed only to particular lawyers in the firm, the firm must abide by that instruction.

(C)   Incorrect. To facilitate a law firm's practice, its lawyers may share client confidential information with each other, even though doing so may increase the risk that the information will be disclosed to third parties outside the firm, because clients generally understand that this is done and implicitly consent to it. Law firms take other measures to minimize the risk that the information will be disseminated to third parties. Therefore, except when the client instructs otherwise or there are special reasons to limit disclosures within the firm, client information may be shared, as in this case, among the firm's lawyers for legitimate business purposes.

(D)   Incorrect. Disclosures of client information may be made within a law firm to carry out the representation, but that is not the only circumstance in which disclosures may be made within the firm. In general, they may also be made for the purpose of facilitating the law firm's practice, such as for billing purposes or for the education of young lawyers or, as in this case, to familiarize the firm's lawyers with the nature of each other's practice.

Question # 57

(A)   Incorrect. Although the judge acted officially in the lawsuit before resigning from the bench, she was not restricted by Rule 1.12(a) because she did not participate "substantially" in the matter when she entered an administrative order changing the courtroom. Comment [1] to this Rule provides that "the fact that a former judge exercised administrative responsibility in a court does not prevent the former judge from acting as a lawyer in a matter where the judge had previously exercised remote or incidental administrative responsibility that did not affect the merits."

(B)   Incorrect. No rule prohibits a former judge from appearing on behalf of a party before a judge of a court on which she previously sat.

(C)   Correct. Under Rule 1.12(a), the former judge may represent the plaintiff because she did not participate "substantially" in the matter while she was an acting judge. She merely entered an incidental administrative order unrelated to the merits of the lawsuit.

(D)   No, because any information that the judge learned about the case while acting as a judge was a matter of public record.

Question # 58

(A)   Incorrect. Under Rule 1.8(h), a lawyer may not limit his liability prospectively unless the client is independently represented in making such an agreement. Whether there is consideration for the agreement is not relevant.

(B)   Incorrect. Under Rule 1.8(h), a lawyer may not limit his liability prospectively unless the client is independently represented in making such an agreement. The reasonableness of the proposed fee and the quality of the work are not relevant to the propriety of the agreement.

(C)   Correct. Under Rule 1.8(h), a lawyer may not limit his liability prospectively unless the client is independently represented in making such an agreement.

(D)   Incorrect. Under Rule 1.8(h), a lawyer may not limit his liability prospectively unless the client is independently represented in making such an agreement. The form of the agreement is not relevant to whether the agreement is proper.

Question # 59

(A)   Incorrect. When legal fees are paid in advance, they must be kept in the clients' trust account until earned. When the representation ends, the lawyer must return the unearned portion (here, $1,000) to the client. The lawyer may withdraw fees as earned except when, as in this case, they are disputed, in which case they must be kept in the clients' trust account until the dispute is resolved. Rule 1.15(e).

(B)   Incorrect. Both steps are wrong. The $600, which represents the amount in dispute, must be kept in the clients' trust account until the dispute is resolved. The remaining $1,000, which represents unearned fees, belongs to the client, and must therefore be returned to the client. Rule 1.15(e).

(C)   Incorrect. The lawyer is right to disburse $1,000 from the clients' trust account to the client, since that amount represents unearned fees and therefore undisputedly belongs to the client. Rule 1.15(e). But the $600 that is in dispute must be kept in the clients' trust account until the dispute is resolved.

(D)   Correct. Rule 1.15(e) requires that when the lawyer has a dispute with a client over funds in the lawyer's possession, the lawyer must deliver to the client the funds that undisputedly belong to the client and hold the remainder in the clients' trust account until the dispute is resolved. Therefore, the attorney is required to hold in the clients' trust account the amount of disputed legal fees ($600) and return the remaining $1,000 to the client.

Question # 60

(A)   Incorrect. The Model Rules do not prohibit a lawyer from asking others to post advertisements concerning the lawyer's services.

(B)   Correct. Model Rule 7.2(b) prohibits a lawyer from giving anything of value to a person for recommending the lawyer's services. Subsection (4) of that rule provides for an exception for reciprocal referral agreements with other lawyers or with nonlawyer professionals. Because the restaurant owner is not a professional, however, this exception does not apply.

(C)   Incorrect. A reciprocal referral agreement constitutes an agreement to give something of value in return for recommending the lawyer's services, and any such agreement is prohibited by Model Rule 7.2(b) unless the agreement is with another lawyer or a nonlawyer professional. The attorney's promise to display the restaurant ads and to mention the restaurant to clients seeking a recommendation is something of value.

(D)   Incorrect. If the reciprocal referral agreement had been with a lawyer or a nonlawyer professional, these facts would have made the agreement permissible under Model Rule 7.2(b)(4). That exception, however, does not apply to the restaurant owner, who is not a professional.

About the *Supreme Bar Review MPRE Review*

The *Supreme Bar Review MPRE REVIEW* is more than just a book. It includes FREE access to our comprehensive web-based video lecture.

You have discovered the fastest, easiest, most convenient way to prepare for the Multistate Professional Responsibility Exam (MPRE).

Don't just read it. See and hear it, with our comprehensive MPRE Video Lecture delivered through our FREE online classroom.

For the price of the book, you get online access to the most up-to-date MPRE lecture anywhere.

How do you access the FREE web-based video lecture?

Includes Web Video Lecture

Simply visit:

http://MPRE.SupremeBarReview.com

Made in the USA
Charleston, SC
30 April 2014